APOLLO & THELMA

APOLLO

& THELMA

A TRUE TALL TALE

JON FAINE

Hardie Grant

BOOKS

Published in 2022 by Hardie Grant Books, an imprint of Hardie Grant Publishing

Hardie Grant Books (Melbourne)
Wurundjeri Country
Building 1, 658 Church Street
Richmond, Victoria 3121

Hardie Grant Books (London)
5th & 6th Floors
52–54 Southwark Street
London SE1 1UN

hardiegrantbooks.com

Image copyright as indicated with pictures where applicable. Every effort has been made
to confirm the provenance of images used. Gratitude to the Anderson family and others
for supplying images from their personal collections, and to photographer David Johns for
capturing Apollo's memorabilia in digital format. Thank you to the Estate of Frank Hardy
for granting permission to reproduce the cover and excerpts from *The Unlucky Australians*.

The moral rights of the author have been asserted.

A catalogue record for this
book is available from the
National Library of Australia

Apollo & Thelma
ISBN 978 1 7437 9708 2

10 9 8 7 6 5 4 3 2 1

Typeset in 12/18 pt Adobe Caslon Pro by Kirbyjones
Printed in Australia by Griffin Press, part of Ovato, an Accredited ISO
AS/NZS 14001 Environmental Management System printer.

The paper this book is printed on is certified against the Forest Stewardship
Council® Standards. Griffin Press holds FSC® chain of custody certification
SGSHK-COC-005088. FSC® promotes environmentally responsible, socially
beneficial and economically viable management of the world's forests.

Hardie Grant acknowledges the Traditional Owners of the country on which we work, the
Wurundjeri people of the Kulin nation and the Gadigal people of the Eora nation, and
recognises their continuing connection to the land, waters and culture. We pay our respects
to their Elders past and present.

Aboriginal and Torres Strait Islander readers are advised that this book contains names and
images of people who have died.

To my parents, Solly and Eva,
who taught that you finish what you start.

CONTENTS

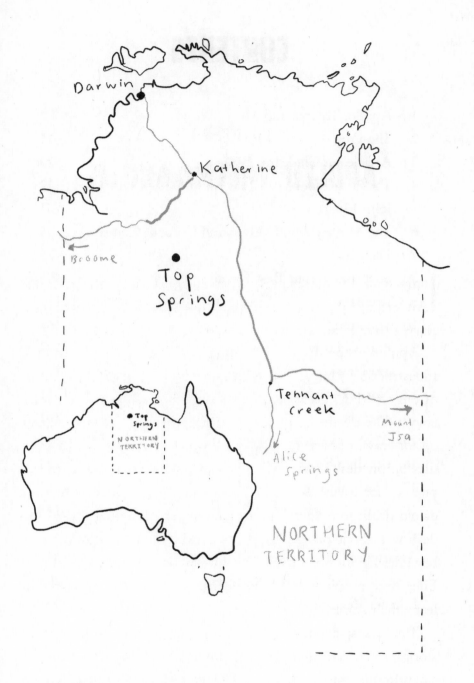

A map of the Northern Territory
showing the location of Top Springs.

CHAPTER 1

APOLLO, THELMA AND ME

I only met Thelma Hawks after she died. Her brother Paul Anderson, 'The Mighty Apollo', introduced us. To tell their story, I have to tell some of mine.

Apollo, the 'Iron Jaw King of Strength', 'Australia's Indestructible Man of Steel' and sometimes billed as 'The World's Strongest Man', became my favourite client when I was a baby lawyer. The Estate of Thelma Cecilia Hawks kept me busy on and off for years. Because of Apollo, I learned to never forget that the files on my desk were not only about the law, not just about the money, nor solely about the documents or corporate structures or old deals gone sour. Fundamentally, each bulging file on my desk was about people, in all their vanity and weirdness, their bewildering irrationality, their naivety, their flaws and failings. Files were people – and to represent them properly, you had to learn their stories.

The inescapable contradiction was that in order to hear those stories, you had to charge for the time it took to listen to them. To sit enthralled for an afternoon to listen to Apollo while I charged him $350 an hour was plainly wrong. Trying to filter out what

Paul Alexander McPherson Anderson, The Mighty Apollo, in his Hawke Street gym surrounded by trophies and antiques.

was work and when yarns became pleasure was not just awkward – it was nigh on impossible. He did not organise his thoughts in neat stacks with labels attached. People never walk into your office with all the legal issues packaged and flagged for attention. They tell a story, and the legal knot to be unravelled is buried somewhere within.

Thelma Cecilia Hawks, born Anderson.

In 1981 Apollo and his three teenage sons unexpectedly inherited Thelma's modest wealth, tied up in a remote pub in the Northern Territory. I soon realised that I was more interested in their unconventional story than the legal problems. This seems obvious now but was shocking to me then. The tussle about money was getting in the way of hearing him tell of breaking world strength records, surviving an elephant standing on him, tugging a tram down the street by a toggle clenched in his teeth and lavish accounts of his life as a 'carnie' touring around the nation decades earlier. As I heard more about Apollo, so too did I become more intrigued about Thelma, a formidable solo woman running a rough outback pub.

Although a strongman, Apollo was in some ways quite weak. While undeniably physically impressive, he was a fragile soul, insecure and anxious, only comfortable with himself while crushing an opponent in a wrestling match or a strength contest on stage. Away from showbiz, he struggled. Just as many comedians suffer from depression, and escape their sadness by making others laugh, so Apollo used his muscles to avoid his demons. His authority came from performing, his energy drawn from the applause and admiration of crowds. His comfort in the spotlight was matched by his discomfort away from it.

When Apollo first 'introduced' me to his recently deceased sister Thelma, I was a naive law graduate, goggle-eyed on joining the world of work. The seductive lure of money and corporate power was opening up a tempting future, and I had glimpses of what my life could become. By the time the estate was finally sorted, seven years later, I had shed that skin. Like so many young lawyers, I decided to chance my arm at something else instead of losing sleep looking after other people's money. Despite learning the trade of a streetwise litigator, I detoured from law to the sceptical and judgemental faux world of the media. I always expected the detour to be brief. It lasted thirty years.

Even after the file was closed, Apollo's unique tale and Thelma's ghostly presence remained constants in my life. My favourite client kept popping up at the most unexpected times. Long after the estate was wound up and the money distributed, threads remained. I felt obliged to tell their story and that obligation came close to an obsession.

Apollo and Thelma grew up in the tough working-class streets of Melbourne's inner north in the 1920s. The squalid and filthy lanes of their childhood were populated by sly grog peddlers and even slyer bookies, gangsters and thugs, standover merchants and debt collectors. The descendants of English, Irish and Scottish migrants, the Collingwood and Carlton gangs fought each other and the world, plotting and scheming their escape from crowded poverty and homes that were little more than slums.

Apollo chased fame, and the secretive and enigmatic Thelma sought fortune. Apollo was never satisfied, no matter what level of celebrity and adulation he reached, while Thelma cannily accumulated her riches in the most harsh and unforgiving landscape this continent can offer.

Thelma cannot be found in the official histories of the Northern Territory and is barely mentioned by any of the flamboyant tellers of colourful outback yarns. If she is mentioned at all in the occasional memoir penned by a Territorian old-timer, she is mentioned as the ex-wife of her entrepreneurial husband, Sid Hawks. Her pioneering role as a solo woman publican, ruling the roost for decades at Top Springs, in one of the most remote pubs in the country, should be acknowledged. While she relished and cultivated her local notoriety, her ghost would disapprove of the embellished stories told about her and savoured by those who stopped for a warm longneck beer all those decades ago.

Apollo is the opposite – he spent his entire life seeking the spotlight, craving fame and the 'legend' status he was eventually granted. The veneer of his public and performing life is amply documented, recorded in official archives, his exploits magnified through his enthusiastic – even narcissistic – pursuit of media attention. But beneath, there is a deep sadness. His three proud sons, fiercely protective of their father's professional legacy, are less effusive about his qualities as a parent. But whatever his failures, any critique of Apollo pales to insignificance beside their entirely scathing memories of their mother, Rondahe, who abandoned them and shot through with her younger lover when they were small boys. The eldest and youngest brothers are determined that the painful truth about their mother is told, while excusing their father his shortcomings.

All lawyers are governed by the rules of confidentiality. I have the permission of my former clients to tell their family story. The three now-adult sons of Apollo, who were the ultimate beneficiaries of the estate of their aunt Thelma, have participated fully and generously in so doing and insisted on only one condition – that I not try to contact their mother. I was assured that it would be detrimental to her health if ancient wounds were opened. I reluctantly agreed.

Gaining their trust and permission in the telling was one essential ingredient. The other was far more complex and much closer to home. In fact, it was at home. Without realising it was happening, immersing myself in the lives of Thelma and Apollo made me see my own family afresh, and especially one particularly emotional part.

Thelma Hawks' outback pub at Top Springs in the Northern Territory is an improbable springboard from which to educate myself on the truth about Indigenous massacres and colonial atrocities, but learn I did – and with a personal motivation I have until now kept private. My own son's Aboriginal heritage was always important to all of our family, but I never really appreciated or understood how profoundly everyday casual racism impacted his life. Unscrambling Thelma's story was a catalyst and revealed to me terrible things that happened a long way away – but not that long ago. It forced me to acknowledge how little I knew about Australia's true origin story, unrecognisably different to the scant history we were taught at school.

Wandering back to find out more about the pioneers of the Victoria River district of the Northern Territory, I learned true tales that were compelling, confronting and sometimes too sad to absorb. They were not suppressed; but like a family secret, they had been tucked away from scrutiny. It forced me to recalibrate my understanding of that local history, to acknowledge the deep prejudices upon which modern Australia has self-consciously built itself. We were not taught about massacres and rapes of Indigenous people in high school – we were taught myths and lies instead of the truth. We still look the other way and do not acknowledge the full horror of colonial settlement and the impact it had on the lives of our First Nations people. When those stories collided with my own family story, I felt that pain in a new and acute way and felt compelled to draw the link.

Blatant prejudice in contemporary Australia is evident and profound. Cowardly apologists for racism brush off colonial savagery as an irrelevant historical artefact, with no bearing on the present. But it is undeniable that the impact of racism is felt across Australia every day, seen with my own eyes as the protective father of our Bundjalung son.

Our country is belatedly and slowly changing, and for the better. As my eyes were being opened over the last forty years, so were those of many others. This must continue. To keep pretending these atrocities did not happen is to perpetuate a cover-up, to be complicit. Even if we did not know then – there is no excuse now.

Although Apollo and Thelma principally taught me to be a more sensitive lawyer, caring about my clients as people and not just piles of paper, they also somewhat circuitously led me to enquire about Australia's troubled past, our foundation myths and my own responsibilities as a father.

Apollo, the world's strongest man, made me stronger too.

NOTE TO READERS

Transcribed passages of direct speech are as spoken; an approximation of punctuation has been applied to retain the conversational tone.

In writing this book, I have borrowed from sources and interviewed people who freely use the racist and offensive terms 'half caste', 'lubra', 'gin' and other similarly horrible descriptions. After much thought and guidance, the original language has been retained for veracity. There are also obscenities quoted, but only where relevant for context. The vernacular is retained to highlight, not to trivialise or excuse, the inherent racism and sexism of those times. Most of those using that language were white, some were Indigenous.

Much of that language is not and should not be in common usage today and none of that language is included in these stories to in any way encourage it – precisely the opposite. Nor is it used just to shock readers, even though it is often shocking. It is used to authentically show the sensibilities of the times and how much has, thankfully, changed. Cultural and social change continues – it cannot stop now. We still have a long way to go.

But change is neither inevitable nor linear – it is up to each of us to make change happen, and a sharper appreciation of our history is a catalyst for more change, and faster progress.

Some events recounted are crimes but were never treated that way, despite being reported and occasionally scrutinised by police or other authorities. Invariably, perpetrators escaped punishment altogether. It is too late to pursue them for criminal responsibility, but it would be a fresh crime if we were to ignore what happened back in those days, now that accounts have emerged.

Many of these events were within living memory – they are historical truths, not ancient history. They did not happen thousands or even hundreds of years ago. Although survivors and eyewitnesses are unlikely to still be alive, their children and grandchildren certainly are.

Indigenous readers are forewarned this book contains names and references to and borrows words from people who have died. Wherever possible, permission has been sought. I apologise when it has not been known to whom that request should be addressed.

I include this painful history to ensure we urgently repair the damage done and free future generations from the burdens of recent history. Our grandchildren must not still be arguing the case.

CHAPTER 2

THE FROG

Policeman Kevin Dailly was gaoled in 1982 for 'larceny as a constable'. He stole $28,550 from a dead woman and was dobbed in by a frog. I should thank that frog. Although I was 3000 kilometres away, the frog not only dobbed in the thief but introduced me to the Mighty Apollo.

The stolen money was part of the inheritance of three teenage boys in Melbourne, sons of Apollo. I became their lawyer. In May 1981 they inherited the Wanda Inn pub in Top Springs, 800 kilometres south of Darwin, on the sudden death of their publican aunt, Old Ma (Thelma) Hawks.

A more remote pub you would struggle to find. At the intersection of two red-dirt rutted roads, the roadhouse was the only watering hole for miles around, relied upon by an occasional optimistic tourist but mostly local stockmen, drovers and truckies heading to the Victoria River district, dotted with cattle stations the size of small European nations.

Rising from the surrounding open grassland like a pile of Lego, Toppie offered brief respite from the heat and dust. A local drunk described it as being 'as cheerful and welcoming as an empty coffin', offering just the basics – beer, rum, fuel, fags or food. And fights.

The local Aboriginal population could buy takeaway grog but never ventured inside – they knew they were not welcome and drank their beer and rum in the shade of the nearby trees, keeping well clear of Ma Hawks and her vicious dogs. Not dogs that you wander over and pat, but a Rottweiler, Doberman and an enormous snarling Alsatian trained to make a mess of anyone in their way.

Thelma Hawks had been the publican and unofficial Queen of Top Springs for thirty years. Each morning, her loyal sidekick and barman, the skinny, aging, occasionally shaven Pom Norm Douglas, would open the day's proceedings with a customary breakfast beer, lubricating his perpetually dry throat. Tiny, ferocious and authoritarian, Thelma would emerge perfectly groomed, plaited hair in her typical bun, hoping forlornly that it would increase the visual impact of her 5'2" frame. Her uniform was a white shirt, buttoned high to hide any glimpse of cleavage, and a pair of short shorts, cuffs turned to highlight impressively muscled thighs.

On Sunday 10 May 1981, confounding the locals – both of them – Thelma Hawks did not make her way down the concrete stairs from her private – very private – flat. Norm had never known a single day where she did not arrive to imperially issue orders and commands to him.

Although he had worked with Thelma for over twenty years, Norm had never been into her rooms. Ever. No-one joined her upstairs since her husband, Sid, had left in the 1960s. This Sunday morning, when, for the first time, she did not come down the stairs, Thelma's discreet henchman was at a loss.

Lunchtime approached with still no sign of Thelma, so Norm conferred with the only other permanent resident of Toppie. Doug Stillson was a huge man, with the appearance and demeanour of a giant. He was only ever seen in a filthy torn blue singlet and ill-fitting greasy shorts that only just immodestly straddled his beer belly, leaving skinny legs poking out below like matchsticks. An alcohol-ravaged nose split his rheumy eyes and with fist-sized hairy ears the entire package was utterly unattractive. If Norm's routine was dominated by the ever-present bottle of beer, Doug took it to the next level. Anchored at one end of the brick bar, wedged into the corner, Doug transacted his life entirely within these walls.

The rumour was that Doug had been a lifeguard in Sydney in his younger years but had been in a bar-room brawl where a man had died. He was not at Toppie hiding from the law – the police were regular visitors – but could better be assumed to be hiding from himself. His range of conversation was limited to the weather or the character and drinking capacity of local truckies. He handed his pension to Ma Hawks each fortnight and simply drank it away. He occasionally helped out pumping petrol, but otherwise just held up one end of the bar.

After deliberating with Doug, Norm went to check on Mrs Hawks. He gingerly made his way up the stairs and knocked loudly on her door, calling out. After a few more attempts, he opened the unlocked door and let himself in. Nothing. Fearing the worst, Norm did a quick inspection of the crowded living room, then bedroom, before he found Thelma in the bathroom. She was slumped on the toilet, head against the wall, eyes bulging, an out-of-date asthma puffer at her feet. Norm gently shook her body, then swore. Thelma Hawks was already stiff and cold. For the first time since he was a child, he wiped a tear from his eye.

Norm called Katherine Police and reported the death to Sergeant Paddy McQuaid, explaining he had found Thelma, eyes bulging 'frog like'. He surmised she had died from an asthma attack. McQuaid instructed Norm to lock everything and wait for police. Norm returned to the bar to tell Doug and the only other customer – a contractor – the news. The shock was best soothed by cracking open a few more beers.

Sergeant McQuaid referred Thelma's death to Wave Hill Police Station, a mere two hours' drive from Toppie. The sergeant there had been transferred elsewhere weeks before, and Constable Kevin Dailly was, for the time being, running Wave Hill solo – his only companion a new puppy, named Len after the senior sergeant at Katherine, Len Pryce. The mongrel had turned out to be untrainable and a nuisance; just days before, Dailly told a mate he would have to summon up the guts to shoot it. Dailly enthusiastically agreed to go to Top Springs to investigate the publican's death, grateful for a break in the monotony. His mate William Purdie, a stock agent, came along to keep Dailly company and score a few free beers at the pub.

Around 13:30hrs Dailly pulled up in the police Toyota LandCruiser 'Troopy', big whip aerial shimmying. He found the Top Springs population in 'a distressed state due to the death of Thelma Cecilia Hawks', according to the Wave Hill Police Journal. Carrying the assumed authority of any man in uniform, Dailly assured Norm that he should keep the pub and petrol pumps trading. Dailly, Purdie and Norm went up to Thelma's flat, but Norm found it too distressing and left. Purdie helped Dailly place Thelma into a body bag and they carried her down to the cool room. They returned to the flat and emerged nearly two hours later, carrying some garbage bags they put into the police vehicle. A funeral contractor arrived from Katherine and took Thelma Hawks' body away. Dailly told Norm that Thelma's valuables and personal effects were secured in cartons and bags for the Public Trustee. Meanwhile, the pub should shut early – a moot point as there was no-one there. Purdie's quest for free grog was not disappointed and they settled in for the night.

Late the next day, having urgently driven the seven hours from Darwin, the Northern Territory Public Trustee John Flynn and his assistant John Hyde arrived. Dailly showed them upstairs and explained he had found a substantial amount of cash, stored in biscuit tins and a locked briefcase. Flynn thanked the policeman, took the valuables, then set about taking stock of the pub. He assured Norm that he should keep trading, because if the pub shut, the liquor licence lapsed, and the value of the entire business would evaporate. The Liquor Commission required a licensed person to be in charge at all times. Barely literate, Norm was not suitable to be even a temporary licensee. Flynn had to look further.

Dick Philip from Montejinni cattle station just 15 kilometres down the road had been flirting with buying the pub from the aging but wary Thelma Hawks. Her idea of its value was vastly different to his. She was banking on a rumour that a Malaysian sultan from Sarawak, who had just purchased a local cattle station, was planning to open an abattoir. If its road trains came through Toppie, she would hit the jackpot. Philip was sceptical, but Thelma would not drop her price. On her sudden death he readily agreed to a temporary lease at bargain rates and asked for an option to buy.

Back in Darwin, John Flynn wrote a letter of appreciation to the Police Commissioner praising young Dailly: 'He has been most helpful and co-operative, outstandingly so'. Thelma's brother in Melbourne was notified of her death, but could not make it to Katherine in time for her sparsely attended funeral.

Norm kept things ticking over at the pub, the only difference being the absence of Ma Hawks. As there was no part of the daily operation he could not manage well except the paperwork, life maintained its boozy Top Springs rhythm.

Six months later, in mid-December, at Wave Hill Police Station, an Aboriginal gardener was watering its tiny patch of lawn and tending the forlorn yard. A frog on the path was casually swept away and hid in the leaf pile, in front of Constable Dailly's puppy. Len chased the hopping frog into a crevice and tried to dig it out. As Len scratched in the soft red dirt, the glossy edges of a plastic garbage bag were revealed, then banknotes. The astonished gardener chained the dog and ran into the police station.

'Senior, come quick – money in the ground, money in the sky ... that there frog ... he find money,' he told the incredulous copper, who brushed him off, muttering something disparaging about the entire Aboriginal race.

The gardener ran back to the hole, grabbed a few $20 and $10 notes from the still-buried bag and showed them to Senior Constable 'Bob' Bruce. Wide-eyed and apologetic, the cop came out to see for himself. As a passing willy-willy swirled across the yard, scattering banknotes into the air, Bob Bruce pulled the bulging garbage bag from its crevice. How had tens of thousands of dollars come to be buried outside Wave Hill Police Station? He had his suspicions.

Bruce radioed his superiors in Katherine to alert them to a problem for which there was no guidance in the police manual. He next called in his sidekick Dailly.

'Mate, I need you back here ... straight away,' said Bruce, without mentioning the money.

With Dailly back at Wave Hill, Senior Constable Bruce confronted his mate and asked determinedly if he knew where the money came from. Poker-faced, Dailly denied any knowledge. Bruce was unconvinced so with neither evidence nor confession he called headquarters in Darwin.

The next day, an irritated Detective John Maley flew in from headquarters. His chief concern was that his planned Christmas holiday might be interrupted by this case so he was keen not to waste time. He interrogated Dailly with all the banknotes spread out on the table for theatrical effect. Dailly's denials crumbled once the experienced and no-nonsense detective applied the blowtorch.

'Shit, when we saw the old lady was dead, we started to go through everything. There was all this money in a biscuit tin; we thought she didn't really need it and no-one would ever know. I divvied it up with my mate, we didn't even count it, just made equal piles. We left half for her and divided the other half between us. Am I still in trouble if they get the money back?' is how Maley remembered Dailly's eventual confession.

The record of interview tendered to the Supreme Court at the trial was somewhat toned down, with the prisoner 'making full admissions after his initial denials and was quite frank about how he came about the money and readily admitted he was aware of his duties'.

Dailly told his assembled police colleagues, 'I was going to shoot that dog ... it's a mongrel, but I felt sorry for it ... now it has betrayed me'. Maley wondered if the dog sensed he was going to cop a bullet and had done Dailly in first!

Maley noted that the young constable Dailly 'was a pushover, not some mean and nasty bastard, and once he knew he was caught he did not try to wriggle out of it'. Maley could not hide his disappointment that a policeman would breach the ethics of the force so cheaply.

In custody in Darwin, Dailly dobbed in his mate Purdie as recipient of half the money, but Purdie refused to answer questions formally or informally. His lawyer flat denied any crime and suggested a counternarrative – that Dailly squirrelled away all the missing stash and was using Purdie as a smokescreen. Detectives checked if Purdie had been on a spending spree of late and established that although Dailly had arranged to buy a car for cash next time he was in Darwin, no similar transactions or mysterious bank accounts were found to confirm Purdie's probable windfall.

To avoid a brewing public scandal and media coverage about 'thieving coppers', the top brass arranged Dailly's court appearance for late on Christmas Eve. Dailly was suspended without pay but allowed bail – an unusual liberty. No information about the theft leaked out until April 1982 when Dailly pleaded guilty before Mr Justice Gallop in the Supreme Court.

Reading the court transcript, it must have been an amusing day for everyone except Dailly. The judge was given the entire story, frog on the path, dog and all. The Crown explained that *'the general opinion of the deceased is that due to her thrifty business ways, she was in possession of a considerable amount of cash, coins, old bank notes and valuable jewellery'.*

The Crown conceded that other than succumbing to this temptation, Dailly carried out his duties in a *'proper manner'*. The money stolen was the second stash of notes, discovered after he had followed police procedures fully with the first.

Dailly was described by the prosecutor Mr Tiffen as a 24-year-old, originally from Scotland, who arrived in Australia aged nine. He had left school in Doveton, Melbourne, after completing only Year 3 of high school and worked as a labourer and truck driver. He had been a policeman in the Northern Territory for less than three years and had struggled to get through the basic police training. The court was told he had been depressed since being charged and would be dismissed from the force.

Mr Peter Ward appeared for Dailly and explained 'I'm from Melbourne and was admitted to the Territory yesterday' by way of introduction. He had little to work with but told the judge that, after initially following procedure to the letter, this immature, inexperienced and unsupervised policeman *'fell across a gold mine'.*

'His education is not the most appropriate for someone who had to discharge the onerous responsibilities that my client had … His lack of academic skills would have exacerbated the pressure in this difficult undergoing of his duties … This greatly tempting situation of a 23-year-old fairly new constable confronted with over $52,000 cash and valuable jewellery, old bank notes … an astonishing find. He finds himself in a situation far beyond where he should have been …

PC gets jail over buried $28,000

DARWIN. — A Northern Territory police constable who stole $28,000 from a deceased estate and buried it in a garbage bag in the backyard of a police residence has been sentenced to six months' jail.

The court was told the money was dug up by the constable's pet dog while digging for a frog in the backyard seven months after the bag was buried.

Constable Kevin Dailly, 24, who was suspended from the force after he was charged, pleaded guilty to larceny.

Mr Justice Gallop in the Northern Territory Supreme Court sentenced him to two year's jail but ordered that Dailly be released after serving six months on condition that he enter a $5000 two-year good behavior bond.

The crown told the court that Constable Dailly was the only policeman stationed at Wave Hill, 820 km south of Darwin, in May last year.

He was sent to May 10 to the Wanda Inn at nearby Top Springs to take possession of the assets of the proprietor, Mrs Thelma Hawkes, who had died.

The Crown alleged that the next day, Public Trustee officers arrived and Constable Dailly gave them $52,000 in cash and a quantity of jewellery.

The Crown alleged that Dailly had a further $28,000 and buried it in the backyard of his police residence at Wave Hill.

The court was told an Aboriginal tracker attached to the police station saw a large amount of money scattered about the yard while he was watering trees on December 14.

He had reported this to Katherine police.

Senior Constable Robert Bruce said he went to the police residence and saw a garbage bag, which appeared to be torn in a hole.

He said there was a frog in the hole and Constable Dailly's pet dog was nearby.

Senior Constable Bruce said he believed the dog had uncovered the money while digging for the frog. He said the money added up to $28,450.

The court was told Constable Dailly initially denied all knowledge of the money when questioned, but later admitted he had found it at the time of Mrs Hawkes' death.

Herald May 1 1982

succumbing to temptation, with no pre-meditation and of course Your Honour should take into account that this was a career-ending move.'

Mr Ward emphasised to Justice Gallop that his client only earned $15,000 a year and chanced upon an amount vastly greater than that. Ward told the judge that Dailly's years with the police had been the happiest of his life and he was facing ruin because of one bad decision. His wife had just given birth to their second child and there were great stresses in their lives. Dailly's pensioner father had flown in from Melbourne and testified how shocked the family were as Dailly had always been an honest and reliable son until this one terrible mistake. Ward pleaded that his client not be sent to gaol.

The next day, the judge recited the unusual facts in open court to the delight of the few journalists present.

'In the scale of larceny as a public servant the offence committed by the accused loomed large and grave. Not only did he succumb to the temptation to take the money, he furtively hid it and perpetuated the breach of trust. His crime was only discovered accidently. I am told it is inevitable that he will be dismissed from the police force with all the disgrace and dishonour appropriate for that dismissal. There are strong grounds for leniency, but I believe that the general public would expect a custodial sentence to be imposed in the circumstances of this case as a general lesson to police officers or other public servants who have committed breach of trust reposed in them by their office ...'

Dailly was sentenced to two years' gaol, to be released after serving six months, the remainder to be converted to a two-year good behaviour bond. The NT Police press release emphasised this was a rare example of police abusing their office for personal gain and claimed, counterintuitively, that the integrity of the NT police had been upheld by the prosecution and sentence.

And back at Wave Hill, when the news about the policeman going to gaol filtered through, the elders in the Aboriginal community all nodded with understanding and told anyone who would listen: '*That there frog? You know that frog, he the spirit of Old Ma Hawks.*'

CHAPTER 3
ARTICLES OF CLERKSHIP 1981

Fresh out of Monash University, I had just started work in a city law firm. It surprised many that I got there.

I was not celebrated for my commitment to my university studies. I was more of the 'do as little as you need to in order not to get thrown out' type of student. My father was a doctor and professor at the same university, with a distinguished medical academic career, and he and my physiotherapist mother were highly ambitious for their children. Both my parents were driven by typical migrant ambition. My father's parents both came from Russia but met and married in New Zealand. My paternal grandfather started his working life making leather bags and straps for the tramways. My father was the first in his family to go to university, and education was regarded as the key to success and status in the 'new world'. My mother's parents were shopkeepers before fleeing from Germany, and she too was the first to get a university education. Having just escaped from Hitler's Holocaust, survivor guilt dogged her to her end.

My slack approach to study was not in any way approved of by my parents; it was viewed as a frivolous indulgence – which it was.

Both my parents were appalled by my attitude and vociferously disappointed by my disinclination to chase academic excellence. Halfway through my final year of high school, they somewhat abruptly advocated it would be better for me to beat the school leaver rush and look for a job instead of sitting the final exams and crashing out without proper preparation. If they wanted to motivate me, their tactic succeeded, but it left me resentful of their lack of faith in their youngest child.

I left boys-only Melbourne High School with my HSC but was ill-equipped for the novelty of sitting next to girls in lectures at university. First year of university was the unhappiest year of my life. I was crippled with anxiety, desperate to feel I belonged. Almost no-one from my school group had gone on to Monash, and although there were lots of Jewish students at Monash Law School, they seemed to all know each other and formed a clique that was a carry-over from the Jewish secondary school they had all attended together. Most of my friends deferred the year, leaving me wandering around lonely and lost. I nearly dropped out a few times, only persevering out of terror at the parental reaction if I did, and barely cared about the formal studies. My results in the law subjects were terrible – in one assignment I was given 2/20 and the tutor suggested I rethink my choice of course. The Arts Faculty was more welcoming, and I preferred politics and history.

Second year improved when the gorgeous Debbie became my girlfriend and shared her affections with me for a while – she must have taken pity. University was not so much about studying, but it was definitely educational in a less conventional sense. It was where I went to smoke joints while trying not to cough, tried to master the five-string banjo, learned snooker, threw frisbees and protested over the dismissal of the Whitlam Government, which happened at the end of my first year. I still lived at home with my nagging parents, but having passed my driver's licence and blown $375 of my bar mitzvah money on a rusty, unreliable 1962 Renault 4 meant I could spend as much time away from them as I could manage.

After scraping through second year, and against parental advice, I deferred for a year. I worked in a local grog shop and then as a storeman at the corporate headquarters of Hertz Rent-a-Car, saving money to travel. I needed to grow up, and this was one way to do it. Work hours at Hertz were spent wrapping brochures, uniforms, stationery (to this day I still use paper clips and staples stolen from the Hertz storeroom) and advertising materials for dispatch to car rental depots around the nation. A good day was being seconded to take a truck or a new car out to the airport.

One day that August, my boss at Hertz surprised me by inviting me to the pub for the daily lunch special of a steaming bowl of barely edible spaghetti bolognese and the inevitable pot – or two – of VB. Ernie Pittorino was bespectacled, very short, very round and balding. He wore floral shirts with straining buttons over his belly and shiny brown trousers held to his overflowing arse by what must have been a magic belt. He waddled around the building all day, leering at the women in his employ. Our usual lunchroom conversation was his lewd speculation about which of the accounts clerks would be most likely to pleasure him, the inescapable truth being that none of the dozens of mostly gorgeous women, hired for reasons other than their professional credentials, were in the slightest bit interested and mocked him behind his back.

Slurping spaghetti at the pub, Ernie asked me if I was happy running the storeroom. 'It's running better than ever. You've got a great future in stores, Jon,' was his sincere and undoubtedly well-meaning career advice. My head spinning from his assessment, I reimagined my life overnight. The next day I gave Ernie a fortnight's notice, bought a round-the-world airline ticket and re-enrolled for the following year at university. Years later, the auditors uncovered that Ernie Pittorino was defrauding Hertz and he was sent to gaol.

While I was travelling in the US, my mother choked on a sliver of chop bone at a barbeque at home and suffered critical lacerations in her throat. Emergency surgery saved her life. As both my sisters were living overseas and had commitments and I was totally free, I rushed home to help my father with her long and slow recovery. It meant I got to spend hours and hours talking to them both – especially my mother – as adults, not as parents. Something good came from something bad.

When I resumed uni in 1978, as a 21-year-old third year who had grown up a bit, I moved out of home, found my tribe, smoked too much dope, learned to flirt and went to too many late-night concerts. There were more chaotic but stirring protests – Sir John Kerr and Malcolm Fraser were preferred targets ever since the Whitlam dismissal – and we had a lot of fun. I even started to appreciate my studies – a little. The law part of my course slowly started to make some sense alongside the Arts degree.

My first share house was in Elsternwick, a three-bedroom half house with rising damp, mouldy mushroom-coloured carpets and a tiny kitchen that we hardly used, and if we did it was to heat up a tin of soup. My co-tenants were my friend Robert, a psychology student who played a lot of guitar – very well; and Tony, a uni dropout and part-time taxi driver who, unbeknown to us, was also a full-time marijuana dealer.

One evening, after driving home from Monash, Robert and I were greeted by a large 'For Sale' sign attached to the front fence of our home. We had been given no warning whatsoever of this awkward development. As I was the resident law student, Robert expected me to know what this meant for our tenancy. Did we have to move or could we stay? Did we have to let prospective purchasers tramp through all the time? I had no idea, but I did know our rights if a passing steam train set fire to our haystack or a dam burst uphill from our farm. We were not taught anything particularly practical in my course. But I had recently discovered that some of my fellow students were volunteers at the Tenants Union Legal Service, so the next night I drove across town to get some advice from them.

I walked into an overcrowded waiting room at 80 Johnston Street, Fitzroy, a shopfront free legal service, and was greeted by someone I recognised from my Property Law lectures. 'What are you doing here? Have you come to help?' sighed a busy Alison, and shamefully I had to admit that I was there to seek assistance – from student advisors who were no further advanced in their degree than I was. How come they could provide advice but I couldn't? 'I need help, but it can wait – tell me what I can do?' was the only creditable reply possible, and she promptly handed over a clipboard and told me to take names, addresses and to establish the category of problem of the stream of distressed clients coming through the door.

From that night I volunteered every week for the next five years, and my law classes were never the same again. That 'For Sale' sign and discovering the Tenants Union Legal Service changed the course of my life.

Overnight, uni lectures gained meaning as I was now motivated to use my newly acquired knowledge to help the underdog – real people with pressing problems. More significantly, I met inspirational colleagues who are still friends forty years later. When I got the advice I had come for, I discovered that we didn't have to move house, but Robert and I soon went our separate ways anyway. Drug-dealing Tony was never seen again.

As the next few years of half-hearted study (but full-time student activism and shit-stirring) progressed and the end of my law course approached, applying for jobs in the city became more and more urgent. I never even thought about going to the country or even suburban firms – they simply were not on the radar. Snobbish as it seems, the hierarchies were clearly delineated and city law firms were the only measure of success. Putting on my ill-fitting suit and a thin blue stylish tie 'borrowed' from my father's cupboard, I endured sobering interviews with puffed-up law firm partners in intimidating wood-panelled offices. I was even once asked how much my parents were worth and would I be bringing any clients with me if offered a job. Hilarious.

In the final year of Monash Law, it was optional to spend a semester as a student advisor at the fairly new Springvale Legal Service, for which double points were awarded towards the degree. Following on from the recently established and radical Fitzroy Legal Service, this innovative clinical program was breaking new ground, providing the community with a valuable service at the same time as training law students in the practical realities of law. My first-ever client was a woman who had been savagely beaten by her husband the night before, could not go home and desperately needed help. I have never felt more useless, but the semester was invigorating and it was far and away the best subject the law school offered. It was much more interesting than tedious tax lectures, where I sometimes found myself sitting next to a Young Liberal activist called Peter Costello, one of a gang of precociously ambitious future politicians cutting their teeth on student politics.

The legal service experience was invaluable in learning the language of the law and using that lingo to impress during increasingly desperate job interviews. Eventually one envelope arrived that contained something other than a polite rejection letter, and I could relax knowing that I had at least secured a start on the career ladder. My new employers were to be Barker Harty & Co, a prestigious city firm that enjoyed a reputation for aggressive commercial litigation.

Meanwhile, I was spending more and more time volunteering at the legal service. It became a weekly reality check about how blunt a tool the law really was. Instead of examining the entrails of the rules of covenants, perpetuities and estoppel, I could use my skills to help someone avoid eviction or force a landlord to make urgent repairs.

The highlight of my last year at Monash was when a small group of us stirrers organised a protest in Canberra to coincide with an official visit by Queen Elizabeth to open the new High Court of Australia. As freshly committed legal aid activists, we were outraged to learn that more money was being spent on the

High Court of
Australia Fan Club
T-shirt.

one-day event in Canberra than the entire annual budget for
legal centres nationally. We decided to try to embarrass the then
Fraser Government into expanding the budget for legal aid by
offering free legal advice from a tent outside the High Court
while the lavish official ceremony was happening inside. With
housemate and fellow law student Bryce Menzies, we invented
the High Court of Australia Fan Club, sold T-shirts imprinted
with a cartoon of an ass in a judicial wig to raise money, and
stole headlines with street theatre based loosely on the musical
Oliver, featuring an impoverished legal centre worker begging for
more money for legal aid. Bryce's girlfriend and our housemate,
Stephanie Bunbury, delighted in the distraction from her
Honours thesis on semiotics in film and penned the lyrics, as
well as taking the role of Her Majesty the Queen to officiate
at our unofficial opening of the High Court. We hired a real
donkey and paraded it around the crowds, adorned with a mop

on its head to represent the judicial headgear, and, together with the street theatre, 'Please sir, could I have some more?' made it into all the media that day. We only regretted that we never even thought to fill the High Court fountains with bubble bath, which the police apparently expected us to do.

HCAFC
demonstration.

I finally finished at Monash in 1980 and moved to pre-trendy Fitzroy in Melbourne's inner city with Bryce, Steph and some other uni friends. In the last class on the last day of five years at Monash Law, I looked around the horseshoe-shaped lecture theatre and wondered which, if any, of my coterie I would consult for advice if I was in any trouble. I suppose my fellow near-graduates were wondering the same about me.

* * *

Barker Harty & Co was a ruthlessly commercial outfit. It was the first law firm in Melbourne to introduce time billing and was renowned for dropping clients who did not pay their bills on time. The partners were unapologetic that they were running a business alongside being top-shelf lawyers.

Each weekday morning, I would wake bleary-eyed and gobble down breakfast in the hectic share house where ten of us were negotiating the transition from student life to the workforce, much like caterpillars become butterflies. The huge George Street double terrace was a former ashram but became our sanctuary. We formed a wonderful clan, an eclectic replacement family of a few teachers, public servants, three fledgling lawyers, a journalist and then a few more whose occupations I still do not know. Huge parties gave the house an almost-deserved stellar reputation. Our home became a destination, a meeting point, a community. As we acclimatised to a 9–5 routine and the responsibilities that came with our work, the attendant need for a more disciplined lifestyle caught up and slowly snuffed out the remnants of our student years.

I would take Bryce's brother's unregistered and unroadworthy blue Honda 400/4 motorbike, kitted out with the desirable four-into-one exhaust, and blast off into Gertrude Street and then into the city, weaving around the traffic jams, past the white-gloved police on crossing duty. They obligingly waved me through each day, oblivious to the multiple offences I committed just by riding to work. As I sputtered down Collins Street on the poorly muffled illegal motorbike, my suit coat and tie flapping behind me, it seemed to me no impediment at all that I also did not have a motorbike licence. Rebel without a clue.

I usually tried to arrive early – to impress I am not sure who. Emerging from the lift onto the 26th floor with popping ears, I would usually greet Lynne, the heavily coiffed receptionist, and we'd have some small talk about last night's TV shows or the weekend's football games. Office banter about football and the ritual of the tipping competition was a social lubricant and key ingredient to survival. Some of the lawyers were rudely dismissive of the reception and secretarial staff, but I rapidly overcame my snobbery as I learned how invaluable were the small army of hard-working, savvy women.

Jack Harty, my 'principal', was the president of the lawyer's union – the Law Institute of Victoria. He was the firm's senior partner and a property lawyer, which is a glorified way of saying he did land conveyancing. Despite openly boasting that he did not know any actual 'black letter' law at all, he was very successful at looking after a huge portfolio of loyal clients ranging from sometimes-dodgy property developers to mostly elderly widows with lots of money to invest. Barrel-chested and balding, he strutted

Jack Harty in 1983,
Law Institue of Victoria.

around the firm in a tightly buttoned waistcoat and precariously balanced half glasses. He appeared fearsome, but in time I learned he was one of the funniest people I would ever meet and could charm the wallet out of anyone's pocket. Once asked, 'What did you do with your first million?', his instant response was a curtly snapped 'kept it'. The perfect reply.

The day I started in 'his' firm, he took one look at me, then opened his desk drawer and removed a pair of new long-nose pliers. 'Where is the earring, young Faine?' he chortled as the shiny chrome tool was waved high for my scrutiny. I had taken the precaution of already removing my earring so as not to offend his sensibilities, knowing full well that what had passed as cool at university – my signature green plastic elephant dangling from a sleeper – was not in any way acceptable in town. 'If it ever makes an appearance in here, I am ready ...' he said with a gleam in his eye.

My first week was spent mostly in the strong room, a windowless space lined floor to ceiling with a mess of archived files and thousands of envelopes containing old wills and property titles. No-one had cleaned it up for years and someone decided I would be the bunny to restore some order to the disarray. Had they spied on my CV that I had worked as a storeman? Maybe that is why I was employed in the first place. By day three of my glamorous new career as a trainee city lawyer, I was wearing overalls to work and went home filthy dirty and aching from lugging boxes and trolleys back and forth to storage. By week two I was entrusted with the footy tipping competition. By week five I was allowed to carry files and briefcases to an actual court and sit with the barristers, occasionally dispatched urgently to the court library to fetch volumes of law reports and tasked with the almost pointless routine of furiously trying to transcribe everything said in court by the witnesses, the judge and even the barristers. Although official transcripts were generated, they took 24 hours to appear, so my scribbled notes were sometimes the only reference point to what had been said earlier that day. I do not recall any occasion where anyone needed to check them, and it was just as well.

The mix of power and money was intoxicating, and I felt like a sponge, soaking it all up. The etiquette was fascinating, the clients almost all weird and the lawyers seemed wise beyond their years. Any encounter with a judge, no matter how remote, was terrifying. The ritual of Friday after-work drinks was a chance to hear war stories of triumphs and disasters from the twenty or so lawyers in the firm, all lubricated with a pre-commute scotch and ice or two.

For my first eight months, I shared a tiny office behind the reception desk with one other articled clerk. 'Chloe Handbags' I will call her. We could not have been more different. She had attended a posh private girls' school out in the eastern suburbs and made sure everyone knew it. I had been to a high school, albeit a selective one. She still lived with her parents and was a graduate of the establishment University of Melbourne Law School. I came from the younger, less prestigious Monash, a hotbed of student radicalism. Apparently, in her world, these were distinctions to which were attached great significance. To me, it was as important as which socks I was wearing.

Chloe arrived each morning at exactly nine o'clock, not a moment before or after. Perfectly styled hair, fingernails glossed, she dressed every day as if going to the races and brought three pairs of shoes to the office, two pairs tucked in her designer bag. One moderately formal pair was worn on the tram-ride into the city, another pair – white sneakers – were for comfortably walking around the office during the day and the third (at the cutting edge of fashion) were just for going out at lunchtime and meeting friends. As the year progressed, her negotiations for longer and longer lunches occupied most of the morning, and preparing for her looming engagement reception and regular dinner parties occupied most of the afternoon. As our desks were almost touching, there was no avoiding being privy to her endless telephonic prattle with friends and florists, which tediously seemed to get in the way of her actual work. By the end of her year as an articled clerk, she was managing just one file, an absurd piece of litigation about the unexplained death of an entire consignment of day-old chickens dispatched from a poultry farm. Inexplicably, and to the irritation of our bosses, she had amassed tens of thousands of dollars in costs for a Magistrates Court dispute worth but a fraction of that. I gave up trying to help her. Sorry, Chloe.

As my apprenticeship year was finishing, there was a massive dispute within the partnership and one day, with a slamming of the boardroom door, the two most junior partners suddenly quit. Within what seemed like mere minutes, a locksmith had appeared and all the door and filing cabinet locks were changed. A memo promptly appeared on all our desks to simply say that Guy Jalland and Roger Donazzan had left the firm and no further comment would be forthcoming.

Overnight, I was plucked from the articled clerks' broom cupboard office and moved into Roger's expanse, complete with views across the city. My immediate task was to go through all his filing cabinets, full of cases and advice he had abandoned, and provide memos about what needed doing and whether or not I thought I could do any of it. Anything complex or worth a lot of money, or that I could not understand, was to be handed over to my new boss, the senior commercial law partner, Peter Burden.

I could not believe my luck and sensed a once in a lifetime opportunity as I settled in behind a gigantic desk in the absurdly well-appointed office. My new routine was to arrive even earlier most mornings, utter a polite enquiry of the boss's secretary Elspeth about her ongoing affair with a married man, and then hit the files hard. The small office library became my friend as I had to instantly bone up on all the commercial law that I had deliberately avoided at university. I also discovered that the various long-serving secretaries knew almost as much as the bosses and were only too happy to teach me, seemingly pleased to be acknowledged. All of this had to happen before Peter arrived, so I could pretend I had been slaving away for the glory and enrichment of the partners of Barker Harty & Co since dawn.

My sense of self-importance was magnified by having not one but two telephones on the return attached to my desk, as well as a cassette-fuelled Dictaphone, its multi-buttoned microphone attached by a tightly sprung coil that endlessly wound itself into knots. My boss would direct files my way, usually with a long memo outlining specific steps required, as I slowly became proficient as a commercial litigator. When I was not distracted by the almost model railway–scale view of the city laid out so far below, I was masquerading as competent to commercial clients, who brought everything to us, from debt collection to building disputes, copyright claims, trademark applications, probate, partnership collapses and company director squabbles.

It was the lot of the most junior lawyer to have to do weird things that no-one else wanted to do, and Lynne, the telephonist/receptionist, started to use me almost as triage for enquiries and calls for assistance that did not readily fit the specialised diet of other lawyers in the firm and might waste their time. My daily workload ranged from arranging a barrister for the drink drive charges of the idiot son of a wealthy property developer to recovering substantial funds from a self-styled meditation guru who had established his own sex cult, preying on his patients in his unregistered counselling practice. I got a kick out of feeling useful.

I had been an apprentice, an articled clerk, in reality just a baby lawyer, for not even a full twelve months. I occupied a big office, shared a secretary, and clients telephoned – oblivious that I was still a trainee – and I was not in a rush to disabuse them of the conceit. The year flew and I was invited to stay on – my first year as a real solicitor. Chloe was politely thanked for her efforts and left for a job at the courts – as the associate of a judge who was a golfing companion of her father. Despite her lack of both enthusiasm and aptitude for the law, her new job meant she was immediately earning quite a lot more than I did. It stung a little.

At the end of the year, like all articled clerks, I prepared the swathe of documents required to prove my qualifications to be admitted as a real solicitor, not just a pretender. I would soon be able to appear in court, administer oaths, swear affidavits, wear pinstripes and posture with the rest of them. It required being officially certified by no less an authority than the Chief Justice of the Supreme Court of Victoria to 'be of good fame and character'. I deliberately inserted a typo into my official certificate and, as nobody picked it up, I may be the only person ever declared by the court to be of 'good frame and character'.

April Fool's Day is the traditional day for office pranks and in 1982 was also the day of the ceremony for my admission. I figured I could take some liberties and have some fun. Together with Fiona Low, the new articled clerk, we snuck into the office late the night before and left some traps to be discovered in the morning. As I would be going straight to the swearing-in ceremony, I would not get to witness the reactions when our bosses and colleagues arrived and discovered we had swapped around all the partners' framed degrees (it took weeks before anyone noticed) and that we had rotated the desks so that knees hit modesty boards when sitting and desk drawers were on the opposite side. One partner had a huge tropical fish tank along his office wall, and we tore the corner off a $1 note and laced it like bait to a fishing line and dangled it into the tank. I gambled I would be forgiven any indiscretions but was told later it was a close call.

I put on my best suit – dare I admit one of two, the other being from a charity shop – and matched it with an unfashionable tie again taken from my father's cupboard. I greeted my relieved but proud parents on the steps of the historic domed court complex. I never asked, but I suspect they doubted this day would ever arrive. Their annoyance with my shunning of any attempt at academic excellence had not waned.

My 'admission to practise' was to be 'moved' by a bewigged and gowned Tony Lawson, the chief lawyer at Fitzroy Legal Service, the anti-establishment free legal centre that pioneered what we called 'poverty law' in Australia. My anti-establishment streak had first drawn me to its embrace and, along with the nearby Tenants Union Legal Service, I was now a fully committed subscriber to all they stood for – equality before the law, access to justice, civil liberties, holding power to account. My evenings volunteering were much more spiritually rewarding than anything I did in Collins Street.

Tony had frocked up on my behalf to appear in the ceremonial courtroom before the ancient Chief Justice and two other bored judges to '*move that Jonathan Eric Faine be admitted as a barrister and solicitor of this Honourable Court and I so move on the certificate of the Board of Examiners*'. Then we all went out to lunch.

It was ritual to prepare a 'brief' to counsel who 'moves' your admission. The world of legal mumbo jumbo, code and unwritten etiquette shrouded in mysterious conventions had begun to shape me.

The documents confirming the right to join the profession ought to constitute the barrister's brief, and for the purpose of a ceremonial appearance like this one, it typically consisted of but two vertically folded pieces of paper contained within pale pink legal ribbon, just sufficient to ensure the name of the new lawyer is announced correctly to their Honours ensconced on the canopied bench.

I am embarrassed now to admit that my brief to Tony was wrapped up in a vivid red lacy thigh garter, not legal ribbon, and contained the original of every letter of rejection from the ninety or so other law firms where I had applied for a job. Buried within the folds of those letters was a large and badly rolled joint. It was my seditious hope that the illegal surprise within the bulging package might reveal itself only at the last moment as Tony stepped forward to address the judges and then and only then opened the brief.

He didn't and it didn't. Besides, none of my ultra-conservative bosses had bothered to come to court so the prank would have been somewhat wasted.

The next day, my first as a real solicitor, the office furniture was restored to normality, nothing was said about our prank and the files were all still there. My workload increased but at last

I was now paid more than a pittance. Gradually, I was allowed to interview clients solo and run my own files, and slowly was trusted with more and more complex cases. The partners even started to think I may one day be useful. I used them while they used me.

Not often did Peter Burden invite me to sit in on his initial conference with a new client. The day I started work on the Estate of Thelma Cecilia Hawks triggered an adventure and curiosity that persisted for years.

CHAPTER 4

THE 26TH FLOOR

The corner offices in any prestigious law firm are reserved for the most senior partners. Each corner of the 26th floor of 459 Collins Street hosted a ruthless champion who ruled over their empire. One corner was property law – conveyancing and mostly looking after land developers and builders. Jack Harty and his ever-present waistcoat kept it all humming along, a team of paralegals and solicitors servicing the procession of lenders and borrowers, buyers and sellers who came through the door. As a young bloke, boasting a total of a couple of hundred bucks to my name, I struggled to relate to the transactions and their significance. My first attempt at a conveyance cost the firm several hundred dollars because I failed to do the right calculations, and I was firmly instructed to never go near another one. I was very happy to oblige.

Diagonally opposite was family law – divorces, ghastly disputes about property and occasionally children, managed by the extraordinarily organised and authoritative Michael Taussig. His mind was as orderly as his handwriting, which was so neat that his perfectly penned memos were almost indistinguishable from typed ones. I got to glimpse one celebrated instance of an acrimonious divorce arising from the well-heeled couple's matching extramarital affairs, resulting in a bitter disagreement about who got the convertible Rolls-Royce and the mink bedspread. The lurid and mutually explosive affidavits were handed around for everyone's amusement at Friday evening drinks in the boardroom. They read like the plot outline for a tawdry soap opera. I desperately wanted to sneak off and make photocopies to entertain my friends back in the Fitzroy share house, but did not dare.

The often-locked door on corner three was tax territory. Graham Smorgon was the entrepreneurial partner who ran the business of the firm, as well as leveraging his reputation for innovation into a thriving tax practice. From a famous industrial dynasty, Graham up-ended the traditional conventions attached to being a genteel practitioner of the law and commercialised the firm along US attorney lines. Graham unemotionally policed the tyrannical time-billing system that divided the entire day into six-minute units that had to be allocated to a client, no matter what. Even a one-minute phone call had to be logged and was charged out as a minimum five-minute unit, meaning you could make five short calls and theoretically generate twenty-five minutes of fees in any five minutes of the day. Graham would demand that bills be sent monthly, overdue accounts settled within fourteen days, debts collected and clients threatened if they did not pay on time. 'Money in trust up front' was the usual mantra, but as cases rolled on, our bills kept flowing. If the client did not pay their bill on time, the strict rule was to advise them that you had to stop working on their file until the account was brought up to date. It was hard to balance a friendly and productive relationship with a client while at the same time threatening to discontinue working on their case unless they paid the bill. As well as corporate and personal tax minimisation, Graham's specialty was family trusts and succession planning for high-wealth individuals, of which the firm collected many. It was not unusual for a millionaire to ascend in the lift, sign a few papers in the office to establish a trust or other complex arrangement and then descend the lift technically penniless.

Rainmakers – high fee earners – magnetically attracted much more work than the partners personally could do and, in the purest form of capitalism you can find, they would shovel it out to the underlings like me to complete while the clients were charged what seemed to me to be massive hourly rates for the work. The partners made good incomes with no apologies for 'so doing', as the more pretentious of the legal profession say.

The fourth corner office housed the main commercial partner, my boss. Peter Burden sat behind mountains of paper and always conducted his lengthy telephone calls on speakerphone. He was a generous teacher with endless energy – bounding around the office on the balls of his feet – and rightfully enjoyed his reputation as a brilliant commercial lawyer who had an astonishing command of obscure legal principles and precedents. He was regularly consulted within the firm almost as an in-house brains trust.

Peter relished a challenge and, among other major clients, teamed up with a young Christopher Skase, as the then highly regarded entrepreneur rapidly expanded his empire. Skase was a former finance journalist who decided that he was just as clever as some of the people he was reporting on, quit journalism and went into business for himself. He seemed to rapidly make a fortune by juggling multiple enterprises, but the truth eventually emerged years later that it was all an unsustainable mirage based on massive debt. As the scandal broke, he fled overseas with his wife Pixie and fought a long-running extradition battle until his premature death in exile on the Mediterranean island of Majorca.

I was entrusted with litigating an absurd and costly dispute between Pixie Skase and her kitchen renovators, who had sued her when she refused to pay them – for a range of reasons, most of them petty, like a few crooked tiles. The most absurd element of the court case was the Skase family's outrage that the designers had provided an inadequate exhaust fan for the indoor barbeque in their newly renovated Toorak mansion's kitchen.

A substantial chunk of Peter's office real estate was consumed by his vast slab of a desk, as well as two huge soft leather couches on opposite sides of a low coffee table. The walls were lined by a bank of matching filing cabinets and bookshelves, all enveloped by huge tinted windows with eye-popping views out to the maritime traffic silently moving through the docks and Port Phillip. How anyone could concentrate with that distraction I have no idea, but being invited to sit in on a conference, while exciting and quite serious, was always a challenge; I just wanted to look out the window instead of take notes or listen to the clients.

Mid-morning on Tuesday 30 March 1982, I was dispatched to reception to usher new clients into Peter's office. Lynne nodded towards a group of four, perched nervously on the waiting room chairs, made up of three casually dressed teenagers and who

I correctly assumed to be their father. I tried hard to appear confident, announced myself and was greeted with a finger-crushing handshake by Paul Anderson, a short but square-rigged man in a dapper jacket and old-fashioned tie. The teenagers stepped forward, and in descending order of height and age shyly introduced themselves as Paul junior, Mark and Bruce. As we settled into Peter's couches, I could not help but register how incredibly uncomfortable they all seemed in this cosseted environment. I was barely used to it myself.

Cups of tea were offered. Mrs Thoms was summonsed, the unofficial cultural guardian of Barker Harty & Co. Ancient even by their standards, the diminutive tea lady pushed a creaking wooden trolley around the offices all day, keeping the entire staff caffeinated and biscuited. The etiquette for the tea trolley was rigidly imposed and regulated by the always cheerful Mrs Thoms, who seemingly pre-dated anyone in the firm by about ninety years.

The top deck of her trolley carried a triple-tiered biscuit tray, and her biscuit hierarchy was not open to dispute or appeal. The bottom tier was layered in scotch fingers and shortbread, strictly rationed for secretaries and articled clerks. The middle tier had Monte Carlos and 'cream-betweens', more generously granted to 'professional' staff, while the top tray had chocolate biscuits – Tim Tams and Mint Slices – which were dispensed without limits but were the exclusive privilege of the partners. The day after I was admitted as a solicitor, I clearly recall Mrs Thoms, false teeth whistling and clacking, excitedly inviting me to select my first Monte Carlo from the middle tier – after slogging through five years of law school plus a year of articled clerkship, I had arrived. I prided myself in often distracting her enough to steal a Tim Tam.

Peter Burden had been given the briefest of details about the Andersons before our conference, information provided by the accountant who had referred them to us. We only knew that Paul Anderson senior was the brother of the deceased, Thelma Cecilia Hawks, formerly Thelma Cecilia Anderson, who had died in May 1981. We had been told that she owned and ran a remote pub and roadhouse at a place no-one had heard of: Top Springs in the Northern Territory, described in the file note as being 'between Katherine and Darwin'. A search in the office library atlas left us none the wiser – it was too small to be marked. I later visited a map shop in the city and by consulting a larger-scale detailed survey map of the NT soon established that Top Springs was not between Katherine and Darwin – it was a speck on the map well south of Katherine and at the point where two occasionally used rutted red-dirt minor roads intersect.

The Northern Territory was so remote, and was virtually unknown to any of us in Melbourne – a mystical place: the wild north, a land of crocodiles and Aboriginal Australians. The Andersons' accountants had forewarned that there were multiple complications to do with the frozen estate, including a claim for a share lodged by a business partner, and years of arrears of tax not paid. Our client Paul Anderson senior was described as being a gym operator and fitness trainer, which I later discovered is akin to saying Phar Lap could run a bit, not that I knew anything about him back then.

As the discussions progressed, led by Paul, it became clear that although ten months had passed since his sister had been found dead at her pub, there was little progress in clearing any of these disputes and no sign of any distribution of her considerable estate. The family, who had been told they inherited the bulk of it, were impatient. Paul explained that they did not know why the estate was frozen, did not trust anyone up north and were convinced something suspicious was happening. The details were all vague and the lawyers they had initially consulted were unsurprisingly refusing to hand over any documents to them or us until they were paid their outstanding fees.

My notes of the conference – which I still have forty years on – show scant but scribbled details, names and phone numbers, and some speculation of what the estate may be worth. There was much mention of an act of 'larceny' – a garbled almost unbelievable tale about the police stealing a bag of money from Thelma's home after she was found dead. The amount stolen was $52,000 cash, which in 1982 was an extraordinary sum – enough to buy a comfortable family house in suburban Melbourne. Only half of it had been recovered. We were shown a copy of a letter from the NT Public Trustee, who was managing the estate. As Paul senior sought our advice, I was taken by his thin pencil moustache, his square shoulders and upright bearing, as well as his bear-like hands. He struck me from the start as a self-educated, no-nonsense fellow who spoke his mind and had little time for pleasantry or small talk. He was convinced that some evil forces were at work to rob his sons of their rightful inheritance, and we were tasked with urgently sorting it out. The three Anderson sons said next to nothing throughout the meeting and as Peter wrapped it up, he made various assurances and then astonished and ambushed me as he told them that 'Jon will be looking after you and will keep you informed'.

I showed the family out as far as the lifts. Excited to be getting my teeth into something new and different, I bounced back

NORTHERN TERRITORY OF AUSTRALIA

DEPARTMENT OF LAW

OUR REF

YOUR REF

TELEPHONE: 819311
P.O. BOX 470
DARWIN, N.T. 5794
TELEX: NTLAW AA B5436

THE PUBLIC TRUSTEES OFFICE
47 KNUCKEY STREET,
DARWIN

18th May 1981.

Mr Paul Anderson Snr.,
Guardian of Brian Anderson,
431 Elizabeth Street,
<u>MELBOURNE 3000</u>.

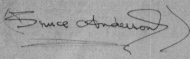

Dear Mr Anderson :

Re : Estate of Thelma Cecelia Hawks - deceased

Please accept my sincere sympathy in your recent loss. As
you have probably been made aware, Mrs Hawks left a will
dated 8th May 1967 in which she names the children of
Rhondahe Anderson and Alexander Anderson as the residuary
legatees, the 3 being Paul, Mark and Brian. I should first
like to make some comments on the will:-

1.   There may be a later will and we are currently
     enquiring with all solicitors and banks within the
     Northern Territory.

2.   Mr Leon Clancy has been appointed executor and whilst
     this clause has been deleted and signed by the Testatrix
     it has not been properly executed and is still effective.

3.   We are endeavouring to locate Mr Clancy but I do not
     think our chances of finding him are good.

4.   You must remember that your entitlement will only
     take place if the estate is solvent and if there is
     sufficient money in the estate to make the pecuniary
     bequest of $10,000.

5.   The bequest numbered 6 in the will to Norman Douglas
     is not effective as there is no business being carried
     on under the name of C.J. Hawks & Co. and nor is there
     any business being carried on on the Special Purpose
     Lease 89 which lease was surrendered many years ago.

2/ ....

The Public Trustee's first letter 18 May 1981 about the Estate of T C
Hawks, addressed to 'Brian' Anderson, not Bruce.

into Peter Burden's office and was immediately given a primer on disputed deceased estates. I had been working on probate files for some months already, but none that were contested. A better teacher I could not have asked for, but my head was soon spinning with concepts new to me such as 'remainder men' and 'residual beneficiaries'. I needed to hit the textbooks and in a hurry. At least I knew enough to appreciate that it would be rash and unwarranted to do anything without getting hold of the file from the previous lawyers, whereupon I could digest the history in appropriate detail.

In the meantime, we sent a telex to the Public Trustee of the Northern Territory in Darwin, John Flynn, to introduce us as the new lawyers for the Andersons and ask for any information he could provide.

I had no idea that my new client, the polite and demure Paul Anderson senior, the father of these three boys, he of the short frame but crushing handshake, was a living legend. This softly spoken but clearly determined man was famous – but in a world that was utterly foreign to me. Still ambitious and driven, even in his early seventies, his constant search for fame by performing death-defying feats of human endurance was only made possible by calling on some inexplicable inner strength, none of which was apparent on his visit to Barker Harty & Co.

The world's strongest man had just sought my help. In his world, he could do just about anything he set out to. In our world, he had no power at all. He was dependent on me – a nerdy, puny junior lawyer who he could effortlessly crush if he was minded 'so to do'.

CHAPTER 5
JOHN FLYNN

Within a few days, a parcel arrived from the Andersons' previous lawyers, the now vanished small city firm of Gill, Kane & Co. The NT Public Trustee had settled their fees, and they sent me their slim file – letters and telegrams back and forth to Darwin and, most importantly, a copy of the Last Will and Testament of Thelma Cecilia Hawks.

A degraded photocopy of a photocopy, originally typed on a wonky typewriter, it was in parts so faint that I struggled to make out the words. Most wills are unremarkable documents, reciting standard clauses that authorise someone to be responsible for initially sorting the affairs of the deceased and subsequently giving away their treasure. Thelma's last will was technically no different but came with some complications. Somewhat curiously, a crucial paragraph was emphatically crossed out with seven or eight heavy diagonal lines crisscrossed over the page with a pen. The target clause that must have caused some offence was unremarkable – it was just a typical recital where the person making the will appoints an 'executor', the trusted person charged with the solemn task of sorting everything out when you die and implementing your wishes.

John Flynn around 1982.

In 1967, Thelma had consulted a Darwin solicitor, Leon Clancy, who had prepared this will and, in typical fashion, was also appointed to be her executor. Lawyers preparing wills are often named as executors – it is a great income stream for them to handle the estate when their client dies. But for who knew what reason, and who knew when, someone – presumably Thelma herself – had defaced the will and tried to erase just that clause from the document. There was a signature in the margin next to the change, superficially identical to the signature at the bottom of the will, both showing a flowing, curly hand. In strict black letter law, and as the Public Trustee had already advised the Andersons, to countersign a handwritten alteration to a cheque, a contract or a lease may be a valid way of making a change, but it cannot work with a will.

Without going into the weeds of the law of succession, absolutely any alteration to a signed will can invalidate the entire document. The slightest mark, writing, annotation or even accidental damage calls into question the will-maker's intentions and can undo the document. So, what happened here? Why the exaggerated erasure and change of heart about her lawyer Leon Clancy? Living in as remote a place as she did, Thelma may well have decided that since she could not readily visit a lawyer to formally reframe her 1967 document, this modification was better than nothing, but why?

Neither Clancy nor any law firm with his name was in the phone book. Hoping to find where Clancy had moved to,

Flynn had called the NT Law Society and discovered that Leon Clancy had been struck off as a lawyer in 1970 and sentenced to six months' in prison for stealing money from his trust account. He was last recorded to be a patient at a 'mental hospital'. Presumably sometime after it became public that he was disgraced and that his ticket to practise was cancelled, Thelma had seemed to take matters into her own hands and had wisely decided to scrub any role for him from her will. But by doing it in the way she had, she created a bigger problem. If she had just left the clause alone, it would have been simple for her family to seek the unremarkable formality of substituting someone else in place of the disgraced lawyer. But by interfering with the integrity of the will, the entire document was now under a cloud. The Public Trustee would administer the estate, and no doubt John Flynn would take into account the wishes and intentions she had expressed in the now invalid parchment. But technically, any bequests in the will had lapsed and theoretically none of the gifts Thelma made needed to be fulfilled. Instead, her entire estate could be claimed by her family – our clients.

In her will, Thelma bequeathed ten thousand dollars jointly to her brother Paul Anderson and his wife, Rondahe Anderson. There had been but a brief mention of the existence of a Mrs Anderson when Paul and his sons had visited the office, but it had not been made clear what had happened to her. It was obvious that they were no longer together, but beyond that we had not been told anything about her. Nor had there been mention that she was the recipient of not just money but *all my watches, jewels, trinkets, personal ornaments and wearing apparel* as well. The valuations obtained by the Public Trustee for the purpose of administering the estate stated that the jewellery was worth over $25,000, an enormous amount back in the early 1980s, enough to buy ten new Holden Commodores.

The 1967 will went on to bequeath Thelma's share in the company that owned the pub at Top Springs to a Mr Norman Douglas, also of Top Springs. The remainder of her estate, whatever it amounted to, was bequeathed to the children of Paul and Rondahe Anderson, but only once they turned twenty-one, which none of them had yet done. The final provision in the will said, '*I exclude my husband Cedric James Charles Hawks from the benefits and provisions of this my Will he already having been provided for during my lifetime*'. There had been no mention whatsoever of a Mr Hawks in conference with our clients a few days before.

At least we now had a start. The kids got the bulk of Thelma's estate once we could work out how to deal with and resolve her debts and any claims, whatever they were. I asked Lynne at reception to book a long-distance call for a chat with John Flynn in Darwin. I had no idea what to expect, but I knew he controlled the estate purse strings. Apart from anything else, and uppermost in the mind of my boss, he would pay for my time and Barker Harty & Co's fees. I scoured the previous lawyers' file over and over to glean any clues that would help me maintain the fragile façade of seeming to be across things when Flynn and I spoke for the first time.

In the file were several long letters from Flynn to Gill, Kane & Co in which he explained how confusing Thelma's affairs were and how many knots had to be untied. Firstly, the business of the pub had to continue uninterrupted or the liquor licence could be cancelled by the NT Liquor Commission.

Secondly, the 1967 will gifted her share in the company that then owned the pub to her employee Norman Douglas. He was the only other shareholder – two shares, one each. However, by the time Thelma died that company no longer existed. A new company with a different name had been substituted years before, and that entity now owned the pub and the valuable liquor licence. Therefore, Mr Douglas was left with nothing. Had Thelma done this deliberately? Had she disinherited Norman Douglas or was it just the unintended consequence of a change in the way the business ran?

By way of simple example – if your will specifies that you want to leave a Holden to a relative, but in the time between making the will and dying, the Holden has been replaced with a Ford, then the relative does not inherit the Ford. The bequest is specifically for a Holden. If you leave 'my car' to someone, and do not specify the make, then the Ford does get passed on. Likewise with shares in companies.

Flynn explained painstakingly in his letters that Mr Douglas had hired Darwin lawyers who, unsurprisingly, insisted that whatever the technicalities, Thelma's intention in 1967 was clear – if she died, he got to own the pub in recognition of his many years of service, much of it unpaid. He claimed it was an agreement between them that he would work unpaid but eventually be rewarded when either she died or the pub was sold. On the other hand, the Andersons' previous lawyers argued that Thelma well knew what she was doing and it was a deliberate move made in the full knowledge that a change in the company that ran the pub and owned the licence would undo the bequest in her outdated will. Norm was not entitled to anything was their assertion.

Thirdly, neither the business nor Thelma had paid tax for years and the ATO wanted to be informed about how the estate was intending to bring the considerable arrears up to date.

Another problem was that Thelma had for some years been collecting an age pension – to which she was not entitled. In the same way that the tax officials were poking around asking questions, so too was the social security department.

The final complication was an astonishing array of people coming forward claiming that Thelma owed them money, some claims going back for years and with little to no supporting paperwork or documentation.

Her estate, to put it politely, was in disarray. The debts and claims against it could eat away much of the value, leaving little for the teenage nephews.

My eleven pages of astonishingly neat handwritten notes from my first call with Flynn take me right back there. I was perched behind my newly acquired ostentatious desk, executive-style swivel chair pulled in close, fingers clenched over the silver Parker pen that I had been given as a bar mitzvah present but until then had never used. Moving into a real office and working as a proper lawyer meant the old plastic Bic biros with chewed ends were no longer good enough. I had adopted the first affectations of a smug city lawyer.

John Flynn spoke deliberately, with a broad country accent, and struck me as a fast-thinking but slow-talking wise owl. I had no idea of his age, but imagined him to be ancient. Trying hard not to show how thin was my understanding of the intricate details of estate law, and how shallow my knowledge of accounting tricks, there would have been a lot of audible nodding and hints of agreeing at my end as Flynn led me patiently through it all.

Flynn spent some time giving me context to the problems of Thelma Hawks' estate – the unique challenges she faced from living in such an isolated spot and why that had such an impact on everything we needed to do now she was dead. He walked me through the remoteness of the pub, the logistical complications of that location, the thirty years' work that Thelma had invested to build a business in such an unconventional setting as Top Springs. He explained to me the decades of devoted service by Norm Douglas and pointed out that in all those years, Douglas had not been paid a wage – other than in board and beer. A lot of beer. To my query as to why anyone would do that, he said and I noted: 'That is how it is in remote pubs … .' As I was to discover, there was more to it than that.

We talked about the money stolen by the policeman and how it was complicating the winding up of Thelma's estate. The policeman was due in court in just a few weeks; after the trial the court would return the 'exhibit' of the stash of money to the estate and Flynn would bank it in his trust account. But counterintuitively, the mere existence of such large amounts of cash sloshing around created a problem. Cash could only be explained as undeclared takings from the pub and we knew the tax office was after their share: the more cash was disclosed, the higher the potential tax bill.

Thelma's receipt of the age pension for some years was causing a headache. When she died she was still one year shy of being eligible for a pension and was working full-time, running a lucrative business. Therefore, as well as anticipating an assessment of several years of arrears of income tax, the government was likely to claim repayment of years of pension and penalties. Flynn explained he was also trying to make sense of a web of interlocking loans from related companies, bank accounts with substantial deposits randomly established all over the nation and mystery transfers and transactions that seemed to serve little purpose other than to confuse anyone – especially the tax office – who wanted to know how profitable her pub had been.

The details of claims from suppliers for unpaid bills were extensive. They covered everything from grog, food and fuel to even the architects who had designed the pub when it was rebuilt around ten years earlier, claiming they were still owed $7197. That claim was so old it was regarded as 'stale' and statute barred from being recovered through the courts.

Flynn anticipated a guilty plea at the looming court hearing in Darwin for Constable Kevin Dailly, who had admitted stealing only $28,550 from Thelma's flat. The police alleged that when Dailly had stolen the cash he had found much more – and the sum over which Dailly had been charged was only half the total stolen. The other half had vanished – along with Dailly's good mate Purdie, who was alleged to have trousered it. We tossed around the dilemma. If we sued Purdie – if we could even find him! – it could cost us more than we gained. Whether we got anything back from him or not, the estate would be assessed for income tax on the amount claimed. We could end up with an additional tax bill of about $10,000 whether we got Purdie's $28,000 back or not. Flynn recommended forgetting about it – writing it off altogether. It was a huge amount of money to forgo, much more than I would earn that year. It was maddening to have to even consider letting someone get away with such a substantial theft.

For the time being, Top Springs pub had stayed open with a short-term lease and licence granted to neighbour Dick Philip, who Flynn had appointed out of desperation and necessity. As the reputedly wealthy local from a nearby cattle station had been in negotiations to buy the pub from Thelma, he was the logical candidate for a stopgap operator. Philip was still keen on the pub, as talk of local roads being sealed to attract tourists and construction of a long-proposed local abattoir had never gone away.

Flynn also asked me to authorise a formal property valuation of the pub so we would have an independent idea of a fair sale price, and to avoid any concerns that he might sell it too cheaply. As he explained, in the city or even in a large town like Katherine, it would be simple to organise an auction, but for a unique asset like the Top Springs roadhouse it would not be suitable. It was so remote, hardly anyone would travel that far to take a look. Only locals would understand the nature of the business on offer, and they would likely talk to each other and collude to avoid genuine competition. If there was little interest and no bids, then there was no floor for future negotiations.

The accounting details were tedious. Thelma's Darwin accountants had arranged the business to minimise tax, as most accountants do. The pub was an entirely cash business, long before credit cards and EFT were invented, but the nearest bank was in Katherine, a seven-hour round trip away. That there were large bundles of cash sitting in a tin waiting to be banked on Thelma's infrequent visits to Katherine was unsurprising.

Over our extended phone call, we studied an inventory of the estate, with Flynn talking me through a list of six bank accounts with term deposits lodged at different banks all over

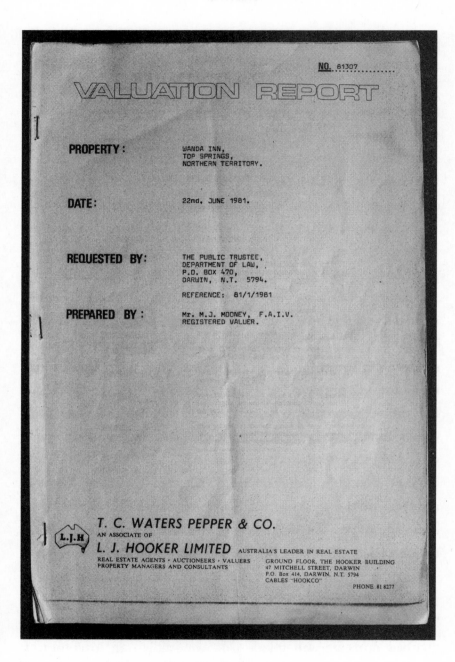

Flynn commissioned the first valuation report of the Top Springs pub in June 1981.

Apollo and his two older sons visited Thelma's pub after her death in 1981.

Australia, equipment at the roadhouse, pumps, fridges, trucks and utes, food and grog supplies down at the pub, her jewellery, a Browning automatic pistol and so on. With a slightly raised tone of excitement in his voice he told me there was a stash of old banknotes – pre-decimal currency, mint notes in series – that would be of some considerable interest to collectors. There were thirty-one ten-pound notes in sequential series, and almost two hundred pounds in other pre-decimal notes, many of these in mint condition. It was fifteen years since decimal currency had been introduced, and these were not just leftover takings from the pub; Thelma had bought and kept these as collectibles.

Flynn next discussed the considerable jewellery that in Thelma's will had been left to Rondahe Anderson, who had barely been mentioned by her ex-husband Paul. Flynn was very guarded in his explanations, but after enquiries had made contact through an intermediary and found the former Mrs Rondahe Anderson was living interstate. He would not tell me which state or any other details whatsoever. She did not want her ex-husband to know her whereabouts, and Flynn was under strict instruction to not even tell me how he made contact with her. 'She's terrified that if her ex finds out where she is, he will track her down and kill her ...' he said, without the slightest hint of drama in his voice. Apparently, there had been an acrimonious split years before, when the sons were very little, and he knew of no contact since. Mrs Anderson had left to start a new life with another man and Mr Anderson – my polite and softly spoken client – was thought to be capable of terrifying violence if he found her. I thought the insistence on absolute secrecy was somewhat melodramatic but said nothing. In hindsight, I am ashamed at my lack of curiosity about such a claim.

As we wrapped up the briefing, and as I thought I had managed to scrape through without making a complete fool of myself, Flynn surprised me.

'The only way you can really get this thing sorted in any reasonable time frame is to come up here to Darwin as soon as you can and eyeball some of the people involved. If you won't come, then I need the Andersons to indemnify me for any deals I strike without you,' said Flynn, as if flying to Darwin on business was something I would do all the time. I nearly fell off my fancy chair!

I gingerly presented myself to the adjacent office, where my boss was on the phone. Hopping from one foot to the other, I told his secretary Elspeth what had happened on the call with Flynn and that I was being called to depart as soon as possible to Darwin. Elspeth was not just smart as a whip but also the office party girl, enthusiastically organising after-work drinks and weekend parties, or a trip to the snow or the beach. She was

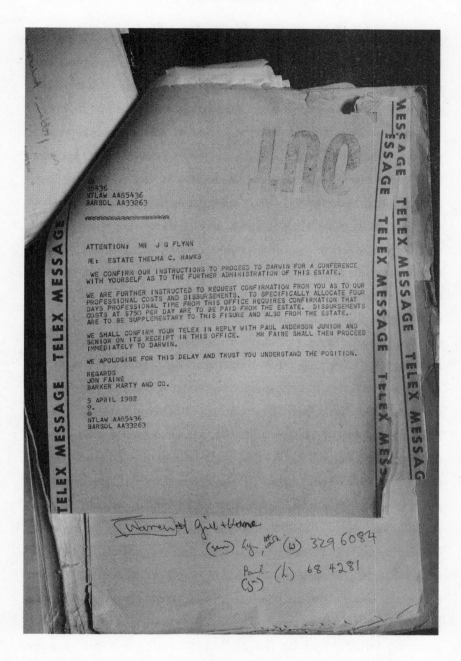

Barker Harty & Co telex to John Flynn in Darwin, 5 April 1982.

glamour personified, ruthlessly efficient, relied upon and trusted by the most valued clients. She snuck a quick hug, told me how jealous she was and slipped a note under Peter's nose that I needed five minutes with him. I was soon waved in.

Peter greeted the suggestion I go to Darwin with a loud guffaw. 'Why can't it be done over the phone?' was his first challenge, which gave me a chance to impress him with how much I suddenly knew about remote outback pubs and their unique challenges. 'That's exactly why I didn't run this file,' he said after my recap. 'As long as they cover your fees and you get that watertight and in writing from the Public Trustee ... then off you go. Have fun.' I detected a slight twang of envy in his upbeat words. But it seemed that I was on my way, and I could barely contain my excitement. If high fives had been a thing in 1982, I would have hit Elspeth for a double on the way out the door.

That night, back in the Fitzroy share house, I was hyper-excited. This is the life, I declared to my curious and, I suspect, envious housemates as we scoffed tasteless overcooked spaghetti or stir-fry chicken with rice or whatever disgusting concoction was passing as dinner that night. I remember the rush of adrenaline, the slightly altered self-regard with which I held myself, and the growing realisation that I was no longer the class clown and wannabe lawyer. What a buzz; only just freshly admitted as a solicitor and immediately trusted enough to be jetting off on a junket, summoned to the exotic Northern Territory. I would be away less than a week and scoured my inadequate wardrobe, guessing what might be the clothes a visiting hot-shot lawyer should wear to a meeting in the provinces. If I had owned a safari suit and a pith helmet, I would have packed it.

CHAPTER 6

THE MIGHTY APOLLO GYM AND COMBAT CENTRE

As soon as my Darwin trip was confirmed, I visited Paul Anderson, to ensure I knew what would be an acceptable outcome for his three sons. There were so many loose threads; the more I could understand what he thought was reasonable, the better to represent their interests up north. The notion that a lawyer would visit the client rather than the other way around was bordering on the unprofessional according to my bosses, but I had a sense that Paul Alexander McPherson Anderson, fitness instructor, was not like any other client I would ever represent. He had an aura, a mystique that piqued my interest. My instincts were not wrong.

The rapidly thickening file and a pad of Barker Harty letterhead notepaper were stuffed into my op-shop leather briefcase and I headed off with one of the tightly rationed taxi vouchers to a three-level warehouse in Hawke Street, West Melbourne, a semi-industrial and down-at-heel area on the fringe of the CBD. It was unfamiliar territory for me, a part of

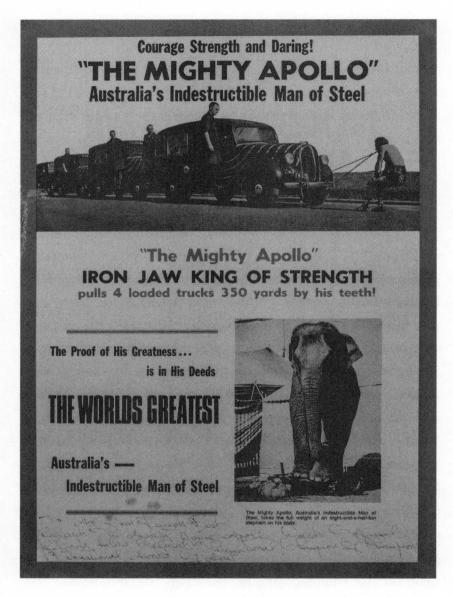

One of the many posters promoting The Mighty Apollo, this one autographed.

Melbourne I had never visited, even though it was only a twenty-minute walk from the office.

The warehouse was surrounded by panel beaters' workshops and auto mechanics' yards, but a signwriter had years before done a great job plastering 'The Mighty Apollo Gym' across the top tier of the yellow façade in chunky black letters. Expanding on the oversized ad for the gym were more signs in huge fading letters alerting passers-by to the martial arts centre, sauna, karate studio, bodybuilding and 'Commando and Unarmed Combat' classes offered within.

It fleetingly crossed my mind that I was about to enter another world, but I was so focused on the need to play the flash, competent young city lawyer that I barely hesitated. I had acquired the self-confident shell, the cocky veneer of superiority, that infects so many who inhabit high-rise towers. My working life had become a diet of legal combat, smart-arse tricks, turning aggression on and off as if it was on tap, finding loopholes and trying to extract commercial or strategic advantage when there seemed none. Unsurprisingly, my work diet was subtly changing me without me even realising.

I took the industrial wooden staircase lined with posters and advertising, mostly peeling and yellowing with age, spruiking long-ago boxing matches and wrestling bouts. Signs directed me to the top floor. Through a huge steel sliding fire door, I walked into a vast open space with sawtooth roofing and frosted glass windows. The floor was crowded with bodybuilding and weightlifting equipment and a symphony of noisy customers doing everything from clean and jerk of barbells and weights to hitting speedballs and punching bags. In one corner was a boxing ring, in another a stack of kettle bells, cannon balls,

Apollo displayed his trophies, sashes, antiques and prize belts around the gym.

more barbells, discs the size of tractor wheels, hand weights, chest expanders with glistening springs, and a collection of other devices which all looked deadly. Spread out across every wall was a veritable museum of memorabilia. Aging and fraying banners, posters, huge fading photographs in dusty frames and leather boxing trophy belts covered in tarnished silver badges. Instructional display boards showed silhouettes of men demonstrating technique for squats, push-ups and every imaginable wrestling hold. Most intriguing of all were the shelves of vintage and even ancient weapons of every kind, with swords, battle axes, flintlock muskets, helmets and duelling pistols all on dusty display. Model sailing ships, stuffed birds in glass cases, primitive art from across the Pacific islands and Africa, posters of bullfighting, suits of armour and old military uniforms completed the colourful scene.

Roaming freely between the machines, gently instructing people to 'straighten your legs' or 'protect your back' was the nuggety tracksuited man I'd come to see.

Paul greeted me warmly and ushered me into his office, a partitioned corner of the gym wedged against the windows, sparsely furnished with an old student desk. Either of the two ancient unmatched chairs with torn vinyl seats were offered as Paul boiled the kettle and made us tea. Out of the corner of my eye I saw a single bed, little more than a camp stretcher with a grey army surplus blanket over the top, behind a heavy velvet drape. His kitchen, if it deserved that title, consisted of a tiny gas stove, a single shallow sink with a cold-water tap fed by a wobbly pipe clinging to the wall, and a bar fridge, tucked under the inadequate bench. The overall impression conveyed was an air of bachelor dishevelment; comfortable it was not. There was no sign of his three sons nor anywhere for them to live.

Before we got to the real purpose of my visit, I had to ask: 'Paul, are you the Mighty Apollo?' I may as well have asked him if he was a giraffe. Indignantly, he straightened, and as he said the words, cliche though it may be, he grew taller and bigger before my eyes. 'I was the Young Apollo when I started out, but now I'm not young anymore am I?' he rasped in his gravelly voice. He immediately ushered me out of the kitchen to the gym and granted the first of many tours of the memorabilia and trophies that completely covered the walls. He showed me huge, framed panoramic photos depicting a much younger Apollo in circus big tops with massively muscled men posing in classic strongman positions, arms on slender hips or holding bathing beauties above their heads. There were lions in cages, elephants doing tricks, an impressively handsome young man with a vee-shaped torso in a Tarzan-style skin, and many photos of acrobatic routines involving women in skimpy costumes being tossed and twirled. Wide-eyed with this fresh information, I needed to rapidly recalibrate my understanding of my client.

Apollo's scrapbooks record every part of his career: adagio dancing with Thelma and a Tivoli co-star.

Apollo in his gym was lord of his domain. While he might have looked ill at ease in our office, here it was me who did not fit in. He led me across the matting floor past a few sweating giants who seemed to be the very people I would cross the street to avoid at night. All the customers were massive men, utterly intimidating to me. They reminded me of the Beagle Boys characters from Donald Duck comics. These huge guys, monstering each other in the boxing ring, lifting impossible weights, throwing each other around in martial arts exercises and putting muscles on top of their muscles, all smiled and warmly deferred to and greeted Apollo as he escorted me across the vast cushioned floor. I was certainly safe here with the master.

We stopped by the first glass trophy cabinet and he recited a story to accompany each of the dozens of prizes inside. '*This one was for being crowned Champion of Champions, strongest man in the world and other grandulous* [sic] *titles. I was the King of Strength, and outlived many of those who claimed they were higher royalty than me. They eventually disappeared, but I endure and go on forever as a legend. This trophy was for doing a charity show, where I pulled five cars down the road with a hide toggle in my teeth, even though it had never been performed before and everyone said it could not be done. Have you seen the TV ad which shows me pulling the fully laden tram uphill with my teeth? That made me even more famous, and that led to more television shows. I've been on all the big shows with the biggest personalities – Bert Newton and Jimmy Hannan … This one is of my most famous achievement, a five-ton elephant stood on me – it nearly killed me … I was bleeding from the bowel for months afterwards … no-one else has ever survived that …'* and on the monologue went. The history leapt off the walls as I stared.

It was akin to walking into a museum or memorial, my gaze constantly stopped by some astonishing piece of silverware that told another story, or a poster-sized photo of a leotard-wearing Apollo doing something impossible. It was irresistible.

As Apollo showed me around, he talked about his involvement with the legendary Tivoli theatre, Wirth's Circus, with travelling boxing troupes, to sideshow alley and freak shows. I felt like a

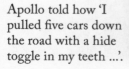

Apollo told how 'I pulled five cars down the road with a hide toggle in my teeth …'.

time traveller back to an era of circus and the already extinct travelling shows. I tried to absorb Apollo's stories but was close to sensory overload – crashing noises from weight machines, sweaty smells, shouted exhalations and throaty grunts, leather on leather smacking sounds and flashes of physicality wherever you looked. I was acutely conscious that I was supposed to charge Apollo for my time, but was already so distracted that I was not even aware of how long this was taking.

Pointing to one of the posters, I asked, 'How do you do these stunts?' Apollo narrowed his eyes to a squint and politely but firmly corrected me. *'Jon, these are not stunts. Stunts are trickery,*

Apollo in one of his personalised track suits.

like illusion, or magic. But what I do is real, these are feats of strength, my inner strength, calling on my special powers, which means I can do things which no-one else can match … no-one, not here, not anywhere in the world.'

Matching Apollo's inner strength was my inner sceptic. I simply could not reconcile the diminutive man in front of me with the claims of incredible strength photographically portrayed on the walls. A circus or sideshow strongman was not five foot and a bit tall (or 162 centimetres) but typically seven feet high and built like an ox. Weren't they? The strongest man on earth was not going to be short, squat, greying at the temples and hanging around West Melbourne. Surely all of this was trickery, or at best just showbiz hyperbole?

We took our leave from the action in the gym and retreated again to his accommodation behind the drape to discuss his sister's estate. Apollo told me he was convinced his sons were being robbed *'by everyone. The copper, the lawyers, the banks – everyone is robbing us and it's not fair, you have to put an end to that …'*

He touched on his own humble beginnings. He'd grown up one of five children in a very poor family, in nearby Collingwood, and once he'd started his showbiz career, his only sister, Thelma, had performed with him. *'She fell for an air force bloke and headed north after the war and although we had stayed in touch, she was so far away – it was hard. She was planning to retire and then reunite us, to sell the pub and move back to Melbourne. She reckoned she would have enough money to buy a house so that we could live with my three boys again as a family. You seem like a decent bloke, Jon; go to Darwin then, and can you make sure we don't get robbed anymore?'*

I was moved by his simple and entirely reasonable request. I told him I would do whatever I could, while acutely aware that Barker Harty & Co would not give a toss about anything except getting paid for my time.

I uncomfortably asked him where his sons lived. '*They don't live here with me – I can't look after them. I would love us all to live as a family but it just isn't possible. There's no room for them here. I have to run the gym and they are better off where they are.*' I do not remember asking what that meant. I had no independent contact with his sons and as he was their guardian, I did not question him about it.

As I went down the stairs, I decided then and there that this was far and away the most interesting file I had and that the Anderson sons and their enigmatic father were going to get red carpet treatment. I wanted to know more about Apollo the man, not just Apollo the client. I wanted to hear the stories behind each and every one of the hundreds of artefacts and posters that were adorning the vast walls of his old-world gym.

CHAPTER 7

DARWIN

TAA flight 480 departed Melbourne Airport at 7 am on Tuesday 6 April 1982. My surprising jet-setting assignment meant that I had hardly slept, convinced that I would miss my alarm. We flew via Brisbane, and I was shocked and then terrified as it became apparent all arriving passengers would have hand luggage searched by airport security. I must have looked vaguely corporate instead of hippie, as the police only glanced into my bag, mercifully not finding the two joints I had stashed in a corner of my leather briefcase in case of opportunity or emergency. My entire career – my life – could have turned out totally differently. Imagine if I had been arrested at Brisbane Airport for possession of marijuana in the era of then Queensland premier and all-round quasi-dictator Joh Bjelke-Petersen. I would have been struck off as a lawyer, sacked from my job and disgraced. The close call left me shaken, so I snuck off and threw the offending joints into the bin inside the airport toilets and thanked my guardian angel. This sliding-doors moment and brush with near disaster was a major contributor to the immature me deciding it was time to shed my undergraduate skin and embrace the new reality, that of a more – slightly more – respectable member of society. The longer leg of the flight to Darwin was far less stressful.

Getting off the plane in any tropical destination is a reality check for anyone from temperate zones. The thick air tickled my nostrils, and my polyester shirt started to stick to my back even before I got inside the ramshackle terminal. John Flynn was waiting to greet me. We had spoken a few times on the phone and he was younger than I expected, around forty to my tender twenty-six. I am certain he was disappointed to meet me in the flesh as I was so obviously inexperienced and not likely to be of much use to him in sorting the accounting and legal technicalities of Thelma Hawks' estate. He must have immediately realised that he would be doing all the heavy lifting. He was a little shorter than me, but trim, and looked sporty and fit in his deep-north uniform of grey knee-length shorts, long socks and black lace-up shoes. His crisp white shirt had epaulettes. His handshake was firm and his gaze direct.

He asked me straight up if it was my first visit to the Territory. Upon confirmation he audibly sighed and said, 'I hope you enjoy your time – it's not like down south. Things work differently up here ...'

Flynn explained, apologetically, that although I was just off the plane after flying most of the day, and even before we went to my hotel, we had to immediately meet with Dick Philip, the temporary publican at Top Springs, who was at the airport but about to fly out to Indonesia. It would be my only opportunity to talk to him, as he would be away the rest of my short visit. I was completely unprepared and felt somewhat anxious at the ambush. Our meeting served as my sharp introduction to the essential ingredient of doing any business in the Territory – ice-cold beer.

Flynn led me across the crowded, hot building and we found Dick Philip at the airport bar. Under the slowly revolving ceiling fans, sweating freely, I met a huge man in a cowboy hat and an open-necked blue shirt and moleskin pants, who put down his beer to crush my soft hand in greeting. He towered over both of us, but Flynn seemed unfussed, so I adopted what I hoped was a similarly nonchalant pose. Nothing at law school, nor what I had picked up hanging around the courts and boardrooms and plush lobbies of corporate Melbourne, had prepared me for this.

Flynn talked through the challenges in managing the pub and its licence and the imperative for Wanda Inn to stay open while negotiating a sale. My contribution was some carefully choreographed nodding and the occasional 'I agree' as I desperately tried to disguise my terror at being exposed as useless. Without much preamble, he asked Dick Philip if he wanted to put an offer to me on behalf of the Andersons, as beneficiaries of Thelma's estate, to buy the property outright. Dick Philip seemed impatient, distracted and non-committal. He made excuses for not being able to even say what he thought the pub was worth.

Undoubtedly, the two locals had been talking to each other before my plane arrived, and their negotiations seemed to me to be somewhat rehearsed. The true purpose of this meeting was not to finalise any deal, but so they both could size me up. I was non-committal on anything except making it clear that the Andersons were in no hurry (not true; pure bluff, they were keen to get things moving) and that they wanted to ensure they could realise as much from the sale of the pub as possible. During a half-hour chat, as I sipped cautiously on a lonely XXXX stubby, Flynn and Philip went through several each as they dissected the commercial opportunity and the complications presented by the pub at Top Springs. Despite the urgency caused by Philip's imminent departure, nothing concrete emerged.

As we left the airport, the humidity squeezed my lungs. Flynn drove me to the oasis of air-conditioned calm that was the Hotel Darwin, and we agreed to meet up again early the next day. At hotel reception I offered up my telex confirming the booking with a lawyerly flourish. Rebuilt after Cyclone Tracy in Christmas 1974, the hotel was already tired, but the ferns and greenery of the lobby and courtyard were delightful amid the bustle. The bar was doing a thriving trade, a meeting point for the Darwin corporate set who needed somewhere slightly up-market for their wheeling and dealing. Soon after unpacking, wanting to stretch my legs, I wandered around central Darwin, everything tightly shuttered after closing, keeping a wary distance from the drunks of all colours, of which there was no shortage.

Darwin was then and still is the most multicultural of Australian capital cities – an invigorating and exciting mix of people with Indigenous, Asian, Islander and European backgrounds, unlike any other part of Australia. Although I had travelled a lot and widely, both with my parents as a child and as a student backpacker, Darwin was a novelty. It was like an Asian or Pacific Island city but within Australia – the smells and sounds were unlike anywhere else I'd been. This was a different Australia and I could feel myself drawn to it. I had no clear idea of the ingredients, but knew straight away that I wanted more of whatever it was. The frontier energy and sense of possibility attracted me. It is a trope of Australian history that this fresh new country appealed especially to those members of the English establishment who wanted to escape the strictures of the class system, who wanted to strike out on their own in a new land built on a meritocracy. Whether true or not, it is part of our national myth. I immediately felt the same way about Darwin.

Next day, we endured a blurring round of meetings, some punctuated by a cup of tea, others by a stubby of beer. Thelma's accountants, the tax department officials, the bank and then the local lawyer acting for Norm Douglas were visited one after the other. None of these discussions ended up with any breakthrough or revelation, nothing extraordinary, and all seemed to follow a pattern. Flynn would set out what the problems were, I would quietly take notes, the contentious issues would be fully ventilated but no-one would commit to any resolution on any of them. It was all shadow boxing, and whenever I was asked what the beneficiaries wanted to do I simply said they wanted to sort out the estate quickly while retaining as much of the proceeds for themselves as they could. It was hardly surprising and there was never a serious attempt at negotiation or resolution of anything by any of us.

Hours were spent with the accountants and bankers trying to unpick the labyrinth of Thelma's commercial gyrations and motivations, projecting onto the balance sheets whatever we thought she was trying to achieve. A consistent thread was Thelma not paying any bills to anyone, even when pressed, while squirrelling away as much as possible for herself. There were bank accounts and investments – not huge but in the tens of thousands of dollars each – in different banks in just about every capital city, and mysterious inter-company loans and transactions that defied common sense but were undoubtedly intended to keep her finances and assets as secret as possible. Whether she was paranoid or just suspicious, it was hard to know. Although there was no convenient bank out at Top Springs, why would someone who lived there deposit cash in banks in Perth, in Brisbane, in Melbourne and so on, always in different banks, for no apparent commercial advantage?

Flynn built up gently to the main event. 'Tomorrow we will head off and drive down to Katherine and then to Toppie. It will take all day ... and since you've never been to an outback pub before, I thought we should stop off at a few along the way so you have something to compare Toppie to ...' Our drive to Top Springs would be a work-related pub crawl. Typically Territorian.

I was disappointed that Flynn was not in a thumping big four-wheel drive when he picked me up the next morning but in his government Holden Commodore stocked with a back seat esky of ice, water and sandwiches. We cruised down the Stuart Highway, first stopping at Adelaide River about an hour-and-a-half drive out of Darwin itself. Our car chat was mostly about the history and politics of the Territory – the push for self-government, cattle barons, the widespread and notorious grog problem that afflicted the Territory and, not unrelated, the seemingly unsolvable problems in local Aboriginal affairs. Flynn had endless experience, stories and insights, and I was soaking it all in as I tried to keep up with his vast knowledge of a part of Australia that was totally alien to me.

Adelaide River offered immediate relief from the relentless highway landscape of low scrub and red dirt. The plentiful supply of permanent water from the river created a lush green oasis and tall eucalypts made an idyllic setting. The birds were deafening, rejoicing in the respite of the water just as much as the humans. The pub sat just off the river bank, its tin roof almost engulfed by thick tropical foliage; the deep verandah offered some relief from the sun. The bar was adorned with what I later learned were typical sets of buffalo horns and old hats nailed to the wall, along with a formidable array of souvenir stubby coolers. A few massive multi-trailer road trains had stopped off, and the cattle noise and the attendant smell were overpowering.

Driving was thirsty work, and back in the day the drink drive laws in the NT – the weakest in the nation anyway – were mostly ignored. Flynn seemed to know everyone in the pub, particularly those behind the counter, and I could only marvel at how much of their communication relied on an almost telepathic understanding. I was used to saying what I wanted aloud, but here the language was grunts and nods as much as words. He

John Flynn on the road to Top Springs, just before our punctured tyre.

knocked back an icy beer, and not wanting to be impolite, but feeling slightly uneasy about boozing at such an early hour, I joined him. Needless to say, and not to labour the point, if two people are having a drink, even mid-morning, and one of them buys the first, it is simple courtesy to return the favour and shout a round.

We jumped back into the government car and motored on down to the next watering hole at Pine Creek, where the same pattern was repeated. More chat, more buffalo horns, more beer.

Next stop, 'The Katherine', the third biggest town in the Northern Territory, after Darwin, now well behind us, and Alice Springs, many hours further to the south. Katherine was then, and still is now, a bustling centre of commerce and a transport hub – freight coming in from Queensland and meat heading back out that way in exchange. Cattle and mining, the twin pillars of the NT economy, sustained the town, as well as tourism centred on the rightly famous Katherine Gorge on the northern outskirts.

We had a lunchtime bite at a pub, washed down with more stubbies of beer, and then briefly stopped for fuel and to check the water and oil. I was already forming a solid impression about the Territory's primary pursuits and proud claims. 'Other than cows, the Territory's main export is empty beer bottles' is one of many local jokes. 'What does NT stand for? Not today, not tomorrow, not Tuesday, not Thursday ...' is another. From Katherine we joined the start of the Victoria Highway and headed south-west. Flynn seemed not to be affected by the beer, but most certainly I was.

The landscape changed dramatically at the same time as the pavement. The bitumen gave way to gravel as the soil turned redder; the ant mounds got bigger and the scrub sparser and meaner. The occasional camel wandered into view in the distance and, at one stage, as we rounded a bend, a scatter of feral donkeys either side of the car created an unexpected hazard. Kangaroos were nowhere to be seen – maybe it was too dry? There was hardly any other traffic on the road. When a truck – usually a road train – came towards us, Flynn pulled off the road entirely to avoid the dust and the inevitable shower of damaging stones that ballooned up behind and threatened to destroy a windshield if given the chance. I felt as if I was some intrepid explorer, a conceit that I harboured throughout our drive.

The reflected heat build-up inside the car, magnified by the glass – to say nothing of the beer – made me drowsy. Flynn was a generous storyteller and our wandering conversations and my ignorant questions about the Territory could not have been met with better or more thorough responses. His fundamental decency emerged, solidly anchored in his unwavering Catholicism. I am not sure he had met anyone who was Jewish before – Jews were vanishingly rare in Darwin – and although I was far from religious, even dismissive of my traditional upbringing and increasingly secular in my outlook, the values clash made for an interesting contrast. We were motivated to do similar things for wildly divergent reasons. His faith told him what was right and wrong. I had dropped my belief in any greater being and thought it was up to me to chart a humanistic path. I hope he did not think me rude in my godlessness.

A solid moral foundation drives many people in public service, and Flynn was one of them. He knew where all the NT bodies were buried, and as we loosened our reserve he was more forthcoming about politicians, the barely concealed racism that underpinned the administration of Indigenous affairs and the skulduggery of local pastoralists and miners. The ethos of the Territory had always been based on survival, and not many questions were asked about how it developed, nor how fortunes were acquired. 'A brawl in every bottle' and the promise of a decent drinking session are fundamental to the local character, and the rough edges of frontier settlers had always been dismissed as more a source of wry amusement than anything else.

We exchanged abridged versions of our life stories – mine dull in comparison to his. Flynn expanded on his commitment to church, community and local charities as well as his cricket club, to which he devoted as much energy as he did to his job. He must have served on every committee and important board in Darwin, as did his wife Katherine, their fingers in so many honourable pies. His was an admirable story.

We turned off onto the Buntine, a highway in name only, and stopped a few times to check tyres, stretch legs and water the soil, and for the first time I experienced that awe for vast and empty space that is so quintessentially Australian. At first blush, the outback seemed empty, but then when I took the time to stop and stare, once I looked out and looked long, and interrogated the dirt, I slowly appreciated that there was so much more going on. I absorbed the smells, the ants, the birds, the clouds and endless sky, and started to marvel at the seeds, lizards, willy-willies and the complex interaction of land and sky in their timeless dance of survival and sustainability.

Here, as anywhere, I had to overcome my default on any trip to be fascinated with the machinery, the trucks, the tractors and the motorbikes. Distractions of the mechanical kind were plentiful up north, but there is a competing demand to pay attention to the surreal physical surrounds, the compelling but subtle tug of the horizon and the bush. Eventually I found a balance, a yin and yang of nature versus machine. The land is so vast, there seemed here to be room for both.

Occasionally, as the miles ticked away, we saw evidence of the many years of pastoralists' or miners' futile efforts to tame the wilderness – some splintering fence posts or a rusty windmill, usually rotting in the harsh climate. There was only an occasional glimpse of any Indigenous presence. In Darwin, Aboriginal Australia was everywhere: people, art and culture in every part of the street scene. Out bush, for the most part, there was just horizon.

The monotony of the long straight stretches of red gravel corridors splitting olive green scrub borders was interrupted suddenly with a punctured tyre. Unloading the spare and the jack, finding something solid to lie under the jack to avoid the car sinking into the sand – the entire process of changing the wheel seemed to test our stamina and take forever. We both got filthy, sweaty and thirsty.

The road got narrower and narrower, eventually little more than a dirt track with deep ruts, more comfortably navigated by four-wheel drives or a truck. These roads were not intended to be negotiated by a standard-issue sedan, far too low to the ground, and sometimes bottoming out on a rut or scraping the exhaust on a bump. We shared that unspoken guilt that accompanies mistreating a government car, knowing that someone else will inherit the problems one day. I did not have a map, so could not begin to imagine where we were. The only measure of progress was by watching the time. Soon after the seventh hour ticked over and well before the dangerous dusk, a time when no-one without a bull bar on the front of their vehicle wanted to be on the road, we saw evidence of an abandoned cattle station. 'Old Wave Hill,' said Flynn, and pointed out the remnants of some tin and timber buildings and fences, skeletal windmills still creaking in the almost imperceptible breeze. 'Everything was built in tin and concrete – it's pretty much the only stuff the ants don't eat,' he explained.

'We're nearly there …' he announced shortly after we passed Old Wave Hill station, and within minutes, a squat brick-and-concrete building with aerials sticking out above the roof and petrol pumps out front loomed into view. Some struggling nearby trees offered the merest hint of very rare and welcome shade and an assembly of wrecked cars and old trucks decorated the landscape beyond. Welcome to Wanda Inn, Top Springs.

Flynn pulled up the Commodore on the forecourt, a concrete apron only partially covered by a vaulted tin roof. The building was square and plain, even spartan, completely devoid of attempts at beautification or decoration, and with only the most basic signage. There was no hint of activity and as the dust from our car settled, we fell out and stretched. Flynn ushered me through the main door, flyscreens banging, to a large saloon, basic in its decor and, if remarkable for anything, it was how stripped-down a pub could be. Along one side was a long, straight and unpainted red-brick bar. Its concrete benchtop was covered in part by threadbare bar towels advertising different species of beer. The lights were dim and the windows were covered in wire mesh. Lazily hovering flies provided a barely audible soundtrack and were slightly buffeted by the greasy-looking ceiling fans turning overhead. Some lonely steel-framed stools along the edge of the room and a table with nothing on it on the opposite side to the door completed the fit-out. There was no-one anywhere to be seen.

We went out a back door, across a large dirt and gravel expanse that was pretending to grow some grass on it and towards another torn screen door that opened into a chaotic small kitchen and storeroom. A wiry balding man greeted Flynn in a still strong English accent. Norm Douglas was introduced and we shook hands. He offered to show us around, and we got a tour of Top Springs, population two plus dogs. I was shown the coolroom, generously stocked with bottled beer and ice; the food storeroom, remarkable for the almost total absence of any food on the shelving; the vital and very valuable diesel generator in its own shed; a shambolic garage and workshop; then up the concrete stairs to Thelma's still-furnished home. We concluded the tour at the hotel rooms out the back where Flynn and I would sleep the night. I was warned not to go around the back of the water tanks as there were dogs chained up there, 'kept for blackfellas when there is trouble ... best you stay away'.

One-star accommodation it was, but I was not expecting the Hilton. The curling mattress on the wire-frame bed reminded me of the worst of school camps. The communal bathroom and shower block was primitive but functional. I put my bag down and wandered back to the bar.

Norm was chatty, and although I was wary of saying too much – after all, we were on opposite sides of a dispute – he was clearly happy to have company. He introduced us to his only other regular companion, Doug Stillson. A less talkative person the world had not seen. Which of us thought the other was weirder? It was hard to know. I lived in Fitzroy, a part of Melbourne renowned for boasting a pub on every corner, and in several of them only long-term locals were welcome. A few were off limits for us newly arrived young professionals starting to gentrify the old terrace houses. One local was a drinking hole for wharfies and bikies and another was a designated 'blackfella' pub. I never dared to go near either of them, but I had seen my share of alcoholics and troubled drunks, or so I thought. Toppie was next level.

It was late, we had been driving all day and Norm offered a choice of a steak sandwich or a reheated pie, either available with frozen peas. There was, of course, a ready supply of bottles of cold beer. He willingly recited the details of his shocking discovery of Ma Hawks' body many months before and the events that followed. Norm also felt obliged to fill us in on the meagre turnover of the pub since Thelma died and Dick Philip took over. One problem was that the local Aboriginal communities now thought the pub was cursed and they would no longer visit. He was not happy.

Norm showed us some fearsome traditional weapons – clubs and spears – confiscated from local Aboriginal men fighting and creating mayhem outside the pub. The typical cycle of drinking and violence reliably coincided with fortnightly pension payments. Thelma would provide overpriced grog in exchange for the pension money paid into bank accounts – which she also administered as the local postmistress, a service that ended when she died. There was no discussion about whether this was fair or ethical, nor why the violence happened, nor whether it could be prevented or avoided. It just happened, frequently, and was a part of life at Top Springs. Any suggestion that Aboriginal people ought to enjoy full equality, even have equal access to the Top Springs bar, let alone something as controversial as owning land ... that was unimaginable.

The original inhabitants – the First Nations people, the custodians of the world's oldest surviving culture, the survivors of the frontier wars – were regarded here as a nuisance, a source of revenue, a pathetic but lucrative customer base for grog and that was all. At that stage of my life, I had barely even met an Aboriginal person. There was only one Indigenous student at Monash Law School, Pat Dodson, but he had dropped out after only one year, and I had no other connection to Aboriginal Australia. Pat is now a senator in the Australian Parliament after a stellar career as a leader of multiple campaigns for Indigenous rights, a career that Monash Law School may well have short-circuited had he stayed! The only other Aboriginal people I had encountered were around Fitzroy. Aboriginal people congregated in the local parks and on the footpaths outside the busy Aboriginal Health Service in Gertrude Street just a block away from where I lived. I had never stopped to speak or engage with any of them in any meaningful way.

After a lousy night's sleep in the world's most uncomfortable bed, first thing in the morning we thanked Norm and took our leave. The unremarkable drive back to Darwin was the mirror image of the trip down, pub stops and all, but no punctured tyre, Flynn yarning the whole way. It became readily apparent that the NT was full of characters, there were no 'normal' human beings;

'Everyone is escaping something,' Flynn said. He expanded with robust and horrific stories of the type readily recited by Territorians to distinguish their struggles from those of urban Australia.

'Have you heard the often told and retold story of the grader driver who worked remote for years, never stopping off in town unless it was unavoidable, sleeping rough and camping out solo in the bush day after day, year after year,' Flynn recounted. *'Never washing, never changing his clothes, never eating proper food, his life was that of a hobo and a hermit disconnected from anyone or community life, but all the while he was making huge money. No-one could understand why a bloke with such solid earnings lived a life of such terrible isolation and unending hardship, totally devoid of any creature comforts or companionship,'* he continued. But then after a chance encounter with someone from his pre-hermit life, *'a local discovered that Grader Jack had never recovered from tragically and accidentally backing his grader over his toddler daughter years before, and could no longer face the world ... his whole life fell apart, no-one could get through to him. He left his wife, went bush and found peace in his grader, when the world offered none wherever else he looked'.* The isolation offered by the bush seemed to attract so many loners.

Flynn also told the oft-repeated yarns about 'Poddy Dodger Tex', so rotten drunk he shot off his own big toe when imagining thieves during the night. Trucking pioneer Kurt Johannsen, credited locally with being the inventor of the road train, ran over one of his own crew sleeping off a big night under the truck. Upon breaking the tragic news to his widow, she said, 'Thank goodness the bastard is gone,' and thanked Kurt because at last the bashings would end.

I had never before heard someone described as being 'too polite to be honest' and even though I cannot recall who it was about, that NT description lodged in my memory and is as apt today as it was then. The saying 'a fight in every bottle or your money back' is not folklore but a reflection on the central role of alcohol in the lives of those who live in the Territory, whether in Darwin or the bush. While himself a 'modest' drinker, Flynn was acutely aware of the problems that grog caused across Territory society. Those in power would never tackle the powerful suppliers, who ferociously protected their lucrative trade. I was not unaware that the only reason I was visiting was because Thelma built her empire on selling grog at massively inflated prices, mostly to people – black and white – who drank far too much.

'Grog runs' were common practice for young Aboriginal men who would pool their cash and dispatch someone (with the most reliable car) to the pub – especially Thelma Hawks' notorious Wanda Inn at Top Springs – to fill up with cases of rum and beer and return to the fringe of the community for a drinking binge, typically on welfare payment day each fortnight. Drinkers would gather just beyond the boundary of 'dry' communities. There was no prospect of policing every community every fortnight, and the damage done and the violence that followed continued unchecked – and still does.

We eventually returned to the welcoming streets of Darwin, and Flynn recommended I fuel my new-found enthusiasm and curiosity for the Territory with a visit to the only bookshop in town, in Mitchell Street, before I caught the plane home the next morning. I was not in any way clear yet how my Darwin expedition made any difference to the resolution of the estate, but Flynn assured me it had. I wandered the streets, visited the historic old stores in Cavenagh Street, the outback supply shops filled with gear for those living remote and the small shops selling some Aboriginal art and didgeridoos to tourists. I bought a book by Bill Harney, a legendary bushman of the Top End, and another by Douglas Lockwood, a veteran Territory journalist and raconteur. I devoured them on my long flight home.

Lockwood's book was full of tales – some of them undoubtedly true – of bushmen like George Fisher, who explored Arnhem Land when white prospectors first ventured deep into the bush, and had been forced to eat brolga to avoid starving. Fisher was disgusted by the 'tough tucker' and opined that brolga breast meat was better suited for resoling boots. Lockwood also recounted the tale of 'Old George Conway', a tough-as-flint bushman who drank two bottles of brandy a day – plus a nightcap – and liked to ride his horse straight into the public bar at Mataranka Pub where he'd order a double brandy, plus a plate of sugar for his horse. Conway was also referred to, in passing, as having participated in an unnamed massacre, which we now know to have been the notorious Caledon Bay massacre where, by his own boastful admission, hundreds were shot down. Lockwood's book introduced me to Phoebe Farrar, the owner of Ban Ban Springs Station, described as a courageous woman and flint hard, like a piece of whipcord, and who kept riding, shooting and working until she died at ninety years old. She was famous for being out on the muster for months with just a 'half caste' stockman and a dog.

I wish I had read Harney's stories about everything Territorian before I visited, not after. They span the niche – when cooking goanna, it is essential to remove the gall sack to avoid a bitter tasting meat – through to the prosaic, detailing the commercial opening up of the frontier by white colonists, predominantly buffalo and crocodile hunters. Amid stories about Aboriginal kinship and skin relationships, Harney explored the most delicate and sometimes taboo topic of all – mixed-race relationships and how they were often unequal and even unwanted. He writes of the lure – regarded by white men as 'irresistible' – of Aboriginal girls, and how often newly arrived white men 'scoffed at' and 'dismissed' the attraction of 'black girls' but soon changed their ways 'again and again', before returning to 'civilisation' as 'strait laced' and pretending nothing had happened. He hinted at scandal and referred to '*forbidden fruit*' and '*black velvet*' and '*gin jockeys*' to describe the not uncommon phenomenon of white men living in remote communities 'taking' Aboriginal women as partners. There were even coarser descriptions with the same salacious implications of sexual adventure out in the remote bush where no-one knows what anyone does and no-one was ever accountable for what happened. White men who partnered Aboriginal women were typically regarded as too lazy, wild or drunk to 'get' a white woman. The other way around was inconceivable. These stories contained not the slightest suggestion of anything resembling consent nor was there any insight into the absence of it. To our eyes today it is shudderingly inappropriate.

Around this time, a momentous shift was underway in the law governing sexual relations. Until the 1980s it was Australian law that a woman's consent was not needed for sex within marriage. No husband could ever be convicted of the rape of someone married to them, no matter what violence or other coercion occurred. Regular stories in the media emphasised how absurd this was and how the law had to be urgently changed. The Northern Territory was the last jurisdiction in Australia to modernise the laws on rape in marriage and did not do so until 1994. The telling and shocking rarity of convictions for rape or sexual assault down south was magnified many times over up north. Rapes of Indigenous women in the NT were even less likely to be acted upon than an identical complaint by a white woman – which itself was very rare. Looking back, it is astonishing that it took so long to change the law and even longer for those changes to start to impact on behaviour. Much has improved but there is always more needed.

I was totally captivated by both Harney's and Lockwood's books, and the other-world they described. This was not the Australia that I thought I knew. I had backpacked through Europe and North America, travelled widely through Asia and the Pacific – but what I'd seen and learned that week struck me as far more foreign. It was absurd that urban, urbane Melbourne could co-exist with edgy frontier Darwin, as if there was some time warp between them on top of the physical distance. I returned from Darwin somewhat more worldly than my shielded years had allowed.

One of the first things I did on my return to Melbourne was bring the Andersons up to speed on what I had learned. Visits to Apollo in his nostalgia-filled gym were welcome relief from the hard slog and late nights of the office. The more I chatted to John Flynn, the more I tried to unpick the knots in the estate of T C Hawks, the more I talked to Apollo – the more curious about Thelma Hawks and the Territory I became.

CHAPTER 8

SURPRISE IS YOUR BEST FRIEND

Returning to a suit and tie meant I had to quickly shed the Territory dust and get back in the city groove. My boss gave me work that was more complex and challenging, and I loved racing back and forward each day to the barristers' chambers and the Supreme and County courts as I immersed myself in the arm wrestle of litigation.

One assignment saw me as the junior bag carrier in a large team at a sensitive public inquiry into whether the planning laws allowed our clients to build a steel mill on a site in Melbourne's inner west. The Smorgon family wanted to challenge BHP's steelmaking monopoly by starting a recycling factory using second-hand machinery they had imported from North America. Their chosen Tottenham site was opposed by the locals. As it was only a few blocks from a primary school, and the residents' expert witnesses asserted the emissions would pose a health hazard to children, our clients were portrayed in the daily media as heartless and reckless. The objectors were represented by friends of mine through the local free legal centre and my allegiances were torn. One day, a youthful Peter

Gordon, later a leading class-action plaintiff lawyer, frontman for the challenge, called me 'Smorgons' bagman' as we went down the stairs after a torrid day of expert evidence. The rebuke stung.

Hopes for a quick resolution for the Estate of T C Hawks were dashed when sometimes weeks and sometimes months would pass between letters from Darwin. We were going around in circles with Norman Douglas and his slowly crystallising claim to be the rightful beneficiary of the shares in the company that owned the pub, and simultaneously we were still hoping to sell the business. I made regular visits to the Mighty Apollo Gym and Combat Centre in West Melbourne to consult because Apollo did not answer letters, rarely phoned and was not particularly easy to communicate with even if he did answer the phone. It was clear that the best, if not only, way to really connect with him was to sit down and talk face to face.

My imposter syndrome was waning. When Apollo and his three teenage sons had first sought help, I had been a freshly minted lawyer, a beginner. Venturing to Darwin on their behalf was the first time I had worked totally solo and been entrusted to make decisions in negotiations that had enormous impact on clients' lives. As the year progressed and my confidence increased, I brashly felt a growing competence about dispensing wisdom and deciding what was in other people's best interests. But in the context of a typically detached lawyer/client relationship it was still beyond my contemplation to enquire about the daily lives of Apollo's sons, the three young men who were about to inherit a life-changing amount of cash, with my attendant concern they would just end up blowing their windfall.

Most litigants only cared about money and obsessed about squeezing every last drop from whatever claim they were pursuing – it was all about the bucks. At no point did it even occur to me to ask whether the instructions being given to me by Apollo were also what each of his under-age sons wanted, let alone needed. I never had a conversation with the three brothers without their father being present. I am not sure whether it would have made any difference if I had.

In every meeting at his gym, Apollo was totally self-absorbed. He loved talking about himself. He was not just the embodiment of vanity – he transcended it. Narcissism does not explain it – he genuinely believed he had inexplicable special powers, that he was a superior being, more than a mere mortal. Some of the time his powers were 'supernatural', some of the time they were 'God-given', some of the time they were 'destiny'. But unlike most narcissists, he was quiet, matter-of-fact, and calm in making his claims. It was so obvious to him that he was special, how could he get everyone else to understand that too?

His physical strength was matched by his vanity. His body was his temple. Early in his career, one of his first performances was as a human statue with 'Muscles in Marble', an early example of strength-meeting-showbiz which later evolved into the sport of bodybuilding. Soon, combining these routines with being a champion weightlifter, he realised his best chance at making good money came from his physique – his strength would be his meal ticket. Driven by a manic determination to become rich and famous, and for validation, he had obsessively sought publicity and then duly recorded into scrapbooks every event he competed in, every trophy, every show, every stunt, whether it broke a world record or just turned a buck from an adoring crowd. He loved showing guests through these bulging volumes. Seeing his life unfold, dutifully recorded in these cherished scrapbooks made it seem literally fantastic, absurdly action-packed, almost super-hero comic-book in its twists and turns.

As the decades passed, the scrapbooks evolved. When Apollo was young and full of ambition, every page was carefully decorated with splendid adornments and embellished with colourful annotations. Many of the photos had witty self-aggrandising subtitles and were captioned in the style of an artistic kidnapper's ransom note – individual words or even single letters scissored from shop catalogues and magazines, assembled into messages about an event. Towards his later years, the elaboration diminished and the scrapbooks served as a mere record, a bare page with just a clipping glued in, with little or no detail.

The enormous journals, hundreds of pages thick, were sandwiched by expandable industrial clamps holding it all together within stiff, gold-embossed covers. Endless clippings of a show in a country town here or a large theatre there, a photo from the newspaper pasted to the page, every mention in any magazine, no matter how trivial. Sixty or more years of showbiz history slowly turning yellow with age, a metaphor for the life of the protagonist himself.

Holding audience in the gym, Apollo told stories the same way he performed on stage. His delivery was theatrical, but always methodical. If he repeated a story, it was almost word perfect the second, third or even tenth time. It was as if he was performing the role of being himself, playing Apollo on the stage of his life. It was not that he was inauthentic, but it seemed to me that he

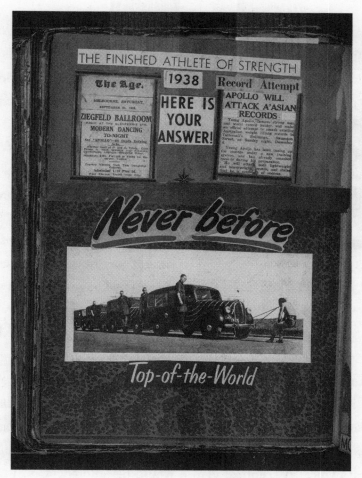

ABOVE: Apollo's scrap books recorded every event he participated in, big and small.

RIGHT: An early Daguerrotype portrait of the Young Apollo performing 'scrolling', circa 1924.

Even as he aged, Apollo performed for the photographers whenever he could.

was guarded about revealing too much about himself beyond what he wanted the world to see. I occasionally tried to divert him from the well-rehearsed and elaborate recital but rarely, if ever, succeeded; his concentration on the storytelling was as intense as his training routines. He had practised and perfected his physical routine and likewise the promotional hype that went with the acts of strength.

Did he know where his drive and determination came from, to say nothing of the unparalleled ability to ignore pain? *I believe that there is an amazing creative power of a higher mental plane that has enabled me to survive ... I was ordained to add lustre to my heritage by the miracle of mind power ...*' Apollo would explain in his distinctive staccato voice. A sceptical glance would be ignored, and in order not to offend I had to keep a straight face. He would keep talking like that until interrupted, an impenetrable word soup. As he mangled ideas and words – 'trepiditious' was a favourite – I would struggle not to interrupt, to challenge him about his philosophy, but his brow was furrowed, his concentration strong, and he was utterly serious, with not the slightest hint of a smile. This was his life we were discussing, his livelihood – his very identity. Without his feats of strength, he was just another weightlifter running a gym instead of being the Strongest Man on Earth.

He imposed upon me to read his diaries and a rough manuscript he had written, which he hoped I could help get published. Incredibly, for a man with almost no formal education, a battler and self-taught author who left school early, he had persevered and completed a memoir, scrappy though it was. He seemed to think that all he had to do was ask me to arrange it and then within a few weeks or months a bestseller would just happen and he'd be happily signing copies. With great ceremony he lifted a shoebox out of a trunk, unwrapped a silk scarf from around some handwritten exercise books and bundles of dog-eared pages held together with bulldog clips. Apollo was convinced that he had penned a New Testament, a fresh bible for the ages, a manual of the secrets of strength or something similar. He treated his writing with a reverence that was entirely consistent with his approach to all his teachings and sermonising. He thought he had a gift, and, as the custodian, the keeper of that secret, he ought to share it.

The script was flowery and decorative, his distinctive curly writing wandering over the page, the pen pressed heavily into the paper. Although deciphering it was not quite the Dead Sea scrolls it was slow going. Not only was the handwriting hard to follow, so were the thoughts and ideas. '*The mystical motivational force by a directive channel of mind consciousness ... The principle is certainly a dualistic one interacted by scientific procedure ... Creative thought is inspired by the elements of my preordained destiny ...*' and so on, sometimes for pages without any punctuation.

Every incredible feat was 'preordained' or the result of 'God-given powers' or derived from his deep faith. At the same time, he wrote that his success was because of '*cosmic powers, mind control, mystical forces, the supernatural*' and '*other forces we mortals will never understand*'.

I thought it was unreadable, and he would not contemplate any changes to his flowing thoughts. Buried within were some precious gems and pearls of insight, especially when he advocated meditation and visualisation before attempting anything difficult. Some aspects of his philosophy, as reflected in his writings, were ahead of their time, and his belief that there is untapped potential in all of us is undoubtedly true – but it was heavy going. Too heavy for me. I was impressed that he had even attempted the task, but had no idea how to tell him it was miles from being suitable to be published. I eventually said it was too hard to find anyone who would do it justice, to give it the treatment it deserved. I was a coward.

When I agreed to read and appraise his life story, he wanted to tell me about it even while I was there. I listened attentively, but then later when reading the diaries and manuscripts, it was amazing how closely the spoken version had matched the written page. It was as if he had memorised it or, conversely, the prepared and memorised version had just been transcribed into the books.

* * *

Born as Alexander McPherson Anderson in 1910 in Clifton Hill, he was the second of five – Terry, Alexander, Thelma, Thomas and Cliff. Apollo moved with his family shortly after to adjacent Collingwood, in Melbourne's inner north. The young Alexander was dubbed 'Young Apollo' in the press and later adopted the title for showbiz, then chose to rename himself 'Paul' as it was close to 'Apollo' – whose physique he shared. In Greek mythology Apollo was the god of almost everything – light, sun, poetry, music, healing and dance. He did not give himself the Apollo name. '*I was given that name, I earned my name Apollo from my death defying acts – like a soldier earns a medal*,' he would quip, always with an eye for self-promotion.

His father worked as a blacksmith and his mother a seamstress. He claimed that his father performed as an acrobat and a '*fabulous hand-balancer*' and often said that his maternal grandmother was '*a Spanish señorita descended from aristocrats*' and his mother was '*a psychic to some degree*' without any hint of evidence to support these impressive claims. Apollo aggrandised himself with the embellishment – although years later a possible explanation was unearthed as to why he felt the need to adopt the Spanish legend.

Apollo's darker complexion may have needed to be explained away in those deeply racist times. Later, family history research conducted by his son Paul revealed that the Andersons had an African-American ancestor who came to Australia in the gold rush. Thomas Byng fought as a 'Black Royalist' in the US War of Independence, in exchange for freedom from slavery, but had to flee to Canada as he had fought with the losing British Army. His son John left Nova Scotia and sailed to the colony of Victoria for the gold rush, and 'Black Byng', as he was known, was active at the Eureka Stockade. He later built the first pub at Mount Gambier. One of John's children, Jane, married Thomas Crowle and their daughter Mary was Apollo's maternal grandmother. Mary Crowle undoubtedly knew her grandfather, but did she keep his blackness a secret from her own grandchildren? Did she substitute her African-American heritage with something more 'acceptable' for the times, like a Spanish señorita, or was that done later down the family tree? We will never know – the genealogy only brought the Byng connection to light long after Apollo's death.

Apollo said his parents taught him *'that when you become famous, as you will one day, people will judge you by the way you talk and your social rank in life will become great. If you can coordinate fantasy with motivation, then fairytale dreams become reality'.* Whether they genuinely made those prophecies, or it suited his image to invent parental inspiration, we will never know.

The family tree shows Apollo's father's family were Scottish, from Lanarkshire, south-east of Glasgow, going back generations. That lineage, about which less is known, features at least one circus performer, hinting at a rich pedigree for the future Mighty Apollo.

He would speak fondly of his father, Thomas, even emotionally – his voice cracking a little as he remembered a tough but kind man who taught him the value of hard work and physical resilience. He told of being bullied at school because of his small size and how he learned to hit early and hard if he thought there was going to be a fight.

'Don't wait, Jon, surprise is your best friend,' he declared, in the well-rehearsed tone of a teacher going through a lesson for the thousandth time. He claimed he first put on boxing gloves at the age of five or six and took them to bed the way some kids cuddled a teddy bear. He told of being jumped by a group of school bullies in Collingwood while still one of the little kids in primary school; he'd been hopelessly outnumbered and copped a beating. His response was to obsessively and secretly start strength training and shadow boxing at home; then, when

feeling strong enough, he went to knock on the door of each of his tormentors one at a time. When the door was answered, typically by a mother, Alex (as Apollo was) would politely ask if Freddie or Johnny was at home and said he had something to give them. On them coming to the door, he would not say a word and simply punched them in the face as hard as he could. After his house-to-house, *'they never troubled me again and I got some respect. I learned you had to stand up for yourself – no-one else ever will. I kept a book with their names and a list and ticked them off as I went door to door ...'* He also decided that being *'short of stature'* was no barrier to *'being strong in the mind'*, a mantra that he repeated in one form or another for all his eighty-four years.

Well-rehearsed, any telling of his life story always began with his father and uncles improvising a gym in the stables at the rear of their home in Collingwood. His uncles held local wrestling and boxing competitions and used Apollo's father's blacksmith equipment as weights. He had started performing as a *'mere stripling'*, when his determination to fight off the school bullies brought him to the attention of his pugilist relatives. He would come home from school and improvise by lifting bags of sand or bluestone, progressively making them heavier, to build his strength. Crouching on the ground, Apollo would loop a rope around his neck, attach sandbags to either end and lift them to strengthen his back and stomach muscles. As that became easy and to challenge him more, he would put another sandbag on the nape of his neck. Eventually, as he grew stronger, his youngest brother, Cliff, would sit on his shoulders while he lifted weights with his teeth to strengthen his jaws and back. His singlemindedness was remarkable, particularly for a teenager.

'*My dad's forearm muscles looked like a corrugated tin roof; he could bend steel bars with his bare hands. In performance it is called iron bar scrolling, and I wanted to impress him so I learned to do it too ... Even as a young boy I was a marvel.*' Apollo pulled a fire hose up the street with his teeth at ten years old and loved the attention. Not unusual for the times, he left school at thirteen, infected with a strong desire for fame. '*You have to keep proving yourself ... my daredevil feats are a way to make a living. I can accept pain as a way to make money, and I can block pain like no-one else can. When I was just fifteen one of my first feats of remarkable strength was when I carried a horse up a 32' ladder ...*' He carried a horse – yes, a horse – in a harness up a ladder.

If anyone else boasted they carried a horse up a ladder – at any age, let alone as a teenager – they would be laughed out of town to a chorus of 'bullshit'. But Apollo would make that claim, and, when doubted, produce a photo or a clipping from a magazine documented in his scrapbook to prove it. He delighted in challenging entire teams to a tug-of-war or juggled cannon balls that most people struggled to budge on the ground. The walls around the gym were plastered with ample evidence that anything that seemed impossible to others was not impossible to him. Time and again, scepticism would be demolished by photographic proof.

Melbourne's inner suburbs in the 1920s were slums; a tough place at a tough time. Apollo was determined to find a way out of struggle street – to lift himself out of poverty, literally. Newspaper linings inside worn-out shoes, hand-me-down clothes, going hungry and the shame of being poor all sharpened his ambition.

He turned to boxing and weightlifting as formal disciplines, broke his first record at his first competition and claimed to have smashed records at every competition he attended. He simultaneously held the featherweight, lightweight, middleweight and heavyweight lifting titles. '*My amateur days were highly valuable and gave me great confidence to smash records in devastating style whenever I tried*,' he recounted. Apollo's first cousin was Tommy Crowle, Australian featherweight boxing champion, managed by the legendary Melbourne gangster Squizzy Taylor. Tommy Crowle taught all the four Anderson brothers to fight, and Squizzy offered to manage them if they showed potential – but he was murdered in 1927 before any of them matured. After a period doing 'security work' around the clubs and pubs, Apollo found a safer way to make a living and started to bring flamboyance and showbiz flair to competitions, adopting a Gladiator theme with embroidered robes and Roman soldier–style high boots. He said it helped to psych his rivals who were always bigger and enjoyed a weight advantage. He needed to even the scales somehow and simple self-taught psychological tricks helped achieve '*a birthright, a destiny; I was invincible as I had these gifts*'.

Showbiz proved more glamorous and lucrative than either security work or sport, so Apollo, brothers Tommy and Cliff and sister Thelma started performing as adagio dancers locally and then at the Tivoli, the biggest stage in town. Adagio was a predecessor to gymnastic dance and a great money spinner, combining strength with grace, staged to music for a theatre audience. His most famous routine, originally with Thelma but later with '*the beautiful Noela De Milo*', was to kneel on the stage and have her stand on his open palm. He would then slowly

Tommy, Thelma, Apollo and Cliff, the De Milo Troupe.

stand and lift the upright beauty straight above his head to a full stretch. *'I would lift her on my outstretched hand from the floor to the heavens, and then she would leap into the air ... and I would catch her on the way down ... then throw her and catch her again behind my back ... the audience would all gasp ... It was all done to music, working across the whole stage ...'* It established him as an individual performer, not just part of an ensemble. *'I dressed as a millionaire playboy, a master showman, the theatre became a guideline to my creative ability.'* Like so many before and since, he thrived on applause, lights, music and the troupes of beautiful girls. The natural showman blossomed.

He was as successful a storyteller as he was a strongman, adagio dancer and weightlifter – 'The Mighty Young Apollo, the Great Embellisher' could have been his motto and it all amounted to the perfect ingredients for showbiz. As well as regular shows with the Tivoli, Wirth's famous touring circus was the biggest show around, and Apollo signed up. He claimed to be the only person to have a contract that included the waiver that 'I accept full responsibility for my death-defying acts'. It was a brilliant marketing tool and convinced the ticket-buying public he was putting his life on the line every night. He would soon play in the centre ring and even headlined the bill.

Issuing challenges became a self-promotional guarantee. Apollo publicly offered a thousand pounds to anyone who could match his feats of strength. If no-one took the challenge, he boasted that he was unchallenged.

He starred in 'Alf Broadway's Variety Stars', a marquee tent show, which travelled the east coast with a big top and sideshows, visiting dozens of major towns and country shows. He challenged every strongman at every town and never lost. A German strongman challenged Apollo while on tour in Innisfail in Queensland, responding to his thousand-pound challenge – an absolute fortune for the times. *'In a booming voice this fellow says, "Where's this Apollo, I have come to challenge him?" and I said "my challenge is to the whole world; if Atlas took the world on his shoulders then I do that too. I was spat out of the mouth of a volcano, not born naturally", and the challenge was on. He was a huge man and I'm only a little man so I walked up to a barbell and did the one-handed lift which was my specialty and I said go ahead, if you can do it too … and he stared at me and I said, "Go on, you're scared of failing aren't you? Look at you, your Adam's apple is jumping around and you are wiping your hands with your towel, and you won't look me in the eye. You're scared because you know I will do to you what happened to the dinosaurs" and I kept going and he couldn't match me and the crowd went crazy … I showed again the ability to conquer, to use the mind as much as any other weapon.'*

The new picture houses, showing the novelty of feature films, were booming. At the Orama Theatre in Footscray in Melbourne's western suburbs, the live show struggled to compete with the new picture theatre down the road. Apollo staged a stunt to not just draw a crowd, but also to hold them out the front of the theatre until after the movie started, to distract them until they missed the beginning of the film. If the start of the feature film was missed, the hope was that the crowd would opt to stay for the live variety show instead.

He adapted a strength routine from his childhood, but with a difference. He became his own spruiker, huffing and puffing, telling the crowd no-one has ever been able to do what he is about to attempt, then pulled a taxi the length of the street by a rope held in his teeth. After the classic circus build-up, and like a circus procession and using every trick of sideshow banter, keeping everyone excited and involved, he 'pulled a crowd' – until they went straight past the movie theatre and stopped at the front door of the Orama. He was appropriately awarded for delivering the crowd to the variety show.

Karl Gaines was a friend of his father and a feted veteran circus performer, using the stage name 'Hercules Roma'. A wonderful and generous mentor, he shared his showbiz smarts with Apollo, teaching him routines that had been handed down to him from generations of performers. Hercules Roma also gifted Apollo two circus artefacts dating back to the nineteenth century – a much-decorated and already well-travelled bed of nails and a Tomb of Hercules board used as a shield for strength

Working in the circus meant a ready supply of exotic props.

tests. This was the golden era of 'the showies', where diverse acts worked together in travelling tent shows that toured the nation, cities and country towns alike. Snake charmers, knife throwers, tattooed ladies, tent boxers, 'freaks' who traded on their ethnicity as well as any physical peculiarity – the shows had it all. 'King Chong with Chang the Pinhead Boy' were regulars, together with giants and 'pygmies', and together, Apollo's troupe eked out a living. Legends like Tommy Castles as 'The Great Kahara' performed as an illusionist or magician, sawing people in half or levitating before the audience's incredulous eyes. Together with a rotating cast of sword swallowers, fire eaters, ever-popular push penny shows, archetypal rotating clown heads and slug-gun shooting galleries, it promised a great day out.

Sharpening his business instincts all the time, Apollo introduced his routines to rural communities with 'The Mighty Young Apollo's Non-Stop Variety Stars'. Photos of his truck and caravan boast elaborate signage: 'Iron Jaw, Dare-Devil,

The Mighty Young Apollo's Non Stop Variety Stars toured the nation.

King of Strength, Official Records Holder, Here to Amaze You, Death Defying, Reckless, Feats of Strength Never Seen Before, Australia's Muscular Marvel'. Bookings in large venues were hard to secure, so he guaranteed theatre owners that if he did not double their attendance, he would perform free. The offer was too good to refuse; his scrapbook confirms he filled plenty of venues. *'You have to keep them guessing and wondering what will happen next. I wanted to be star of my own show, in my own right, not just part of someone else's. Like the Jolson Story, I want to be the box office attraction and get the people to come to see me, not some other act. That is the heart of showmanship, to have something out of the box, something theatrical. That is real showbiz.'*

Occasionally local toughs wanted to test their strength. In Colac, he was challenged to a fight by not one but two locals. *'I'd rather fight than eat,'* he said and disposed of them both before heading off for dinner.

His troupe hit the 'Great North Run', an established circuit for showies, travelling in caravans up and down the east coast as far as Townsville, his convoy visiting every major town and holiday spot, complete with big top and attendant sideshows. Business was healthy, but towards the end of a tour in the late 1930s, a terrible truck crash nearly ended his ambitions and his career. Apollo's left leg was badly broken in the rollover and he was taken to nearby Warrnambool Hospital with multiple fractures and lacerations. His wounds became infected and then gangrenous. Surgeons wanted to amputate his leg, but he stubbornly refused: *'If they cut off my leg I'd never perform ever again.'* Recovering from the infection, he then undertook nine months of rehabilitation with the only legacy a big dent in his left leg just above the knee.

The serious injury meant he was medically unfit for war service. He lamented not being able to do his part, and when he regained his strength and returned to performing, he dedicated his act to fundraising and appeals as his contribution to the war effort. The shows were good for morale but Apollo was forever conscious that others were fighting and he was not.

As his health recovered, so did his passion for fame, ambiguously shrouded in false humility. *'I would rather have one moment of glory than a long life of mediocrity. I knew my intense physical training, sweating it out day after day in the gym was certainly not for an ego trip but for a real purpose – a place in the sporting pages of history. It is my destiny to become famous. I have a supernatural power, transmitted by the Great Master and I am humbled to be in his service,'* he diarised.

During the war, Apollo's sister Thelma met and married an air force mechanic, Sid Hawks, and when hostilities ended, they moved to Queensland. Nola Nolan replaced her in the siblings' act, taking the stage name 'Noela De Milo'. As it became apparent that adagio was no longer sufficiently lucrative nor exciting, and the audience responded better to danger and suspense, Apollo and Nola ventured more into the strength routines – risk-taking drew a bigger crowd. The relationship moved from professional to personal and their marriage lasted from 1941 to 1952. *'Don't get too close to women, they'll fuck you up,'* he later cautioned his sons, based as much on his later marriage to their mother, Rondahe, as the first marriage to Nola Nolan. In every conversation with Apollo, as was typical of the times, whenever women were mentioned, they were only ever described according to their physical attributes, typically as 'curvaceous'. Nola Nolan, as Noela De Milo, was no exception.

Apollo started referring to God as his guardian and spiritual motivation, although there was no hint of him going to church or participating in any other form of formal religious observance. His talk of a higher being often descended into mysticism. He borrowed freely from diverse religious traditions and sometimes creatively mingled them into his own set of beliefs.

What became his signature routine – pulling a stationary tram along the tracks by a cable attached to a leather mouthpiece firmly gripped between his teeth – first manifested itself in a dream, which cemented his belief in visualisation. *'I dreamt I was going to perform it in exactly the way it really happened. God was without a doubt the power that made this miracle possible.'* When explaining his dream with friends over a cup of tea, in mid-1949, he wondered whether they thought it even possible. *'Come off it, mate, you would need a few very large tractors to budge a bloody tram ...'* was their reply, but, never shy of proving his powers, and instinctively understanding the marketing potential, he set about organising the event at Camberwell Junction tram depot, the first time he performed what became his often-repeated crowd favourite. Never entertaining self-doubt, he *'loved a challenge and to make it even more difficult, I decided to pack it with people, and to take the tram uphill. I had to break the barrier of normality to achieve it. Quite casually I fit my huge rope and attached my teeth grip, then I invited as many people as possible to pack into the tram for a free trip to fame and glory for me and my faith. They clambered on the footboards and it resembled a grandstand at a semi-final football match ...'*

At the Camberwell Tram Depot; Apollo pulling a tram with his teeth.

This astonishing feat of strength, taking the tram three hundred feet with his teeth as the grip point, was an immediate triumph, but as the cheering subsided and he was putting on his promotional robe, accepting the congratulations of the crowd, he was approached apologetically by the film crew. The embarrassed cameraman explained that as the throng surged they had crowded in-between the Fox Movietone News camera and the tram and spoiled their shot. Could he do it all again, please?

The tram returned to the bottom of the slight incline for Apollo. '... *I generated greater power than my previous pull and to the tumultuous cheers of the fantastic crowd I increased the distance ... I thought faith cannot only move mountains but a huge tramload of people ... I not only pulled the tram but a big percentage of Australia's fare dodgers as well ...*'

is how he stamped his showbiz mark on the event. The newsreel footage was widely shown and his fame guaranteed.

Into the 1950s, Nola and 'The Young Apollo' were living in a rooming house in Drummond Street, Carlton, and operating a gym in the larger downstairs rooms. On 20 June 1952, an ambulance was called to the house and medics found Apollo with a gunshot wound. A bullet had pierced his chest just below the heart. Surgery saved his life, and the doctors were quoted in the newspapers as saying, 'any normal person would have died almost immediately'. Investigators quickly concluded that the rifle 'accidentally' discharged while it was being cleaned. He later recounted in his diary that Nola was jealous of his flirtations with another woman recruited to his act. It is plausible that Nola shot him and they agreed to withhold details of the shooting to protect Nola and to avoid bad publicity. Not surprisingly, the partnership of Apollo and Noela De Milo – romantic and performing – was over. In his scrapbooks, Apollo celebrated the shooting, keeping clippings from every newspaper and tagged the pages: '*I will win big – and get back from this*'. Typically, he extracted every drop of publicity possible. Never waste a crisis.

Apollo's other landmark stunt – when he had an elephant stand on him – was a triumph that nearly killed him. Elephants were, he said, to be revered as almost sacred animals, inspirational, the repository of great wisdom as well as sheer strength. '*The elephant is the one animal I respected and loved more than any other.*'

'The elephant' was also the result of a dream, but one that carried a warning of extreme danger and foretold that he would be severely injured. '*However, the message to carry out the supernatural feat was the strongest part of this preordained incident*

Apollo was nearly killed, but his scrap book celebrates being shot as a 'win'.

my higher mental plane had received from the universe. I was excited and wildly stimulated to go into action and to put my life on the line in the most dangerous death-defying feat of my entire career … Here was a challenge worthy of the mythical gods who dwelt on Mount Olympus and I was selected to test my strength and extreme faith to accomplish it …' For inspiration, he called on Sampson, David, Olympian gods, the grim reaper and his recently deceased father, but not all at the same time.

Bullen Brothers Circus was encamped at Burnley Oval, Richmond, on the Yarra River. Already forty-four years old in November 1954, Apollo acknowledged the risks, but had confidence in his power and in the animal wranglers. *'I laid down on the ground and Georgie Wade, a member of my stunt team, put the Tomb of Hercules board on my prone body. This board is aptly named because so many strongmen had been injured or died using it for death-defying support feats. However, nothing had ever been attempted with it in such magnitude as this. The circus owner got the elephant lined up and then said to me, "Do you want to change your mind? Nobody will hold it against you". Irrespective of the circus owner's expression of concern I was all psyched up and anxious to get underway: this was the moment I had been created for. I shook my head and answered, "No, get on with it!" In response he simply replied, "Christ, man, you are game". I guess the mention of that name assured me here indeed was my power.'*

There were two assistants, with short-hooked elephant rods, front and back. *'I was quite confident and calm, all psyched up for the occasion, as usual, the killer instinct was riding high and my mind super positive – the breakthrough to cosmic power was operative. The huge crowd who somehow had heard of my attempt certainly were not calm, especially the women …*

'As the elephant was led forward, I could feel the vibrations as his feet struck the ground with every step that brought him nearer. Then, before he stood on me, his huge bulk blotted out the sunlight, and sure-footed he stood completely on my body. The pressure of the weight was so intense I felt as if my body would crumble into a shapeless mass and then the miracle eventuated ... as I whispered God's name I felt a wave of power and I was able to resist the terrific pressure. As this happened, the crowd surged forward and women fainted ... when a camera flash went off, a girl screamed and the elephant panicked and threw his trunk up in the air. He shifted his weight, leaving his two huge front feet poised over my face and nearly crushed me ... the circus owner barked "use the hooks" and immediately they were brought under the elephant's feet. Only intervention by the expert handlers saved my life.'

The following morning, he repeated the act in order to complete the challenge and cement the occasion in the record books. Because the elephant had nearly trodden on his head the day before, the Tomb board was placed lower down his torso, and the elephant's weight was concentrated on his abdomen, groin and knees. 'This time everything was perfection and I succeeded without incident.' The record was his. However, because of the lower placement of the board, Apollo suffered terrible injuries. 'I thought my kneecaps were going to explode and I was like a tube of toothpaste being squeezed. A fortnight later I suffered my first reaction ... my genitals swelled up and I started bleeding from the bowels. I visited the hospital and when they asked what was wrong, I told them an elephant had stood on me. They were not in the mood for funny remarks and told me in no uncertain terms. I produced photographic evidence of the feat to their sheer amazement and they remarked, "It's a miracle

Apollo survived being stood on by an elephant.

you're alive. Anything could be wrong – raptured [sic] *spleen and many broken ribs, just to give you a few minor details".*

Apollo not only survived, but the Newsreel and newspaper coverage was priceless and he was dubbed and, forever after, known as 'The Mighty Apollo' instead of the now out-of-date 'Young Apollo'. His fame spread and, over time, he polished the story, but, even with all the hyperbole stripped away, it is simply undeniable that he did have an elephant stand on him, and he did live to tell the tale. Sitting in the gym years later, casually flipping through his scrapbooks, reviewing his career and telling tale after tale, the story of the elephant was undoubtedly the highlight. He sat back in his chair, played with his moustache and stared out the window for a while before the crashing of weights in machines

Apollo's scrap books
celebrated every feat.

Fire trucks and double-decker busses were all used to test Apollo's strength.

brought him back to the task at hand. *'No-one else in the world has ever done that, you know,'* he would quietly and modestly declare.

While the tram pull and the elephant stunt were extraordinary, they were not something a performer could do every day. There were other showbiz routines that he could perform over and over. He would bend steel bars with his bare hands; lift phenomenal weights, whether on barbells, kettle bells, cannon balls or lumps of steel; win a tug of war against cars; have bluestone blocks smashed against his back or head; snap pennies with his teeth; and challenge the biggest and heaviest vehicle in town, often a fire truck, to resist his 'iron-jaw' teeth-towing routine – astonishing circus acts that always impressed.

'Coming second has never interested me. First man on the moon is remembered, first man to run the four-minute mile is remembered, no-

one cares who came second. Unless you are first, it doesn't matter. You might as well forget about it. I wanted top billing. I was the first man to have an elephant stand on him. I wanted to be first and I wanted to be famous. I'm a dreamer, and I embarked on a concept bordering on a fairytale. Fairy stories are for children not grown-ups, but my story is going to last forever. When I go out there I'm like a psyched-up atom bomb and out to conquer. I reached a stage where I didn't fear anything and I'd practise for hours day after day until I was invincible. I'm not worried about titles and status or glory ...' he said. These last words were not entirely convincing coming from Apollo, the most determined chaser of titles, glory and status you could ever meet, but it suited him to say otherwise.

His capacity for reinvention and conjuring new challenges seemed endless. The 'helicopter' routine involved two 'curvaceous beauties' sitting in opposite slings suspended on a strong bar that revolved around a pivot on a steel and leather helmet, itself supported by two stirrups that clamped and braced around his massive shoulders. The women would spin, encircling Apollo as he held himself rigid. His head, neck and spine were the shaft for the spinning propeller carrying his assistants. He calmly explained that *'if you wobble, you snap your neck ... you would be in a wheelchair and never walk again if you got it wrong ... I defied physics with that feat'* and of course Movietone News loved it. The women featured *'must be smooth skinned, slim and very shapely, they certainly don't appeal to the romantic impulses of man if they are moulded any other way. Any bulk would rock the confidence of the normal everyday guy ...'* He would never survive today's sensibilities, but we must remember there was nothing unusual about expressing those thoughts in the 1950s and 1960s.

Apollo and the helicopter routine, with Rondahe and another 'curvaceous beauty'.

Apollo was invited to tour the UK and the US around 1955 to promote Spenby chest expanders, but after careful consideration chose not to go. Marketed as the solution to weak chest and arm muscles, the multiple coiled chrome springs – typically in sets of three or maybe four if a greater challenge was required – were attached at either end to sculpted wooden handles. Chest expanders featured in full-page ads inside the back cover of comic books and on the sports page of newspapers for decades.

Apollo claimed the record for stretching thirty springs at a time, which he could do both in front and behind his back, and his idealised torso was thought to be the magic marketing vehicle for promotion of these popular devices. I remember the ads from my own childhood: 'Eighty-pound weaklings transformed into Tarzan-like towers of strength'. 'Sick of having sand kicked in your face ...' was another version of the marketing. Many a puny boy, buried deep in *Superman*, *Phantom* or *Archie & Jughead* comics, had a chest expander hidden under the bed. At a friend's house as a pimply teen, I gave one a tryout. I overextended the springs, could not hold the tension, then had to let go suddenly. The handle flew into my face, split my lip and broke a chip off my front tooth that I can still feel to this day.

Apollo was teetotal, and while working with the famous athletics trainer Percy Cerutty (a vegetarian) in the build-up to the Melbourne Olympic Games in '56, when he was hired to provide strength and conditioning advice, he featured several times in a vegetarian magazine. Although he was paid to promote vegetarianism, in real life he loved a good steak.

He continued to pull cars with a rope gripped in his teeth long after it was suggested he retire. The physical strain was

Apollo, arms around Mark and Bruce, and Paul junior with the stunt team in Apollo T-shirts.

Apollo sandwiched between the Tomb Board and Bed of Nails, under a car.

immeasurable, the toll on his body incalculable. Eventually he claimed a world record of a chain of five tethered newspaper delivery vans being pulled by one short man with a toggle firmly gripped in his jaws! He had progressed from cars to small vans to bigger trucks to fire trucks, then the biggest pumper in the fire brigade – the heaviest in the southern hemisphere, weighing in at 30 tons – and then did it again, with the gleaming truck laden with 'bathing beauties'. Anything that would attract the newspaper and Movietone News cameras.

Another regular and record-breaking performance was for Apollo to lay on the ground, gripping the Tomb of Hercules board on top of him, while a skilled stunt driver would steer a car straight over him. His first efforts needed refinement for theatricality, and he switched positions so that his head was visible to the audience. They wanted to see his face, wanted to watch him grimace and groan as the weight of the car went over his prone body. Future events always had him head out, not feet out.

There were mishaps – a few times a car was driven too fast, too erratically and several times slid off the wooden ramp and drove over his legs. Repainting the boards with shiny gloss paint made them look good, but they became slippery and he suffered some injuries as a result. But it remained a staple in his act and the audiences lapped it up. True to his mantra to 'always keep them guessing' he tricked up the car, and fitted an 'open' or loud exhaust and a police siren. His driver – Ernie Galatalli – would rev the car excessively, creating a sense of menace even while it was stationary. Then he would make a few practice runs towards a prone Apollo, getting closer and faster as he drove towards his unprotected head. Only at the last moment would Galatalli slam on the brakes and skid to a stop just shy of crushing Apollo, who, only after this build-up and suspense would take on the ramps to protect his body as the next pass of the car went right over him.

Over the years, more and more cars and sometimes trucks were added, and by the time he retired in his late seventies the routine had grown to twenty-four cars one after the other, another world record and a feat varied and repeated for charity fundraisers. As if that was not exciting enough, Apollo innovated and added extra spice to the car routine by lying on a bed of nails. His back would be pock-marked with thousands of indentations, raw and red across his shoulders and right down to his waist, testament to the authenticity of the routine and the absence of any trickery. The

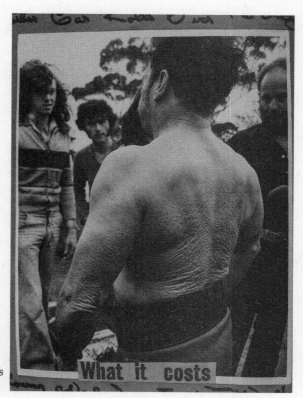

The Bed of Nails leaves
its mark on Apollo.

mental strength required to withstand that much punishment is astonishing, confirming Apollo's extraordinary capacity to ignore pain.

Single since surviving being shot by Nola and then divorcing, Apollo thought himself a playboy and acted accordingly. But the snappily dressed star was lonely. He craved a family, and when another comely assistant, albeit a much younger one, entered his orbit, it was hardly surprising that she soon became his wife.

CHAPTER 9

RONDAHE

Having parted ways with Nola Nolan, Apollo subscribed to the common view of the time that women inhibited a man's career. *'Cut out the dames and go for the fame. When I was young, I chased beautiful women, but the thrill of conquering is more enduring than the thrill of love,'* he diarised in typical candid style.

In 1953 the patriarch of the clan, Thomas Anderson, died, and just a few years later his wife, Margaret, was diagnosed with terminal cancer. Recently widowed and financially struggling, she travelled by 'parlour coach' to the NT to live with Thelma and husband Sid at Top Springs, but died soon after. Apollo felt the loss of both parents acutely. He and his brothers had all taken different paths, and he had little to do with them. Now recently separated from Nola, Apollo immersed himself in the business as a way to suppress his loneliness.

His gym prospered as the marketing impact of regular well-publicised performances delivered customers. He moved from Carlton to a bigger space in the middle of the city, where he could establish a modern, dedicated gym – described in his advertisements as the most advanced in Australia – and courted the press whenever the opportunity presented. He was at the top of his game.

Television was launched in Australia to coincide with the Melbourne 1956 Olympic Games, and Apollo readily adapted his performances and soon popped up on the black-and-white flickering screen. TV producers loved him – his circus credentials readily lent themselves to a variety show format and he became a regular on the new medium. His scrapbooks are peppered with letters of thanks from all the major TV networks, often with personal greetings from the stars of the time as well as the various directors and producers who negotiated his appearances. Performing inside TV studios meant obvious limitations, but he relished the chance to not just lap up applause from the live audience but to relentlessly market the gym.

Around the same time, Rondahe Valerie Camille Smithers crossed his path. A notable beauty and model, featured in local papers as the winner of several beach girl and beauty competitions, Rondahe was introduced to Apollo by Mark and Pam Lewis from the Australian weightlifting team, one of few who trained women. It was they who thought Rondahe a suitable assistant for Apollo. After auditioning at their Cheltenham gym in March 1955, she started as just a performing partner. Promotional photos from the time show a tall, slim woman with long, thick, jet-black hair, perpetually wearing tight leotards which, back then, was exceedingly daring and risqué. She looked confidently at any camera pointed her way, chin up and gaze direct, showing performative instincts, no doubt coached by the media-savvy Apollo. Over a few months, their relationship blossomed. His diary records the rapid progress from 'remember –

RIGHT: Rondahe Smithers was attracting attention even before Apollo started working with her. [*Australasian Post*]

BELOW: Apollo documented Rondahe's success as a beach girl competition winner.

[*The Sun/The Argus*]

to fall in love is to be hurt' in early April 1955 to just a few weeks later *'to be in love is to be inspired'* by May. He recorded lingering doubts in his meticulously kept journal: *'She is too young for you ... it will interfere with your career ... Don't get too close ... women have a tendency to curtail a man's ability to conquer because they soften the stern fibres and destroy the man's killer instinct.'* But fall for each other they did, despite a significant age difference. Rondahe had grown up without a father, so perhaps an older man offered reassurance. Or perhaps she hitched her wagon to the famous Mighty Apollo with the lure of stardom.

Against the wishes of Daisy, her mother, who believed her daughter to be making a terrible mistake, Rondahe and Apollo married on 6 November 1961 in the Methodist church in the city. *'Daisy, our grandmother, was always pissed off that Rondahe married Dad, a showie. She was a social climber and wanted her beautiful daughter to marry a professional: a doctor or a lawyer, or at least someone rich. She thought it was her ticket to high society,'* recounted their youngest son, Bruce.

When they married, Rondahe was just twenty-six and Apollo fifty-one – but told anyone who asked that he was forty, as was recorded on their marriage certificate. He had little trouble maintaining the façade. His physique better fitted a younger man, and when asked about the age difference years later, Apollo said, *'All the women my age were too old for me'*. Eldest son Paul junior was born just five months after the wedding. Three boys in rapid succession between 1962 and 1965 kept them busy – Mark was born nine-and-a-half months after Paul, and Bruce less than two years later – but their marriage lasted just ten years and ended dramatically.

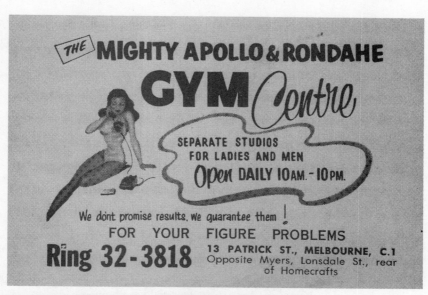

ABOVE: The gym business card: For your figure problems.

LEFT: Apollo and Rondahe, Paul junior on the dog, Mark and baby Bruce on Rondahe's lap, 1965.

'*We lived on the top floor of the gym – that was home. The ground floor was the women's gym, the middle floor was the men's gym and the top floor was for us, as well as boxing and martial arts. We had our living area on the street side, in the middle was space for martial arts and the full-size boxing ring, but the bathroom and water taps were at the back – on the other side. You had to drop your head and go under the boxing ring to get through,*' recalls Paul. It was spartan, but clean and organised, more like camping than a family home. The three boys shared a three-tiered bunk in the same room as their parents. Middle brother Mark claims '*Rondahe didn't like living in the gym. The kitchen had no water supply, so that was very frustrating for her. It was too basic and she wanted to live in a house, not somewhere you had to duck around a boxing ring every time you wanted to go and get the water to cook dinner*'. Bruce and Paul have a different memory. '*My parents decided together not to buy a house because it was better for the business to stay living in the gym,*' says Bruce.

Living in the cramped space beside the boxing ring had some advantages. It saved them money and meant Apollo and Rondahe could always be on hand for their growing workload as well as juggling the needs of three small boys. Unusual for the era, they both worked, and merged beauty classes, strength training and some of the very first local self-defence classes for women. They relentlessly chased publicity about them all. Neither parent made their children a priority, regularly hiring babysitters so they could both work after hours in the gym. Occasionally unsupervised, with the city as their playground, the three small boys explored neighbouring empty buildings and soon learned how to get into cinemas without paying, and other skills. Their unorthodox upbringing and mischievous nature saw them occasionally in trouble – sampling the wares in Myer uninvited, for instance.

Apollo and Rondahe rebranded the gym as the 'Mighty Apollo and Rondahe Gym and Combat Centre' to emphasise and profit from the novelty of classes run by a female instructor. At first, Rondahe concentrated on figure sculpting, and the signage promised 'The Doorway to Strength and Beauty': Apollo was the strength, Rondahe the beauty. When she too embraced the martial arts some years later and her self-defence classes for women became more and more popular, the newspapers and TV loved it – the glamorous mum who was mixing it on the mat with not just women but men, too. A female karate, kendo and jodo (stick and sword) instructor was a novelty in the early 1960s, and the eye-catching Rondahe, whether in a full-length flowing kimono or her white fighting tunic, long black hair arranged for effect, was perfect for endless photo opportunities, with or without Apollo. There are dozens of articles in the scrapbooks featuring her with sticks, swords, ropes and other fighting accessories, in embroidered silk gowns, sometimes barefoot, sometimes in leotards, swimsuits or street clothes. The headlines are consistently and remarkably fixated on her femininity and often her figure: *'Muscles Can Be a Girl's Best Friend'*, *'Shapes up Well'*, *'So Watch It Fellas!'* and so on. The publicity for the era features the same messages: *'Girls, Girls, Girls – Do You Desire a Perfect Figure? Don't Envy the Film Stars, Do Something About It … Special course for business women and housewives'*.

The tabloids loved any opportunity to feature Rondahe in a tight tunic or lifting weights. *'Rondahe – the girl who has given hundreds of disproportioned women an attractive new figure contour –*

and a brighter outlook' was one caption, alongside adverts for figure sculpting. The 1960s were a time of great social upheaval, and the offer of improved personal safety for female customers on the newly liberated streets made good business sense. Asian martial arts coupled with the hit *Samurai* TV show were also tempting ingredients; Apollo and Rondahe capitalised on them both as much as they could.

As Rondahe became more involved in the fighting arts, her focus shifted away from beauty and figure shaping. Apollo thought it better for growth and balance in the business if she concentrated on the more feminine offerings, but she thought she could satisfy both callings. Bruce recalls many years later his father telling him it was Rondahe who made the choice to

Apollo's scrap books celebrate Rondahe's growing profile. [*Australasian Post*]

diversify, even though combat was incompatible with modelling and beauty work. When her modelling work dried up, she rued her choice, and even blamed Apollo for it, quite unfairly according to Bruce. *'She later told me that we collectively had ruined her modelling career.'*

In the mid-60s and into the '70s, some of Australia's most popular kids' TV shows featured samurai culture. The postwar Japanese revival was celebrated as an economic miracle, and Japanese appliances were slowly arriving in local shops. Apollo and Rondahe ran the biggest karate classes in Australia, and Apollo went on his first and only overseas trip in December 1965 to Japan to learn more. *'Dad was the first in Australia to demonstrate karate,'* says Paul, *'and when he went to Japan, they called him The Almighty Apollo. He quite liked that.'* Apollo meticulously recorded and diarised his 1965–66 Japan visit, making sure that anyone who enquired knew that he *'toured to achieve, not to be a tourist'*. Coming to terms with different cultures was *'a Herculean task'* but he *'was confident he could achieve new horizons in my march to glory and fame'*.

His intention was to connect to the *'warrior culture'* in Japan, which had simultaneously appalled and fascinated Australians during the war. Apollo went to great lengths to ensure his reputation preceded him, calling in favours from anyone he knew in sport and showbiz – there would be few indignities worse than being ignored or overlooked. He was not disappointed, and his contacts through the international weightlifting and Olympic communities served him well. He was introduced to officials from various sporting bodies who arranged for friendly media, was feted like a VIP, and fell in love with Japan. He took tea

Rondahe became an expert martial arts instructor.

with Reiso Kano, son of Jigoro Kano, originator of judo and president of the famous Kada Kan, and also met Masatoshi Nakayama, master of karate at the headquarters of the Japanese Karate Association, the Shoto Kan. His host was an ex–US Marine, Donn Draeger, one of the first westerners to be accepted by the Japanese as an instructor in judo. Regarded as the greatest non-Japanese teacher of martial arts and a key interpreter for its western adherents, he had a devoted following in his own right.

To be granted an audience with Draeger was itself an honour. The Japanese had been sent footage and clippings of Apollo's tram pulls and the elephant standing on him, and '*knew of my superpowers and my miracle feats*' and dubbed him 'Tetsu Jin' or 'God of Steel'. They presented him with a jacket with 'Almighty Apollo' embroidered on the chest and kangaroos and 'Tetsu Jin' across the back. He made sure the trip generated considerable publicity back in Australia. At his own expense, he brought Isao Inokuma, winner of the 1964 Olympic Judo Championship heavyweight title, to teach in Melbourne, together with Mr M Nakayama, the chief instructor of the Japan Karate Association, and eventually Donn Draeger himself flew to Melbourne to visit and teach at the Mighty Apollo and Rondahe Gym and Combat Centre. In March 1967, Mr Inokuma started doing work for other gyms, in breach of his contract, and Apollo took him to court. Rather than repay his airfare and other costs to Apollo, Inokuma rapidly decamped to Japan.

His fascination with Japan was not the only example of Apollo's curiosity about other cultures. For a man who had little formal education and left school in his early teens, he had a remarkable breadth of interests. His writings, sometimes impenetrable with his blend of mysticism and jargon, had structure and demonstrated a commanding vocabulary. His peculiar turn of phrase and self-aggrandising aside, he instinctively knew how to craft a story, whether in spoken word or written form. Years ahead of the entire genre of self-help books that explore the same themes with a more conventional vocabulary, he was exploring the mind-body connection way back in the 1960s. He made friends across all races and readily embraced African-American boxers like 'Gentleman Don Johnson' and the famous professional wrestler and emerging TV star Chief Little Wolf. Anyone non-Anglo fascinated him, as did their spirituality, their fighting style and weapons. He often would glean a snippet or a morsel from a different tradition and work it into his routines, making his performance more exotic for doing so. *'Fighting weapons have changed through the ages, but their ability to create destruction has never changed. I developed the ability to master many forms of weapons over the years; a warrior must be able to use whatever is available to him; the ability to know how to fight is the greatest asset a man can have ... Never use the same technique twice as your enemy will study your technique and find your weak spot.'*

Impressed with sumo, Apollo claimed to have an instinctive connection to *'the warrior mindset, the great arts we are learning. The spiritual side of what they do with such grace; it is not just strength. There is a fighting man stance, a mindset, and you have to learn it exactly right, not close to it but exactly right. It's not tiddly-winks, it's a serious business'.*

While Apollo was in Japan, Rondahe completed their negotiations for the lease on a second gym, a mere 100 metres up the road from their home and work in Little Lonsdale Street. As business boomed, they had outgrown the original space and decided to move the martial arts studio to dedicated new premises – to establish the biggest martial arts studio outside Japan was their claim, unprovable but possibly true. Apollo was unsure about the additional financial commitment but was comforted by entering into an arrangement with boxing champions Don Johnson and Lenny Young to run boxing classes in some of the old space. Their media profile increasingly focused on the photogenic Rondahe and her martial arts and self-defence classes, as Apollo became more the behind scenes promoter and businessman. He continued to train clients but, on Rondahe's urgings, he performed fewer death-defying stunts. *'If anything happened to you I'd die,'* she would say. Years later, Apollo would retell the story but finish her sentence: *'Yep, die laughing'.*

Each of the Anderson sons recalls the details of their childhood differently, which is common to all families. But most families do not share episodes as dramatic and traumatic as those that happened as the Anderson parents' relationship deteriorated. *'Some time well before she left, there was a big argument about something, but I don't know what. Rondahe had a Morris Minor and after some argument she wanted to drive off in it. Dad went and picked up the car; he lifted the wheels off the ground and even with the engine running, she couldn't drive away. I guess it could be funny now, but it wasn't then,'* recalls Bruce. *'He said, "Come back inside and we can talk; I'm not putting the car down until you agree to come back inside".'*

The mental picture of Apollo, like Superman, holding up the bumper bar, the engine revving, wheels spinning in the air and Rondahe at the wheel, is somewhat compelling, and unique to

Happier days for the Anderson family.

this family – bridging the gap, as they were, between showbiz and the newly emerging fitness and self-defence craze.

Three spirited boys sometimes getting into mischief did not improve the mood at home. Each of the adult Anderson sons admits that they were individually and together more than a handful. Mark recalls just one example from many that upset their mother, Rondahe: *'She cracked the shits when we were out in the old shot tower. We were always mucking around, nicking stuff ... and we thought it would be funny to tell her Paul had fallen down the tower. I ran home and told her I thought Paul was dead, and she came racing back. He was lying on the ground and we had theatrically put a brick on top of him to make it look good. She was furious and said that was the last straw, even though, before she got to him, I told her it was a joke and he was alright. It sure backfired – we got into heaps of trouble.'*

Bruce remembers their stunt clearly. *'She was furious, and looking back now it was a cry for help by my brothers, a maybe misguided attempt to get some attention. Before that she used to lash us with the electrical cord from the jug. Dad never laid a finger on us and another time even stopped her beating me with a Japanese fighting stick she snatched from a nearby rack. But she did do all that – she had no patience and couldn't handle three hyper kids all tearing around the city, shoplifting and stuff ... we were sometimes pretty wild.'*

Whether it was business pressure, stress caused by three mischievous sons, the age difference, the romantic lure of new love – or some other influence – the marriage came to an abrupt end in 1971 when Rondahe vanished with one of the martial arts instructors, Alex Dudko. The actual day they 'did a runner' is recalled slightly differently by each son, but they all agree it came with no build-up, nor warning. Bruce, although not quite six years old at the time, remembers when she left '*with such clarity that I know what people were wearing. I have the clarity of a child but now with the understanding of an adult*'.

Paul was nearly nine and also recounts his clear memories. '*The business fell apart because the gym was shut after "Incubator" ran off with one of Dad's younger martial arts instructors, Alex Dudko. He was a dud like his name and barely half her age. Dad treated him like he was part of our family and then he did that to us ... runs off with his boss's wife ... what a creep,*' spits Paul, fifty years later, recalling that calamitous day.

'"*Incubator*"? *Yep, that's the only name I can call her ... she was no mother, not to me nor my brothers, and I'm not prepared to call her by her name or anything else. She was just an incubator, and I don't care what people think. I've had counselling for abandonment and trust issues, I have had trouble forming relationships with women and at last, these days, I am happy. But she stuffed me up. Not just me, my brothers too – we are all the same. I can't forgive her, why should I? You bet I harbour a grudge. She violated our trust.*'

The eldest and youngest sons harbour and freely express this deep resentment, tipping into anger, over the loss of their unconventional but usually happy childhood. When their mother vanished with her lover to start a new life is the defining moment in their lives. While they are protective of Apollo's legacy, a special venom is reserved for Rondahe Anderson.

'*Rondahe, the bitch, she ruined my dad,*' says Bruce in a deliberate and measured tone, not taking any backwards step. '*He was at the top of his game when he met her. She emasculated him, ruined him. She did not have a maternal bone in her body. Dad always spoke fondly of her and said she had done all these amazing things, but she was always saying really bad things about him, things that we knew had not happened. She lies until she believes it herself.'* Without the slightest hesitation he recounts the impact on his life of his mother's sudden departure. He opines that his mother enrolled him to start school early (aged five) so that she could get him out of the way and *'skip and run off'.* He was in state care the longest – until he was seventeen-and-a-half years old. He eventually took an apprenticeship as a carpenter so he could get away. *'I never finished school but quit early just so I could escape that gaol. I went to live with Dad for a while but he was thoroughly undomesticated and difficult to live with. If you asked him the time, he'd tell you how to build a Swiss watch. He couldn't help it – that is just how he was, he loved to tell a story; he was always a showman, but it drove me nuts. All he did was work and sleep at the gym, he was totally oriented to trying to make the business work and he had no interest in anything or anyone else. He was an enigma, even to us … so I left. I don't go through life blaming her but I can't and won't forget it. I am not a nut case, but that is surprising with what I had to go through.'*

Middle brother Mark is still in touch with his mother, now well into her eighties and in frail health. *'I ended up with all sorts of problems and anxieties because of going into welfare. I'm pretty resilient now but it has all made me guarded, and I don't easily trust people. I like structure now – it comes from being institutionalised when a kid. It's stuffed up our lives and I can't even begin to tell the pain it caused.'* Mark sighs as his partner comforts him, softening the distress from excavating the most painful years of his life.

Paul recalls the traumatic day Rondahe left in graphic detail. *'Incubator had a green Morris Minor, she called it her freedom car.*

We went to school in Faraday Street in Carlton, up near the Women's Hospital. Early 1971 it was; the school term had only just started. I was nearly nine, Mark was seven, Bruce would have been nearly six. She dropped us off in the morning like usual, but then she started crying. "What's wrong," I said, and she goes: "Remember, Mum loves you very much, look after your brothers, be good boys for your dad, I have to go." And that was it; we had no idea what was going on, we just went into school like normal.' As he remembers that day he stares for ages into the corner of the room, then gathers himself and rifles through a dog-eared pile of publicity photos until finding the one he wants.

'Here he is ...' declares Paul and holds up a portrait of two men in white combat uniforms, coloured insignia belts knotted out front, standing bare feet apart in a pre-fight pose, fists clenched. Apollo stared down the barrel of the lens, comfortable with a camera, typically immaculately groomed and coiffed, thin moustache atop the pursed upper lip, his eyes and mouth with not the faintest hint of a smile. His stance was square and solid – he knew no other. Next to him was a comparatively skinny man, a scruffy beard framing a small mouth and damp sweaty hair falling towards unsmiling eyes. Alex Dudko was Apollo's trusted sidekick, already a highly rated martial arts instructor in his early twenties. In a matching photo, taken in the same batch, Dudko was snapped standing with 'Incubator' and a karate-suited young Paul. All three were smiling broadly. Rondahe had both her hands on her eldest son's shoulders, as Dudko – maybe already her lover? – grinned to the camera. That photo was glued into one of Apollo's scrapbooks, annotated in the unmistakeable flowery hand of Apollo: 'BASTARD' he wrote in capital letters, with a heavy arrow in ink pointing directly to his rival.

ABOVE: Alex Dudko with Rondahe and Paul junior; Apollo added 'BASTARD' on the photo in his scrapbook.

RIGHT: Apollo and Alex Dudko – a contrast in physiques.

Paul hesitates, then recovers and resumes his grim story. '*At lunchtime I was called in to see the headmaster, which was pretty weird, and Dad was on the phone. "Come home ... your mum's gone ..." I'm just this kid, you know, so I got my brothers, and a car came and took us to the gym. Dad went into a fog and lay on the couch and wouldn't eat. I heated up cans of Irish stew for us, but Dad would not move. He closed the gym, wouldn't open the doors to anyone and he just lay on the couch for days. I thought maybe he was dying, so I sat on the couch and put an ear to his chest to see if he was breathing. I knew there was something wrong, but didn't know what to do. I ran out to the street and told a policeman there was something wrong with my dad and they came to check. Basically, he had a nervous breakdown. We found out later that she had already told Thelma she was leaving and that she was starting a new life and wouldn't have anything more to do with any of us. They weren't close, but Thelma had visited and knew she was unhappy. After a few nights at the gym, one of Dad's instructors, Neville Houghton, and his wife took us to their house and Dad was taken to Royal Park Mental Hospital for a fair while – about six months or maybe longer, and the gym stayed shut for about a year. He was pretty sick; he flipped out. He thought there were people being sent to kill us.*'

Rondahe Anderson and Alex Dudko first moved to Adelaide, then Queensland. She did build a new life, teaching horse riding and dressage. When she left Apollo, she was thirty-six and he was sixty. Alex Dudko was in his mid-twenties.

Each brother has slightly different memories of the day of their mother's disappearance. The younger brothers say they were left waiting at the gates after school to be collected, and when Rondahe did not arrive and the school was closing, a teacher called the police, who drove them home to the gym, where their father was beside himself with worry. Memory is an unreliable companion at the best of times and they were small boys, distressed, and it was fifty years ago. Whichever version is correct, the shock of the sudden disappearance of their mother was soon supplanted by the enormity of what happened next.

After a few weeks, as it became apparent that Apollo was likely to stay in hospital for treatment for some time, the Houghtons called for help for the three Anderson boys. '*Our sixty-year-old granny, Daisy Smithers, Incubator's mum, was living in Bacchus Marsh, but the welfare wouldn't let her take us,*' is how Paul picks up the tale. '*Incubator wrote a card to her mother – a bloody card, can you believe it? – and a letter to us which was sent to the Houghtons, who read it to us while we all sat on a couch. The letter said "I don't want to see any of you again and don't want anything to do with Apollo again".*'

Middle brother Mark takes up the narrative. '*Next thing,*' recalls Mark, '*the Houghtons call the police, and on 19 March 1971 a policewoman took us to Allambie Children's Home in Burwood. The welfare said Granny was too old to look after three young boys and to raise us, and the only other relative we knew was Aunty Thelma but she was too far away.*'

'*At Allambie, there are different dorms full of abandoned kids … we were allowed to be together and we knew how to look after ourselves so we were OK, but there are kids fighting, jumping from bed to bed when the lights go out, and so much bullying. I tried to escape but got into trouble,*' recounts Paul. Mark and Bruce have even more alarming accounts of their initiation into state care. '*Allambie Children's Home was draconian, a terrible way of looking after kids. You weren't allowed anything personal, any valuables got knocked off. If you complained about anything you just got clobbered. If you were naughty they threatened to send you to Turana, which was like kids' prison and even worse,'* says Mark.

Bruce remembers in horror as he angrily casts his mind back to their first few nights in Allambie. *'It was awful. First thing we see is ... we are taken to a dining hall and offered some food; and some old bitch with man arms was force-feeding some little kid with a spoon, a pile of peas; and this kid threw up and I swear I saw her scoop up the spew and force it back into his mouth again. That place was hell for us, so I hope Rondahe goes to hell when she drops off her perch. When the cops got in touch with her about leaving, she said to them that she didn't care about Apollo, the business or the kids. I don't know how anyone can say that. If she didn't love Dad anymore and wanted to leave – well, I can understand that, people split up and get divorced all the time. But she broke him, cleaned him out and ruined our three lives as well.'*

After two slow and agonising months in Allambie, the three young brothers were placed into foster care with a family in Hallam. *'It felt like months, but we were put in with a Salvation bloody Army family,'* tells Paul. *'We had to call them Uncle and Auntie and spend Sunday all day at bloody church. Then we were with another family – he was a nasty cunt. He would hang shit on Dad and say, "Your dad's not really strong, it's all fake", and then if we argued he'd make you pull your pants down and hit you with his belt, and drag us by the hair.'* Paul clenches his jaw, squares his massive shoulders and looks through me for a moment. *'If I saw him today, I reckon I would rip his bloody head off. The last time he hit me I was fourteen and I said "if you ever touch me again I will fucking kill you" ... and he said "Oh, big tough man, are you now?" but he never touched me again. When I was not there, he would get stuck into Mark and Bruce though.'*

Mark shudders as he remembers the violence. *'The kids at school in Hallam, they called us "housos" and we were always treated differently to the other kids. We lived in a house on Harmer Road in Hallam and we used to take it in turns to cop a hiding. If anything was wrong or broken, you were blamed for it even if you didn't do anything. You couldn't ask a friend to come back to your place after school, and you weren't ever allowed to go to their place; everything was always controlled. School was pretty rough – there was a bully called Bernard who was much bigger than me and he tried to push me into the urinal while I was peeing and so I defended myself and turned around and kicked him in the nuts as hard as I could. He needed seven stitches, and I got into a lot of trouble, but afterwards we were left alone. Later I found out that Bernard was also a state ward and we became good friends. The first house parents were Salvation Army, and we had to go to church three times a day on Sunday – it was all fire and brimstone and I hated it and it put me right off God, but I loved the band and it got me interested in music. Then there was a family with a dad who was just plain vicious. He used to come into our room with his belt wrapped around his fist, and he'd threaten to beat us. It was horrible. When Dad visited – once he got out of hospital – they would listen in to everything we said. After he was gone we would get into trouble for telling him stuff and they would threaten that we would not be allowed to visit him anymore. When we did go into the city and stayed at the gym he'd lay out all the mattresses on the floor – it was like an adventure. We would sneak into the movies, he would teach us martial arts; but if he was working, it was like the city was our playground, full of vacant warehouses and derelict buildings we would explore. We would catch pigeons and take them back to school after the weekend or the holidays and sell them to kids. Then the pigeons would fly back to the city and we would catch them and sell them all over again. It was pretty good fun.'*

Bruce was in the welfare system for eleven years. He vouches for the brutality, the lack of any affection, and is bitter over the detachment of the social workers who were supposed to be securing their wellbeing. *'They did nothing to protect us from these vindictive and cruel cottage parents who were being paid to care for us. They coached us — actually threatened us — to keep our mouths shut, and we were warned that if we dared complain they would make sure we would not get to see our dad ever again or be sent to kids' prison. I would love to see some of them now as a grown man ...'*

Apollo had shock therapy during his six months in hospital. Although he eventually recovered well and returned to both the gym and performing, he was never quite the same. Whether that was because of the illness or the treatment is impossible to say. Paul reflects, *'He became a harder version of himself — determined to prove he was still the Mighty Apollo and driven to succeed but lacked trust in instructors and particularly women'*.

His sister, Thelma, drove from Top Springs to visit when he was released from hospital, and briefly there was a plan to relocate the family to Katherine where they could all set up house. Mark was told, *'She would still run the pub but we would go to boarding schools — top schools — and we could all become doctors or lawyers instead of hobos, and she would pay for it all. Dad said he would find a way to keep working but then the welfare people put the kybosh on it because it didn't fit their criteria or some garbage. Rondahe claimed that before she left she had spoken to Thelma and had made arrangements for Thelma to look after us and to make sure we would not come to any harm. She was adamant that she had done the right thing and that it was Thelma that had let her down, not kept her side of the bargain'.*

Eldest brother Paul can add some detail to the tale. *'Thelma came down and they said maybe we would go and live with her at Top Springs, and Apollo could open a gym and work out of Darwin and she could get a nanny and we could do school of the air. It all sounded fabulous. We thought we were going to the NT but the welfare changed their mind and had a bad attitude about it and then Dad had a falling out with Thelma. It became obvious that it was just not going to work for him.'*

After Rondahe left in 1971 with Alex Dudko, Apollo initially struggled to recover financially. *'When she went, he was left with so much debt. She must have planned it for ages, because they just vanished. He always said that she cleaned out the bank accounts but I don't really know. He had nothing, that's for sure,'* recalls Mark. Apollo's nervous breakdown and long stint in hospital left him emotionally vulnerable and guilty about his inability to adequately provide for his three sons. But once back on his feet he still chased fame and tried to resurrect and reprise his commercial and showbiz appeal. He returned to his gym, trained relentlessly and worked to successfully rebuild his business, motivated by anger directed at his ex-wife, a refusal to be beaten and his desire to create a legacy with whatever time he had left.

Business looked up and for a while, he made a good living again. His lavish spending habits returned, and he splashed out on exotic antiques that gave the gym the atmospheric allure that so impressed me the first time I walked in all those years ago.

Tribal weapons, African and Aboriginal art, old and possibly rare guns, huge porcelain vases and bronze urns, stuffed animals – an eclectic collection. Paul remembers his father carrying around huge wads of notes, '*rolled up like a gangster. He had a fancy new leather jacket with about $10,000 in the pocket, and one day he left it on the stairs when he answered the phone inside the gym in a hurry, and when he came back out the jacket was gone. Some lucky thief had no idea when stealing that jacket that he was getting a whole lot more*'.

The Mighty Apollo was determined to be mighty again.

The lifting of the veil on the family dysfunction explains the desperation in Apollo's requests at our regular legal-related meetings about his sister's estate. Within this traumatic family context, their father's determination to squeeze every dollar from the Estate of Thelma Cecilia Hawks makes absolute sense. When Apollo and his sons appeared in the foyer at Barker Harty & Co and sat on the edge of the couch in our office, I knew nothing of their back story. It was neither enquired into nor seemed relevant. While I was working my way through negotiations with both John Flynn and Norm Douglas's lawyers in Darwin, unbeknown to me my teenage clients had been through a brutalising time in foster care homes. As they grew older, and were able to leave the welfare system and live independently, their needs were no less urgent. Thelma's estate was a windfall, like winning the lotto, a once-in-a-lifetime opportunity for the Andersons. With hindsight, Thelma's money, if carefully managed, ought to have made all the difference in the world.

When Thelma died in 1981, her defaced and invalid 1967 Last Will and Testament included a gift of all her valuable jewellery and some cash to Rondahe Anderson. It was impossible to know whether Thelma still intended for Rondahe to inherit her valuables after her sister-in-law ran off with a lover, but the gift still took effect.

Flynn did not know how to contact Rondahe, and Apollo suggested he try through Daisy Smithers, her elderly mother. Daisy refused to reveal her daughter's whereabouts, even to the Public Trustee, and claimed that Rondahe and Dudko feared for their lives, believing they would be hunted by Apollo and killed if he ever found out where they lived. Flynn accepted that Rondahe was genuinely terrified of Apollo. Those fears are so often found to be genuine and there is not the slightest doubt that Apollo would have been physically capable of inflicting serious injury or worse on anyone he wanted to harm. But there is no evidence whatsoever that Apollo ever searched for Rondahe or planned to do her or Dudko any harm.

All three sons scoff at the very thought that their father could have been violent to Rondahe. There is no history of Apollo being violent to anyone, not even Nola Nolan when he was shot and nearly killed after they fell out. There is the remote possibility that Nola shot him in self-defence, but there is no evidence whatsoever of that. But over several years, Rondahe was consistent in telling her mother of her fear of Apollo, as was Alex Dudko. We will never know.

Back in the 1970s, the three Anderson boys were dealing with life in brutal institutional care, the after-effects of their father's nervous breakdown, a mother who walked out on them and only occasional contact with their grandmother Daisy. Paul is perplexed these days at his grandmother's deception. *'As little kids, we wanted to speak to Mum and I remember asking Granny where she had gone. I wrote to Incubator and asked Granny to send her the letter but she claimed she did not know where she lived. We knew that wasn't the truth, but we were just kids.'* Bruce snorts with derision at the suggestion that Daisy did not know where Rondahe was. *'When we visited for Christmas or Easter there would be a card in Rondahe's distinctive hand on the mantlepiece; there was no hiding it.'* When word came through in the mid-80s that Daisy was dying with bowel cancer, they found themselves unexpectedly reunited with Rondahe.

'Dad named Daisy "Eagle Beak" – she was a meddler,' recounts Mark. *'She was authoritarian and had delusions of grandeur. Her daughter was too good for our dad, and she had tried to stop them getting together. She never approved of him because he came from the wrong side of the tracks, he was a "showie". Bruce found out Eagle Beak was ill and said we should go to visit her in hospital in Bacchus Marsh, and that Rondahe was going to be there; and he wanted to say his goodbyes and asked me to go with him. It was awkward because I was persona non grata. She had accused me of stealing some stamps from her collection when we visited in the school holidays a few years before. It was utter bullshit but I got left out of her will. Petty and cruel, and I think my brothers got $50 or something trivial anyway, but that is what she was like – spiteful and mean.'* Small issues become big ones in so many families, but something as minor as a few stamps from grandma's collection is a remarkably slight trigger for a woman to disown one of her grandsons, especially given all that these boys had been through.

Mark continues his sad tale. *'It was like a UFO had landed. Out of the blue there is our mother, in the room, quite talkative.*

Remember, we have not seen her for nearly fifteen years and I am only twenty-two, so I had no idea what she was like. I am trying to keep my composure, but there is my grandmother, who I have not seen since she called me a liar and a thief, and she is dying; and then there is my mother who I have not seen since she left us so she could start a new life with her lover. The emotions are pretty intense. It was like I was somebody else watching it happen. I was trying to be polite and wanted to get to know her, and be respectful to our grandmother, but I wanted to talk to my mother about everything.'

Bruce was hoping the death-bed visit to Daisy might improve family bonds and is more generous in his memories of his grandmother. *'We were family – that means something to me. Daisy was our grandma and despite disagreements she always remembered our birthdays and Christmas even when we were in the welfare system, and we would get a card and some money, which for an old lady on a pension would have been a lot. She was strict and old-fashioned but she still loved us.'*

Paul relishes recounting meeting his mother again when Daisy was dying. By then she was a stranger to them all. *'I was around twenty-five when I saw Incubator next ... We went to Bacchus Marsh and I didn't know Incubator was going to be there, and she answered the door. First thing she said to me in, like, years ... 'Oh, my beautiful son ...' then she tried to cuddle me, fake tits poking out. She was one of the first to get them, Dad said they cost a fortune. She said she had to get them so she could keep performing. Fake everything. She did whatever she thought would impress people, but there was nothing real there. I asked her why she never contacted us and she said we were better off in the home and tried to blame Dad for not being in touch, saying he wouldn't allow* it, which I know is a total lie. I don't care if I never see Incubator again; she means nothing to me.'

Apollo also visited Daisy on her death bed, which led to the only meeting Rondahe and Apollo had after the split. Mark explains: 'It was like a cat and a canary – he still loved her and they seemed happy to see each other at first, but suddenly someone said something and it turned ghastly. She lurched at Apollo and was abusing him and he wouldn't take a backward step; Bruce took Apollo away before anything happened.'

Mark contacted his mother again after Daisy died and held out an olive branch. 'She was charming and said how sad she was to leave us – I wanted to mend fences.' As he had no work down south he went to live with her and Alex Dudko in Queensland. 'When she made her new life in Queensland, there was no hint of sons. And then I turned up, and she had to explain to everyone around her that I was her son from a previous marriage. It was awkward. Dudko was a vegetarian and into yoga and spirituality. He died a few years ago, and I never really felt I got to know him. He was pretty quiet and kept to himself. She got into horses and equestrian in a big way. I still see her.'

Bruce also tried to reunite with his mother, in the early 1990s. 'After our grandmother died, she said, "Come stay with me." In my early thirties I spent six months living with her. Right at the start I said that there was one condition, that she didn't go badmouthing our father. I said that I will struggle to call you Mum because you were never a mum to us. Mark and I were there living with Rondahe at the same time, and it was a disaster. One time I introduced her to my then-girlfriend who later was my first wife, and after a cup of coffee, Rondahe said, "My advice is don't have kids, because they will ruin your *life." She says that to my girlfriend who she has only met five minutes before and in front of me. When my girlfriend left that day Rondahe said, "How dare you bring your slut over." What do you say to your own mother if she can come out with something like that? And on my birthday, the first time I had celebrated with her since she had left us, she said, "I wish I had not had kids; I would have had a better life ..." and she says these things in front of us and then is surprised when we get upset.'* He shakes his head and exhales with pent-up emotion, as much a snort of derision as exasperation. The confirmed view of two of Rondahe's three sons – embittered as they are, but not always in total agreement on their shared history – is that she left an irreparable trail of emotional wreckage behind her.

Bruce was and still is fiercely protective of Apollo's memory and his legacy. *'She told us to stay out of her way, even when we were staying with her, and she was always running Dad down. It was character assassination. I hated it, so I packed my bags and walked out and have not spoken to her since. It turned out all the things that people had said about her were true, but I had to see it for myself. I gave her a chance, but she's just not a good person. I hope none of that part of her ends up in me and instead I take after my father – easy-going and give people a chance. She is the opposite and a liar.'*

Two of Apollo and Rondahe's sons denounced their mother in a way that is incredibly rare. All families hold secrets, and relationships can be bitter and often fraught. But not often is the condemnation so clear and consistent. The three Anderson brothers share the same history, the same legacy, and each has dealt with it in their own way. Although the hurt has receded it will never go away. Why would it? Some scars fade, but some thicken into permanent scar tissue over time.

* * *

As Apollo had got older, and the physical demands had increased, he devoted space in his diary to reflect on the clash between *'the circus strongman'* and the *'classical strongman'*. *'The pressure of advancing years is with me. If you can't take the pressure, it is because you stopped thinking positive ... but I am far from being through, or being rated as a has-been,'* he said. *'Dying isn't the worse thing in a man's life – it is just the last thing,'* he believed. He regained some if not most of his former power and prowess and pushed himself to keep performing long after his sons wanted him to stop, seeking equally the adrenaline rush and the cash. The gym had to relocate in 1976 as a new shopping centre was built in the city centre, and within a few years Apollo had to relocate again. He moved from the A'Beckett Street premises to West Melbourne in 1982.

He had been making a decent living again, and regularly volunteered to appear at fundraisers and donated his time to community events. Apollo announced multiple times that he was 'coming out of retirement' or that it was his 'final appearance'. He was still interviewed for TV shows, respectfully recognised as a pioneer, but now regarded nostalgically as something of a relic, a curiosity, a reminder of a forgotten era of circus strongmen and sideshow acts that had all but vanished from the modern world.

In 1988, at the Pacific Body Building International competition Apollo was crowned 'The Greatest Strongman of the Century – a Living Legend, Champion of Champions' and presented to an adoring crowd at a packed Dallas Brooks Hall. In his signature embroidered tracksuit, he received a standing ovation, smiling broadly, but there was a hint of moisture in his eyes.

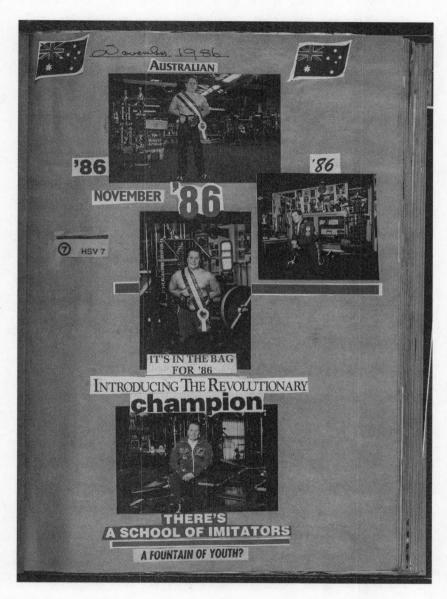

Even as he aged, Apollo celebrated every sash and trophy with another scrapbook entry.

'Becoming Champion of Champions and winning that belt was my greatest honour. When I began my career, I never imagined I would reach these heights and become the proud possessor of these trophies. The formula if you want to succeed is sheer confidence and willpower. Winning is 20 per cent physical and 80 per cent psychological. Use the power of thought to win – keep the positive warrior spirit. When you perform, no matter what it is you are performing, you are selling a product – sure, it is yourself, but never forget that it is teamwork. To the expert, I lack height and body weight, and the huge bulk necessary to do the things I can do ... but bulk is not as important as faith. I was always a dreamer, always emotional to a degree and I responded to inspiration. If people thought the Mighty Apollo should be someone bigger – well, I am big enough for the job. If I was any bigger, it would embarrass me beating the giants who seek my scalp to hang on their totem pole. My super mind polarity enables me, and I can harness the power of hate. My hate complex and my experiences have curtailed my trust in fair play and sportsmanship. I had rivals defame me and try to trick me, to rob me of what I had achieved. But my cosmic power and complete unity with my inner strength made me stronger.'

Apollo talked in one moment about faith and God, but then in the next breath claimed that his ability to do what he did was because he believed in cosmic power and *'the harmonious merger of thought and action, intrinsic energy and mental telepathy in scientific studios'* and *'surging vibrational cosma-kinetics and psycho-astro wavelengths'*.

'God is power,' he would recite to whoever was listening. He was searching widely through nature, religion and science for the words and concepts that might explain his strength, his

power and his drive, to explain it in ways other people might understand.

How could he do the not-doable? In pure physical terms, it remains inexplicable. Apollo always said it can only be explained by his ability to tap and harness cosmic energy and God-given powers, the *'super-positive mindset and energy that comes from visualisation'*. He truly believed that he could visualise and thus control energy, imagine himself to be a giant and foresee the completion of what otherwise seemed impossible.

Surviving being underneath the feet of an elephant, recovering from being shot at close range, rehabilitation from nearly losing a leg to gangrene and to not just recover but to perform feats of strength again and again that nobody in the world could match – Apollo's career exceeded all known boundaries.

The original sign from above the door to the Mighty Apollo and Rondahe Gym.

His was an accurate boast that mere mortals are not supposed to be able to survive what he consistently did. No conventional understanding of the human physique explains his achievements and what he endured. Whether it was divine intervention, cosmic energy, body fields, chakras, frequency portals, energy queuing or an altered consciousness – or all of them – we will never really know.

Whichever way you look at his extraordinary career, his self-belief, physical endurance and repeated exhibitions of sheer power and strength – he just did the impossible. The unbelievable had to be believed. This short, barrel-chested, broad-shouldered man with the pencil moustache, greying hair and elaborate tracksuit tops was unarguably the genuine article – the strongest man on earth.

CHAPTER 10
SQUATTERS

Deep into the second half of 1982, in a startling outbreak of almost responsible behaviour befitting my new-found self-regard as an almost respectable city lawyer, I stopped riding to work on the unregistered motorbike and started catching the tram. Each morning or evening on my short commute I dipped into a slice of Frank Hardy's epic *Power without Glory*, an engrossing tale of corruption and vice in Melbourne of the 1920s and 1930s and a great distraction for me from work.

In an interesting parallel, the daily news was endlessly about corruption – the so-called 'bottom of the harbour' tax schemes. The McCabe Lafranchi Report explained how millions – if not billions – of dollars was being defrauded through dodgy tax avoidance promoters. The scam was startlingly simple – companies would be stripped of their assets, leaving behind unpaid tax and other debts. Sham directors and shareholders who had zero assets and often criminal records would replace the real owners, whose accountants would then send the companies 'to the bottom of the harbour', declaring that the companies were unable to settle their debts. Paying tax became optional for the unscrupulous.

There was also a related Royal Commission underway, headed by Frank Costigan QC, into corruption and organised crime which famously scrutinised the secret financial activities of media baron Kerry Packer, then Australia's richest man. Some of the accountant clients of Barker Harty & Co were caught up in both inquiries, and the firm's questionable links to aspects of the escalating scandals, marginal but still embarrassing, were splashed over the front pages of the newspapers. My own daily diet of disputed debts, probate for deceased estates, collapsing partnerships, leases for helicopters – the commercial law bread and butter – was all far removed from anything scandalous, but the collective anxiety affected everyone on the 26th floor.

Not surprisingly, honest clients did not want to get caught up in the widening net of anti-corruption investigations and anxiously decided it was the perfect time to relocate their legal work. The phones stopped ringing and the office became worryingly quiet. There were days when I literally had nothing to do, and I could smell the fear. The usual office bonhomie and banter all but vanished and the stress was palpable. There were a lot of loud discussions between partners behind closed doors. The lull in work was clearly unsustainable.

On a Friday morning at the start of December I was summoned by Wendy, the personnel manager. She had always been very kind to me, although it was her routine to ruthlessly sack a secretary almost every week. The firm's unsentimental philosophy was that by keeping the staff on edge they would stay focused and motivated, but a lawyer being shown the door was a rare event. Wendy could not look me in the eye as she outlined how difficult things were and then awkwardly handed me a written reference and a month's pay in lieu of notice.

My boss Peter Burden was vaguely apologetic but incapable of any empathy – I felt disposable. I was to finish that same day, and, once the shock subsided I had to sit at my lavish desk and dictate explanatory memo after memo to go with each file I had been working on. The clients I had worked with, forged a relationship with, the friendships such as they were – all amounted to nought. I tearfully handed in my security pass, gathered up anything personal from my desk, pocketed some pens, souvenired the stapler and went down the lift for the last time. No farewell, no speeches, no sentiment. I was barely given enough time to go around the office and say goodbye. The tram ride home was slower than ever as I tried to hide my misery from the other commuters. Overnight, I had become an unemployed first-year commercial litigation solicitor. I felt used, betrayed, bitter and angry. Although I knew why I was being let go, the residual worry was that people would assume that I had done something to deserve being sacked. And how was I going to explain this to my anxious and judgemental parents?

My Fitzroy housemates were reassuringly upbeat and supportive. Over the two years we'd been there, as the group consolidated, relationships had evolved. Andrea, who occupied the room adjacent to mine, became my partner and that was but one of several romances that brought the household closer. It was a remarkably stable community with its own rituals and routines. There were rosters for cooking, cleaning, shopping and laundry. The large courtyard garden lent itself to parties, as did the massive living areas with floor-to-ceiling doors which doubled the available space when open. Ten of us could co-exist without feeling crowded or in each other's way. We all went to see a local band the night I was sacked, and although I remember dancing to The Pete Best Beatles the rest of my beer-soaked memories are vague. The George Street family was a great comfort as I coped with the shock of feeling discarded.

Elspeth, my boss's super secretary, was also let go the same day, and the following Monday, by then in a better mood, we met up for an ironic breakfast celebration of croissants and cheap champagne. Neither of us contemplated being long-term unemployed so we embraced the novelty of being out in the sunlight on a work day. Slightly tipsy and arm-in-arm we stumbled on to the local dole office. Filling in the forms felt only half serious, and the clerk behind the counter looked dubiously at me as I cheerfully presented my degrees and professional credentials. Lawyers were not supposed to go on the dole.

Within a week, a recruitment firm had organised two job interviews and almost straight away I was offered a position at the well-regarded trade union and ALP–aligned firm of Holding Redlich & Co, but not to start until the new year. In the interim I had a month to fill, so the next day I threw some clothes into the tattered leather panniers on my 1955 BMW R50 motorbike and hit the road to clear my head and have a holiday in Sydney with friends. Playing with old motorbikes had become my main hobby, and it was a chance to kick-start my favourite for something longer and much more freewheeling than a Sunday ride.

Heading north, the rhythmic thrum of the air-cooled twin cylinders reverberating through the rubber saddle, I felt exhilarated and carefree – no longer worried about the last job and with no idea about the next one. This was a joyous and rare window with no responsibilities whatsoever. Barker Harty & Co could implode for all I cared. The classic BMW attracted attention every time I stopped, and I took my time whether on the highway or quieter backroads. Not quite *Easy Rider* but the open road on a slow old motorbike was hypnotic and a great tonic.

An overnight stop in Gundagai and a counter dinner at the pub with blokes who turned out to be real bikies left me terrified. I had parked my bike on the street out the front – and inevitably when meeting up, motorbike riders compare machines and tell each other tall tales. The 'lads' were trying to impress Mandy, another traveller who was passing through town, also staying at the pub. She rashly accepted their invitation to share an after-dinner bottle of rum by their campfire, and fearing for her safety I did the only chivalrous thing possible and went with her. A wild night followed, complete with bottles being smashed against heads and idiots riding their motorbikes through the flames of the fire. At peak craziness, Mandy and I contrived a discreet retreat. The entire episode reinforced to me how unavoidably bourgeois I was, no matter how hard I tried to shed the skin. Sampling even one night of the bikies' 'normal' made my routines look dull but safe. Our worlds were so different that I engaged with them much like exhibits at the zoo, curiosities to be kept at a distance. My memories are vague, but I hope no-one was hurt.

My bike and I survived Gundagai and then a sudden thunderstorm and downpour on the outskirts of Sydney where I got so wet that my sheepskin-lined riding boots filled with water like two buckets and were forever ruined. My saddle bags proved not to be at all waterproof and every single piece of clothing that I had was sodden. After drying out I tootled around Sydney for a few days and caught up with friends. One day, after a long and liquid lunch, and showing off as the seasoned long-haul rider, I kick-started my beautiful bike, coolly waved goodbye and accelerated hard away. The still-locked bike progressed about half a metre before abruptly stopping, toppling sideways as the heavy chain reached its full extension. Some of the lunch crowd are still laughing forty years later. The chain ripped out multiple spokes on the rear wheel, leaving the bike unstable and, as I could find no quick repair in Sydney, I had to nurse both my shattered pride and the lame steed home to Melbourne by train.

I started at Holding Redlich in January 1983 and just about my first task was to ask the Andersons to authorise the handover of the Hawks estate file from Barker Harty & Co to Holding Redlich. Although it is hardly a rare event to transfer a file, it can be problematic, but my relationship with the family was by then well established and we continued on together. There were no other clients I cared about as much, and all the other work I had been doing stayed behind. It was a difficult transition to one day be fighting tooth and nail for clients then suddenly cease all contact.

Holding Redlich was such a contrast to Barker Harty. The offices were on the city fringe, just a ten-minute walk from home, low rise, and the furniture was more functional than fancy. The culture was still fundamentally hierarchical, but less formal, and the clients were eclectic. It was obvious that Holding Redlich was a better fit for my values; I was still practising commercial law but in a larger firm with a social conscience.

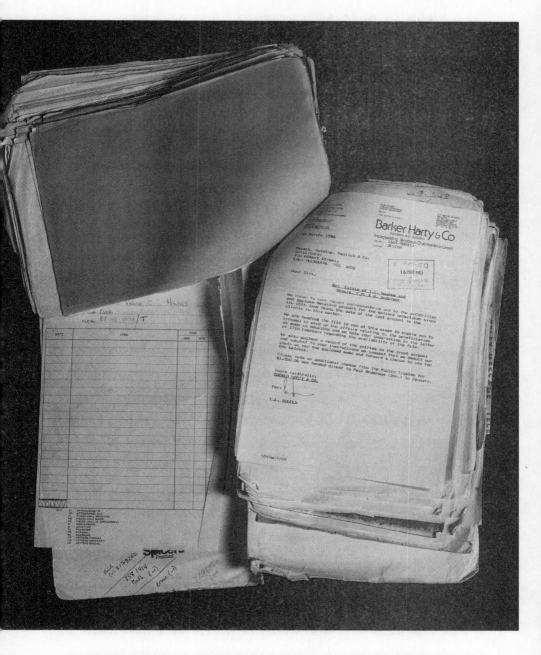

Barker Harty & Co handed the growing file to Holding Redlich & Co in
March 1983.

Clyde Holding, one of the founding partners, had left to become a Labor politician. Clyde's son Peter was one of my uni friends and a housemate at George Street. He acted for workers making compensation claims and gave me an insightful run-down of the internal culture and warned me to beware the foul-tempered but mercurial founding partner Peter Redlich. The first time I met the legendary Redlich he threw a file at my head, but we ended up more than friendly and he was an outstanding strategist.

The majority of the firm's work was representing injured people, whether referred by unions after work accidents or victims of car crashes, slips and falls in supermarkets, defective products – injuries, howsoever caused, were bread and butter. As a commercial litigator, I was part of a small but growing department that was regarded as a peculiarity, a sideshow to the main game of workers compensation and injury claims. My boss, Nathan Kuperholz, had a rightly deserved reputation as a hot-shot 'scorched earth' commercial litigator and legal brawler, and sitting in on conferences with him was frequently breathtaking and like a masterclass. He relished the contest and took no prisoners. I was given enormous responsibility and was determined to demonstrate that it was warranted.

I inherited four filing cabinets full of ongoing Federal, Supreme and County Court disputes over everything from defamation to white collar crime, defective buildings, debts, trade practices, arguments about commercial tenancies and some contested estate claims. Some were worth tens of thousands of dollars and some were worth millions. There were days where I was running simultaneous cases in the Federal and the Supreme courts, dashing around to juggle the needs of the clients and the demands of our barristers. I lived on adrenaline, worked twelve-hour days and, unless recovering from a big Saturday night party, I started going in to the office on Sunday morning to stay on top of the workload.

There was something compelling and exhilarating about my new routine. I had grown up with a workaholic father who spent more time at his laboratory than at home. My physiotherapist mother's work ethic extended even to the intensity with which she would sweep a path. The broom was her weapon, the concrete her enemy. Second best was never good enough, and although I had been a lazy, distracted and unambitious student those days were clearly behind me. Getting high marks had seemed pointless, but there was nothing pointless about real people with actual disputes to be fought, especially if they were the underdog. I wanted to prove myself and had found what seemed the perfect and intensely competitive environment in which to do it. Sharing a mid-trial sandwich with QCs and swapping banter with junior partners provided a road map for what I assumed I would become. It was all about the contest, and the ego rush that came with landing and winning a big case was almost erotic. The promised future financial rewards were not irrelevant and I could feel the seductive tug of the flash end of town pulling me away. But each Monday my stint at the Tenants Union Legal Service would ground me anew in the real world. As my mid-twenties accelerated in a rush, I could feel the changes in my outlook and priorities. Was I selling out or growing up?

Most lawyers specialise in something. Commercial lawyers know little if anything about injuries law and vice versa. Family lawyers are not much chop at resolving an industrial dispute.

Legal aid lawyers are experts at crime, family law, housing and other common concerns of their mainly impoverished clientele. I found the commercial law challenges I faced at work during the day the opposite of those I had to grapple with as a legal centre volunteer in the evenings. At the office we demanded the client deposit thousands of dollars into the trust account before the file would even be opened – money 'up front' before anything happened. Clients were able to pay and understood the benefit of doing so. At the Tenants Union Legal Service, the people needing help did not have a spare dollar to contribute to the running of their cases. We sometimes struggled to even find the money to pay stamp duty to lodge documents to go to court.

Getting clear information for a case was often impossible – legal aid clients were not great at retaining receipts or bond forms. Many clients spoke little or no English, and we frequently needed to press their kids into service as interpreters. Distilling confusing histories into discrete legal problems was the typical challenge – sometimes it was a puzzle to even work out what had happened. Unlike commercial clients, the legal service clients did not present in the office with folders of neat bank statements and copies of correspondence.

Although the same legal skills and tricks were needed to represent the poor as were used for middle-class or corporate clients, it was far more satisfying to win for the underdog – and homeless squatters were about as disadvantaged as anyone could be. It was a legal tussle involving squatters that made me question my direction.

An historic mansion in South Yarra called 'Bona Vista' had for many years been owned and used as offices by Telecom.

It had been sitting empty for some time and the Commonwealth Government wanted to sell it as a surplus asset. Some homeless people had taken up residence and declared themselves squatters. After months of attempting a negotiated exit, the police were called to force them out. A friend from law school, Mary-Anne Noone, was working at Springvale Legal Service and acting for the squatters. She'd advised them that they enjoyed not many but some legal rights – there were specific procedures that had to be strictly followed if the sheriff's officers wanted to move them on, and those procedures had not been followed. The squatters barricaded themselves in and were joined by more protesters in solidarity and to try to attract publicity about the desperate plight of the homeless. There had been no media coverage of the drama and, like everyone else, I was unaware of it.

One Friday I was racing through the glum corridors of the Supreme Court juggling two separate commercial cases. One was to do with a long-running dispute involving dozens of litigants about the blow-out in the cost of the construction of the Melbourne Arts Centre, in which my boss at Holding Redlich acted for an engineer who was the fourth named third party or some such minor player. We were, in truth, protecting the interests of the professional indemnity insurance company who had covered the engineer and thus had exposure to a fractional liability in the biggest juggernaut of litigation the court had ever seen. Each time all the parties were brought together there was barely standing room in court for all the assembled and slightly amused lawyers.

That morning I also had another case running where we were arguing for access to some additional documents in a different building dispute. As I hurried through from court to court, I was surprised to bump into Mary-Anne Noone, looking more than slightly distressed. The Supreme Court was not her typical hangout – she was more used to the local Magistrates Court. She explained that ten protesters – not the actual squatters – at the South Yarra house had been arrested that morning during the eviction process and now were in custody. The judge who had ordered their arrest was Justice Brooking, a crusty and grumpy old judge notorious for his short fuse. He had ordered that the site be cleared and the squatters arrested and detained over the weekend, to be brought before him on Monday. Mary-Anne needed to find a way to explain that the wrong people had been arrested – the protesters were not squatters. She needed to urgently find a barrister who could explain to the judge that the protesters should not be gaoled for three nights for simply being in the wrong place at the wrong time. More easily said than done, but I offered to help.

Together we crossed the road to Owen Dixon Chambers, home of the Melbourne Bar. We just needed someone – anyone – who knew what to do, who could help. Back at law school we had learned about a Writ of Habeas Corpus, where counsel could argue to a judge that someone had been unlawfully deprived of their liberty by the state, but we did not have the slightest clue how you went about getting that exceptionally rare claim heard. I had been involved in litigating several urgent commercial injunctions, so I was at least familiar with the procedures for what was called the 'Practice Court' – where pressing matters were dealt with every day by the duty judge. But this was exceptional.

As we scoured the bewigged and gowned barristers surging in and out of the lobby, I saw a familiar face. Bryan Keon-Cohen had been one of my favourite teachers at Monash Law and only recently had left academia to go to the Bar. He was already junior counsel in preparing what was assumed to be a hopeless long-shot test case which might establish native title for Indigenous Australians for a client named Eddie Mabo.

I had been sending Bryan some work from Holding Redlich as he got established, and this panicked morning he was more than keen to help. Mary-Anne explained the chronology and he immediately studied the court papers, right there in the bustling building lobby.

Bryan's advice was that we go back to the same judge and point out to him that the orders made were far too broad, and even if that point failed, the judge had not authorised the police and sheriff's officers to arrest innocent bystanders: people who had not been in any way involved in the earlier court case. They had been arrested for contempt of a judge's order, but an order they did not know about. It is not possible to be found in contempt of an order you do not know about. It was obviously and undeniably an abuse of power.

The three of us went back to the Practice Court. Bryan waited patiently and then explained his arguments to the judge, asking him to withdraw the arrest warrants and order the release of the protesters. Brooking was intensely irritated at being told his earlier order was an abuse of power and after refusing to hear any more submissions abruptly stood up and stormed off the bench. Mary-Anne's clients, ten innocent protesting bystanders, none of them squatters, were stuck in Pentridge, at least until Monday.

The injustice was glaringly obvious, the errors plain to see, and we were all furious but powerless to force the judge to change his orders. Fuelled by our collective sense of injustice we trooped back to find a sympathetic QC who might have the requisite seniority to be taken more seriously and to turn the case around. Bryan approached everyone he knew and eventually leading commercial silk Ron Merkel QC agreed to take on this example of unjust detention.

Ron quickly got across the facts and the sequence of events and, forming a flying posse, the four of us returned to the Supreme Court late that afternoon. Ron's tactic was to seek the intervention of the Chief Justice, the most senior judge in Victoria. The Chief was sitting with two other judges in an appeal and Merkel led us into their court just as they were finishing for the day. He stepped forward unannounced and addressed their Honours from the body of the court, very briefly explained it was an instance of Habeas Corpus which necessitated this unusual step, and asked them to overrule Brooking's order to imprison the innocent protesters. The Chief Justice heard Merkel carefully for a few minutes, quickly conferred with the other two judges on the bench and, with no explanation, politely declined to hear Merkel any further, before adjourning the court and vacating the bench. We were flabbergasted. We learned later that there was a judges' black-tie dinner that evening and surmised they did not want to be late.

Merkel was so outraged that he recommended we appeal to the High Court in Canberra to remedy such an obvious miscarriage of justice and ram home to the Victorian judges that what they had done – or refused to do – was plain wrong. Within the hour, he phoned Canberra, spoke to the Registrar of

Preparing for the High Court, October 1983; Mary-Anne Noone, Iain Stewart, Jon Faine.

the High Court, secured a judge for an exceptionally rare urgent hearing on a Saturday morning and drafted up the necessary papers. Now all we had to do was find some money for the flights to Canberra, then write and type, format and prepare multiple copies of the affidavits and court documents, notify the lawyers for Telecom and the Commonwealth what was happening and try to get some sleep.

Over the course of that frantic evening, and joined by Iain Stewart, the lawyer at the Tenants Union, we prepared the multiple complex papers for a Writ of Habeas Corpus in the High Court. We worked late into the night, and each time a photocopier broke or ran out of toner we press-ganged friends who let us into nearby law offices after hours, and did the same again. We found the Director of Legal Aid at home well after office hours and persuaded him of the merits of an appeal to the High Court on a Saturday morning – an unimaginably bold event – and got authorisation to spend money on flights. Somewhere along the way, in an adrenaline-fuelled phone call, I checked in with my boss at Holding Redlich & Co, who not unreasonably asked me where I had been all day and what I had been doing. I explained that with Ron Merkel, a QC he did a lot of work with, we were preparing an application for a Habeas Corpus in the High Court for the detained protesters he may see that night on the TV news. I waited for the expected explosion of fury at my prolonged absence and deviation from the work of the firm. Instead, after the briefest of pauses, Nathan Kuperholz expressed admiration for what we were doing and said if we needed additional help to let him know.

On Saturday morning in Canberra, upon hearing from Ron Merkel, the High Court of Australia ordered the protesters be immediately released and expressed disquiet – judicially and politely – at the way the right to protest had been so arbitrarily ignored and the arrest powers of the Victorian Supreme Court misused. Upon a phone call from the court registrar to the state government Minister for Prisons, the protesters were released from Pentridge Prison by Saturday lunchtime.

As a cute footnote, Mary-Anne Noone and Iain Stewart forged not just a professional but also a personal relationship.

My day spent brawling for some imprisoned protesters was more fun than anything else I did in my working week, and triggered a gradual rethink of my direction. Although I was still attracted to making money and the prestige offered by the connection with a well-regarded law firm, I sensed that there was not as much fun to be had along that path.

At Holding Redlich & Co, Apollo was regularly in touch, phoning on average once a month, prodding and probing and making sure that his sons were not forgotten, always gently but firmly enquiring about the delays in resolving his sister's estate. Every step took ages – letters back and forth to the lawyers in Darwin and phone calls that resolved not much but took time. From his point of view, the snail's pace was inexplicable, and he thought *'there is a stronger power behind it'*. His mysticism came to the fore. Everyone was *'too intent'* on taking money off his kids and when it came to the claim from Norm Douglas he said, *'Granted, he was supposed to get the pub, but what about my kids? They're being robbed, right left and centre, by the copper, the banks, the tax people. They're always being squeezed, and my concern is always for them. I won't let them be sold short.'* He had been in a fall at the gym and, ever since, his ability to reason was *'not good, I think I am OK but maybe I am not. Maybe I should pass on the gym to the boys, but I am not capable right now in working things out. I don't mind if I suffer from doing the wrong thing, but I don't want to do the wrong thing by my boys'*.

A few weeks later, while I was trying to cope with the daily juggle of telephones, clients, the endless need to feed the Dictaphone, a bulging diary, court appearances, barristers' briefs and undoubtedly drowning in files and affidavits, Don, the aging but always cheerful office messenger, delivered to my office a trolley load – an actual tea chest – full of plans, specifications and architectural drawings relating to a leaking hangar at Melbourne Airport. Our assignment was to look after an engineer who had been a peripheral advisor on the hangar's construction, and we were instructed by his professional negligence insurer. Apparently,

I was expected to spend two weeks reading every single page and poring over every sheet in the tea chest in order to try to shave one or two per cent off the insurer's contribution to the inevitable payout for the remedial works required on the hangar. There were about a dozen different defendants, all of whom had worked at some stage on the project, and it would be a long slow legal brawl to work out who paid what. I felt ill at the prospect of this crushingly dull task.

Not long after, I was booked to go skiing for the weekend with some friends. Late on a Friday afternoon, I got a call from an important client I had been nurturing who had emerged from a meeting in the nearby Southern Cross Hotel. He ran a plastics factory and asked me to urgently draft a complex contract they needed before Monday. A German company that had invented a system of wheeled rubbish bins had just agreed to sell them the licence for the Australasian market. The German executives – from the Otto Bin company – were leaving Australia the following Tuesday. The agreement was worth an enormous amount, was commercially complicated, full of technical specifications and intellectual property concepts and none of it could wait. I went to see my always generous boss and Nathan's words still echo in my ears: 'Just this once I will do it for you. But do you want to be a chief or always the Indian? This is what is required if you are serious about this game.' My life passed before my eyes, and I knew then and there I did not want to make that commitment. The snow was terrific.

The last straw in my commercial law career was when my boss sacked me one Saturday morning, before being reinstated later that afternoon. My sin was to be quoted on the front page of

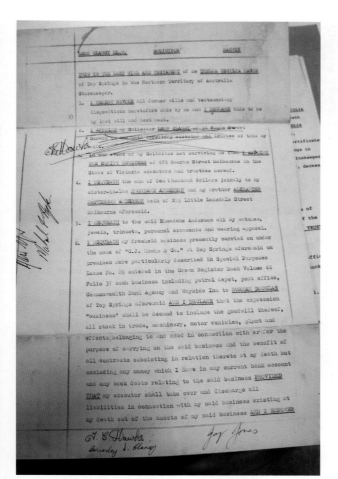

LEFT: Thelma Hawk's will, with Leon Clancy's appointment as Executor crossed out in blue pen.
BELOW: Made from galvanised tin, the Top Springs pub replaced the bark store. Photo circa 1972.

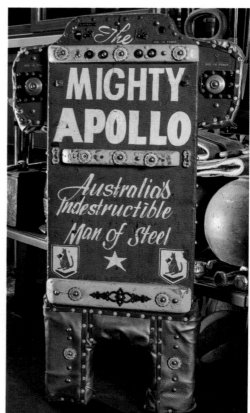

ABOVE: Apollo's historic 'Bed of Nails'.
RIGHT: The 'Tomb Board' used by Apollo throughout his career.

TOP LEFT: Apollo's 'helicopter' helmet with shoulder braces.
TOP RIGHT: Apollo's scrap books, bedecked with a small sample of his medals.
ABOVE: The Apollo Gym building, West Melbourne, circa 1982.

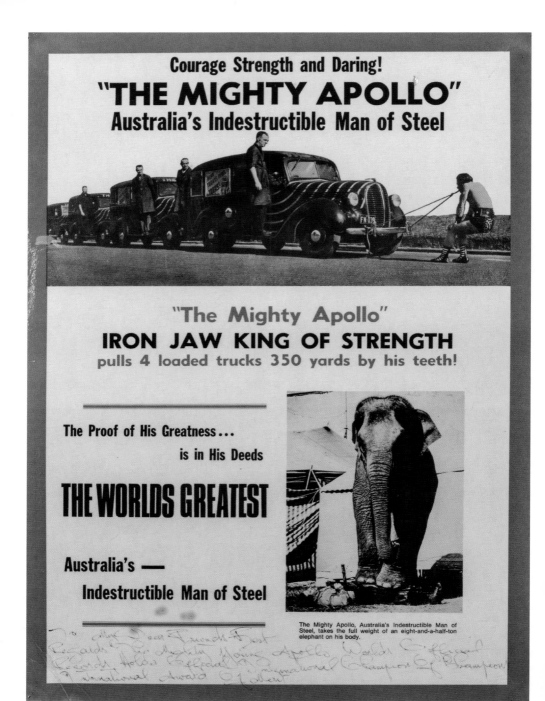

An autographed Mighty Apollo Gym &
Combat Centres advertising poster.

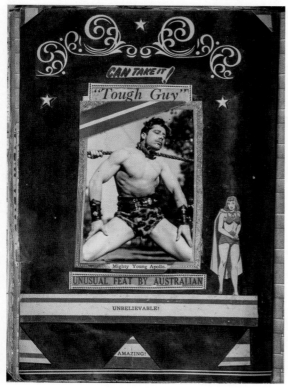

ABOVE: The scrapbook page celebrating 'heavy haulage', the famous tram feat.

LEFT: Apollo's scrapbooks document the changes in his extraordinary physique.

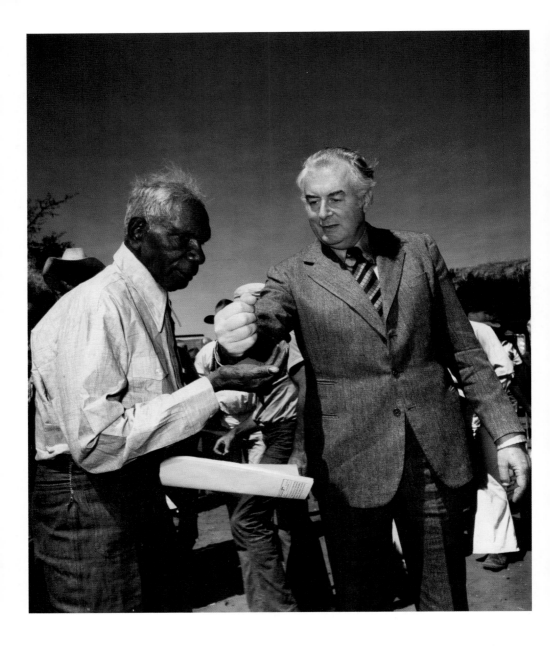

Prime Minister Gough Whitlam pours soil into the
hand of traditional land owner Vincent Lingiari 1975
by Mervyn Bishop
National Portrait Gallery, Australia
© National Indigenous Australians Agency

Gough Whitlam speaking at the
celebration of the life of Frank Hardy,
Collingwood Town Hall, 1994. [*The Age*]

ABOVE: Thelma Hawk's grave, Katherine Cemetery.
LEFT: Apollo's funeral, 1995. Paul junior in black suit at rear of the casket; Mark in a light brown jacket, middle front; Bruce in a dark brown jacket, middle rear; Ron Taylor in front with black leather jacket.

the newspaper as the spokesperson for a newly formed group of employee solicitors and articled clerks agitating for better pay. The group had been convened by a fellow junior lawyer at Holding Redlich, Lindsay Tanner. Years before going to Parliament and becoming Minister for Finance in the Rudd Government, Lindsay was trying to establish a foothold in the very conservative Federated Clerks Union, and decided that a legal industry sub-group would be a handy beachhead. A small committee was formed and given the task to organise a mass meeting of indignant and underpaid junior lawyers. We booked a meeting space at the Law Institute and put flyers around the traps. At Lindsay's suggestion I chaired the small meeting; I was not expecting it to attract any mainstream publicity. On the night, a few dozen baby lawyers gathered, argued a lot and then we all went to the pub.

Come Saturday morning, our meeting was on the front page. The splash quoted me saying that the exploitation of cheap labour in law firms had to stop and that we were charged out to clients for $350 an hour while we were being paid $127 a week – the award wage for an articled clerk. None of my figures were wrong, but an apoplectic Nathan Kuperholz rang me at home. Standing in the hall, cradling the phone to my ear with the market shopping being unpacked around me and music blaring in the background, I could hardly concentrate as Nathan yelled, 'Either you are misquoted and I expect the paper to print a full retraction by Monday or you are accurately quoted in which case you no longer work for me. My clients cannot be left thinking that I exploit young lawyers.'

My efforts to explain that I was not expressing any personal dissatisfaction but was speaking on behalf of others fell on not just deaf but enraged ears. We had become friends, I had been invited to his home for a meal, met his wife and kids and enjoyed his company. Having invested heavily in mentoring and training me for what was assumed by all to be a glorious future in the firm, he understandably felt personally betrayed. The small point that I was being sacked by a union-aligned law firm for the crime of standing up for the rights of workers did not seem to make any impression on Nathan at all. By the time I put the phone down, my knees were shaking and I was all but in tears. My fellow housemates shared in my indignation, but before I could work out what it all meant, I was phoned by Peter Redlich, the most senior of the partners. Peter asked me for the background to the story, told me I had been an idiot, to wait for Nathan to calm down, not to go to the media about being sacked and to turn up as normal on Monday.

I did not sleep for two nights and cautiously arrived early on Monday to try to sneak in to my office before anyone else arrived. I failed and was greeted with incredulity by junior partner Chris Lovell, whose office was next to mine. 'You're a prize goose' was his greeting, and things did not improve from there. It was weeks before Nathan Kuperholz even acknowledged that I still existed and our previously close relationship was soured from that day on.

My heart was no longer in it. It became inevitable that I would have to leave.

A few months later, in late 1984, there was a job on offer at Springvale Legal Service, a free legal centre an hour's drive away that was attached to Monash University Law School. I had loved being a student advisor there in my final year of study, and the prospect of a secure university job but with the legal aid connection was tempting. I took a three-month contract for just one semester as a try-out and started the nearly one hour each way daily commute. I hated the long drive of an already long day so when my friend David Allan, the sole staff lawyer at Fitzroy Legal Service, suddenly resigned and that job became available it was not hard to choose which I preferred. The interview process at Fitzroy was nothing to do with legal skills whatsoever, instead focusing on my position on the conflict in the Middle East and whether or not I was committed to the staff functioning as an autonomous collective. After almost four years in commercial law, I left plush offices and the world of suits and ties behind forever and went to work at Fitzroy Legal Service, Australia's oldest free legal centre.

But what to do with the Estate of T C Hawks? I dreaded the idea of handing over my favourite clients to someone else and contrived a way to continue to look after the Andersons and their aunt's estate. A free legal centre is not the place to be representing beneficiaries of an estate worth hundreds of thousands of dollars, but up the road from the legal centre was a small practice of two fabulous volunteers at FLS, who agreed to be on the record, but let me do all the remaining work. I could draft letters as needed and hopefully soon negotiate a final settlement and take the file through to completion.

**

John Flynn was slowly sorting the remaining issues to do with Thelma's estate. The lease to Dick Philip, the temporary licensee, had been a successful stopgap, but Philip had dropped out of being an interested party for the purchase of the pub. Flynn had written: *'Philip didn't arrive at our meeting, it looks like he has malaria, and when I eventually saw him I have never seen anyone so sick without being dead.'* There had been a number of potential buyers circulating, but the pub, together with all the plant and equipment, stock and associated vehicles, had eventually sold in August 1983 to a Mr and Mrs Suffolk for $245,000, a price that was slightly above the sworn valuation. Now all that remained was to resolve the claim by Norm Douglas before the Andersons could collect their money.

Letter by letter, month by month, the original inflated claim from Norm Douglas was being whittled down. Eventually we got to realistic amounts that would satisfy his argument that he ought to be the rightful owner of the pub. His claim – with much window dressing from his Darwin lawyers – was that over the years he had swapped wages for a share in the business and even lent money to Thelma when she had a cashflow problem many years before. We countered that assertion, pointing out that the transfer of $15,000 from Norm to Thelma was at exactly the same time that Norm claimed a pension and the convenient emptying of his bank balance was more for the benefit of Norm than Thelma. Besides, we pointed out that Norm had been provided with food, lodgings, cars and all the necessities of life at no charge for his entire stay at Toppie, exceeding the amounts he claimed to be owed, and that if he had been paid wages he would not have been entitled to the pension.

The haggling continued into 1985, each step in the negotiation taking months. At their end, contacting Norm – still living and working at Toppie – for instructions seemed to take forever, and there was the same delay each time I had to contact all four Andersons to find out what they wanted to do. Norm Douglas dropped his claim to a more modest and realistic $110,000 and his lawyers said there would be no retreat from that offer.

Later that year, Norm's lawyers confirmed what John Flynn had already told me. Norm was in poor health. While Flynn had made it clear he thought it was not fair to delay paying him out, Norm's lawyers lobbed back: '*Knowing Mr Douglas is not in the best of health and has no known next of kin and without drawing any inferences it is in the interests of the other beneficiaries that this matter be protracted* ...' My combative response was to deny any such improper motivation and assert that the majority of the delay had been at their end not ours. I suggested that out of goodwill more than legal obligation or liability I would recommend to my clients the estate would offer to settle at $90,000 if Norm was happy to walk away. To our relief he was, and he quit the pub and happily bought a home on the riverbank at Katherine. The estate sorted its debts to the tax office and all other claimants and the Anderson 'remaindermen', as Paul, Mark and Bruce were described in law, were each able to collect their inheritance.

The estate of T C Hawks was finally wound up, and after we paid Norm, the legal fees and other bills, bank cheques for $77,000 were handed over to each of Thelma's nephews, adjusted for any advance that had been paid. They all greeted the news and the resultant cheques enthusiastically, as did their dad. He was noticeably aging, and the 'boys' were all growing up. Apollo was still trying to perform, but eventually he had to accept the reality that his routines were too demanding for a man in his seventies. The last footage of Apollo, only months before another breakdown, shows him doing his sledgehammer routine, where heavy hammers are pounded into his abdomen as he ignores and withstands their blows. But the footage also shows that he staggers and wobbles, the only recording of Apollo's entire career where he is anything other than rock-steady on his feet. His sons are the assistants and provide support as he recovers his composure. It is a telling moment. He never performs in public again.

For the first time in Apollo's remarkable life, he had to accept there were limits to what his body could do. Post-divorce, the physical trough was temporary – but this time the changes were permanent. He continued to welcome a shrinking clientele to the Mighty Apollo Gym and Combat Centre, but it was becoming even more of an anachronism. His eldest son, Paul, was trying to make changes, but Apollo would not accept that it was time to hand over to the next generation. He was always proud of his sons, called Paul junior 'Little Apollo', and only ever wanted the best for them – but he was fixed on his own career, not theirs.

After becoming a schoolboy champion athlete, Paul had been accepted into and trained at the elite Institute of Sport. Injuries during selection trials ruined his prospects of competing at the Commonwealth Games and his post-athletics life took various paths, including training as a PE teacher, before eventually he joined his father at the gym.

Mark, the middle son, worked as a photographer with the Defence Department before taking off motorbiking around Australia. He had several times asked me for small cash advances on his inheritance and with some hesitation Flynn had sent him a few hundred dollars here and there, with Apollo's consent. The estate was not supposed to be an emergency bank account and Flynn was reluctant to see him fritter away his inheritance.

Bruce had qualified as a carpenter, played with old cars and eventually, as a change of career, joined the army.

I was sad to close the file, having carried it with me since the start – both of the dispute and also my legal career. I assumed that I would not see the Andersons again and that Apollo would just become one of those surprising individuals you encounter along the way in life. I could not have been more wrong.

CHAPTER 11

FRANK HARDY

Fitzroy Legal Service was a roller-coaster ride. I had worked hard in private practice, but that was nothing like the routine at FLS. I was often at the office six days a week, typically twelve and sometimes even more hours a day. We saw an average of a hundred clients every week, were open to the public from nine in the morning until nine at night, and it was only polite to head to the pub with the volunteers after the doors were shut. Home was around the corner from work, so it was but a ten-minute walk through the high-rise public housing estate to get to the shopfront in Brunswick Street where the legal service rubbed shoulders with Pasquale's coffee shop (Sila, the original Italian café, the oldest in all of Fitzroy), the Tucci family fruit shop and a hairdresser. Across the road in pre-gentrified Fitzroy, still quite poor, were several boarded-up shops used for storage, and around the corner, the local Catholic priest Father Brian Cosgriff provided the single most compassionate and useful welfare service in the city. He literally washed and clothed the homeless and ran a soup kitchen that fed whoever turned up, day after day. I came to learn that Father Brian and his volunteer parishioners

Robin Inglis, Domenico Calabro and Jon Faine outside Fitzroy Legal Service, Brunswick St, 1986. [Wayne Ludbey, *The Age*]

provided more support for the poor than all the government social workers put together.

The commercial skills I had acquired and relied upon in the city were useful but inadequate at the legal service. On my first day I was at Fitzroy Magistrates Court representing an elderly pensioner charged with shoplifting. I had no idea of criminal law procedure, had never been in the Magistrates Court before and had never been on my feet questioning a police witness. My client was a depressed Greek-speaking septuagenarian who had led an unblemished life until his wife's recent death. His clumsy drunken attempt to steal food from a local supermarket was easily seen as a cry for help, which thankfully the notoriously cranky and harsh Magistrate Jack Caven understood. Barely into my submissions, he barked at me to stop talking and offered 'a section 13 bond' to my client. I had no idea what 'section 13' meant, which legislation it referred to or why it was being offered, but my good mate and experienced legal aid lawyer Domenico Calabro kicked me under the table and whispered 'just say yes'. I did, and my client went home having promised to abstain from alcohol in exchange for no conviction being recorded. He was referred to a local welfare service to make sure he had better support in his grief.

My steep learning curve had barely started. Every case taught me something, every client needed more than we could provide, but it was better than nothing. I also learned that the people you did the most for were often the least grateful, while those you did the least for showered us with gratitude. One day I helped a family from Turkey fill in some sponsorship forms required by the Department of Immigration and they then kept us supplied with cakes for months. Conversely, an unpleasant and violent man who the Clerk of Courts asked me to represent at the last minute on his umpteenth court appearance, who was eventually gaoled for persistently ignoring a court order to pay his ex-wife maintenance out of his wages, turned around and blamed me for his incarceration and sued me for professional negligence.

When I asked Darren, a recidivist unlicensed driver, why he continued to drive, risking gaol if he was busted once more, he answered simply that he had several times tried to get a licence but because he could neither read nor write he kept failing the test and now was too frightened of the police to sit a test again. We found a volunteer who could devote time to coaching him, took him along to sit (and pass) the test and supported his effort to work within the rules. He got a job as a delivery driver shortly after. A few years ago, an aging truck driver started yelling loudly at me in what I thought was road rage, until I realised it was Darren saying hello.

The legal service dabbled in some astonishing areas. We were regularly approached by local clients who had been assaulted by the police and wanted to make a complaint against them. Typically, the response to an official complaint was an escalation of the charges in retaliation – suddenly 'resist arrest, assault police' would be added to the original trivial charge and the police would argue they acted in self-defence. Magistrates always accepted the police version, as their mates would corroborate their account. Occasionally we could pierce the façade, but not often. We reluctantly also represented paedophiles – as they could not readily get representation anywhere else and were at risk of turning up to court without a lawyer at all. We also acted for many victims in sexual assaults. The most distressing experience in my three years at FLS was when a young woman had to sit and recite her injuries and trauma in excruciating detail in order to seek compensation from the Victims of Crime Fund. I sat in tears as she told how her drug-dealer boyfriend had significant debts he could not settle, and to force him to pay he had been bound to a chair and she was gang raped in front of him. Whatever money we secured for her trauma was grossly inadequate. Heroin was the main street drug of addiction at the time and we were constantly working with local clinics to keep people in detox long enough to avoid gaol. Several times I had to turn up to court to advise that our client would not be appearing as they had died from an overdose – typically the night before, having one last hit before an expected gaol sentence. The rarefied comforts of commercial law were a million miles away, not just fifteen minutes up the street in the city.

The internal politics of a non-hierarchical community organisation were also unnerving. When I started, I was working solo, the only lawyer on the staff and juggling an absurd workload. Our community development worker was the energetic and creative pony-tailed Robin Inglis, and together we quickly cranked up the output of law reform and community activism, which caused resentment among the support staff. It seemed weird that a legal centre placed so little emphasis on legal work and several of the administrative staff members wanted to run it as a drop-in centre. I had little time for the endless consultation and circular meetings that tied up so much of the day. There were always clients waiting to be seen and letters to write or court documents to prepare – but none of that supposedly mattered if one of the half a dozen colleagues wanted to devote hours to debating whether in the name of fairness and collective solidarity the cleaner ought to be paid the same hourly rate as the lawyer. I was also finding myself less amused by the antics of the eclectic tribe of lost souls who treated the office as somewhere to get a free cup of tepid instant coffee. A core group of six would arrive mid-morning every day and sit around chatting for hours until heading up the street to the free lunch provided by the nuns at Mary's House of Welcome. While being accessible to the community was important, it was hard to get much work done.

The tension in the office eventually erupted. At an emergency meeting of the hundred or so members of the organisation I offered to resign unless there were staff changes made. The standoff was with Jean Melzer, a former ALP senator who was by then heavily involved in the fledgling Nuclear Disarmament Party. Notionally her job was to be the office manager, but mainly she managed to misplace files and not answer the switchboard even when urgent calls were expected. As the practice grew and we got busier, cheques for my trust account were not being promptly banked, which left me in breach of the rules for lawyers and at risk of being disciplined or even struck off if audited. Robin and I, together with a newly employed second lawyer Mandy Glaister, decided enough was enough. When Jude, the incredibly competent woman employed to do the typing and provide secretarial support to the lawyers, announced that she and Jean had together agreed the typing was not that important and she didn't want to do it anymore, something had to give.

Jean, Jude and a few of their volunteer supporters wanted the legal service to stop representing clients altogether and instead just refer them on to local lawyers. I was trying to build a small poverty law practice, had built up enough work to fund a second lawyer full time, and with our rapid expansion would soon be looking for a third lawyer. A grant from the Law Institute had allowed us to buy ergonomic furniture and a new word processor and we were busier than ever. Jean thought that was a bad thing and an unnecessary trajectory away from a future role as a community centre. I thought it was good to be meeting the legal needs of the local community. A few days before the crisis meeting, the logbook which recorded new members of the legal service vanished, only to reappear the night of the crisis meeting with several of Jean's family freshly signed up. The old ALP branch-stacking trick was explained to the wider membership

Former volunteer Premier John Cain launched the Fitzroy Legal Service
Law Handbook, 1987. [*The Age*]

to her acute discomfort. Despite Jean's attempt, the meeting
overwhelmingly decided in favour of the legal service retaining
the law practice; Jean was paid out her contract. The stress was
ghastly. My appetite for conflict was never great, and the toll on
friendships was horrific. There was great relief when the standoff
was over and the legal service could concentrate on the campaigns
and clients instead of its internal ructions.

About this time, I moved from the ten-person share house in
George Street. Years of saving meant I managed to put down a
deposit and bought a house. It was a wreck of a place held up by
structural paint but with what the real estate agent called 'good
bones'. Unbeknown to me when I signed the contract, it was
also in the path of a planned road upgrade. When I belatedly
found out and made panicked enquiries, I discovered that the

government and local council were already well advanced in abandoning the plan to turn my new street into an arterial road, and with reckless enthusiasm I then borrowed the unimaginable amount of $25,000 to get a builder to graft a new but very basic bathroom, kitchen and living area onto the front four existing rooms. As I moved out after six years in the warm embrace of the George Street gang, I broke up with Andrea too – a time of tumultuous change.

Appearing for multiple clients every day in one of the local courts we covered, supervising the roster of volunteers and checking each and every file they worked on, running law reform campaigns, test cases, visiting clients in prisons and youth detention centres, lobbying politicians, chasing funding, editing the Law Handbook, feeding the media – my job was relentless but more fun than anyone was entitled to have. We also established a 24-hour, seven-days-a-week emergency legal help service activated by pager, with a roster of volunteers available for after hours and weekend bail applications. The police hated it as they were suddenly being called to account in the police station for the first time. Working like a demon was easier when doing it for the underdog rather than in a commercial environment doing it for straight cash. Trying to make 'the system' function fairly is worthy but frustrating and, although I threw myself into it, after three exhilarating years with barely a break, it was not surprising when I hit the wall. The ugly signs of burnout were showing – I was on edge all the time, still trying to be cheerful but often impatient with the occasional volunteer who didn't know what they were doing. Sometimes I was just plain rude. When a drug-addled homeless client broke in to the service one night and used the office floor as his toilet I decided that I too had seen enough crap and it was time to move on.

A more pressing reason to spend less time working was that I had fallen in love. My now wife Jan was then the boss at Coburg Legal Centre and it was almost but not quite love at first sight when we met at one of the mostly boring committees we were both on. One night I needed a lift back to Fitzroy and Jan was heading that way. Her kind offer turned comical when she ran out of petrol, but once the car was started we went on to dinner – our first date.

About a year later we decided to live together and along with Jan came her then nine-year-old son, Nigel. At age thirty, with little appreciation of what was really involved, I became an instant stepfather. Parenting at any time has its share of challenges, but step-parenting brings another level of complexity. Nigel taught me many lessons, and still does, but establishing a relationship with a child that is not based on the assumed authority of a parent is deeply humbling. The first time we went together to buy him new shoes was in itself a masterclass in what not to do. He knew exactly which pair of sneakers he wanted: the make, style and colour. Needless to recount they were without any doubt the most expensive pair of shoes in the universe. I had no understanding that shoes were a measure of status, mistakenly thinking they were just an item of footwear. We did not quite come to blows, but it got perilously close.

Similarly, I had to learn how to score at cricket in order to be able to take an active role in his sports-dominated life. When his front teeth were knocked out by a ball while wicket-keeping, I popped the bits of tooth into my cheek and against his protestations that it should wait until the match was over, raced him to the dental hospital. Waiting an hour with the broken shards protectively kept moist and warm in my gums, we then got to see a dentist, whereupon I spat out the fragments in the hope they could be reunited with the two stumps in his mouth. The amused dentist explained that unless they came out with the roots they were just scraps of enamel and to my horror threw them into the bin.

As well as transforming our home, Jan transformed my life. My old skin was shed, and I discovered the beauty of creating a family. I still spent the weekends playing with motorbikes but also worked in the garden – under strict direction. My selfish single lifestyle gave way to sharing. It was increasingly obvious that my non-stop work routine was incompatible with a new and serious relationship, being a decent partner and committed step-parent. I needed to find another way of making a living and was attracted to the vague notion of becoming a barrister, but in late 1987 I resigned from FLS without a job to go to.

I found myself at home in the evenings, which had never happened before. I was lost and restless, unable to adjust to the totally foreign notion of unallocated time. I sometimes paced up and down the house and regularly wondered if I had made a terrible mistake. But as I decompressed from the pressure-cooker of a job that had consumed me, and as a few other offers of part-time and casual work arrived, I relaxed. As Jan and Nigel introduced me to the world of living with kids, it all made sense. Becoming a parent so suddenly – overnight – is the best thing that ever happened. Each summer, Nigel went off to spend the holidays with his father, Ted, and the rest of his family in Brisbane, returning in time to go back to school. While away, Nigel learned more of his Bundjalung Indigenous culture and the Inala family's lifestyle, which was entirely different to the bourgeois Melbourne world of the rest of his life. That he was the only Aboriginal kid at his school, the only Aboriginal kid in his cricket or hockey team, the only Aboriginal kid pretty much wherever he went and whatever he did was clearly a novelty to many – but irrelevant to anyone within his circle. He was just Nigel, and although I started to notice the stares and the occasional comments his very existence attracted, and was appalled that it aroused so much casual racism, I was oblivious to the worst of the discrimination he later told us he encountered in his everyday life.

While clowning around at FLS I had developed quite a few contacts with journalists who had started using me as their 'dial-a-quote' legal commentator. I got a thrill from being quoted on anything from complaints against police to drug law reform. I had been interviewed a few times by Tom Molomby, a veteran figure at the ABC who produced and presented *The Law Report* on Radio National each Tuesday. He was first in touch with Fitzroy Legal Service about a law reform campaign we were involved with and we continued to speak regularly. He found it useful to have input from outside the narrow confines of the Sydney legal bubble so as I prepared to depart the legal service I introduced him to my replacement. Tom asked what I was planning on doing next and I replied somewhat anxiously 'not sure'. He offered me a casual gig straight away, as his Melbourne 'stringer', not that I knew what a stringer was, but he promised that someone at the ABC could teach me. He also needed a sidekick at the rapidly approaching Commonwealth Legal Convention in Perth, a major event with dozens of concurrent sessions, too big for one person to cover. He offered me paid work for a week, travel and all expenses covered, an offer that was impossible to resist.

Within just a few weeks of being a legal aid activist and troublemaker at FLS I found myself in Perth in the massive Convention Centre, lugging around an ABC branded reel-to-reel tape recorder. The Hawke Government Attorney-General of Australia, Lionel Bowen, was in the crowd and with the ignorance of protocol that only a novice can get away with, I went straight to him and asked him to explain the funding shortages in legal aid – something legal centre lawyers had campaigned about for years without any impact. The AG smiled at me and made solemn promises into an ABC microphone, the exact assurances that we had spent years trying to secure through politely writing letters and other more conventional methods. Although it was not yet money in the bank – that took many more years and budget cycles – I immediately realised that this ABC logo I was hiding behind was rather useful – microphones must have magic powers.

Within the year I was making regular contributions to *The Law Report*, while juggling some other part-time tribunal work, and, shortly after, in mid-1988, Tom Molomby resigned to go to the Bar in Sydney. I applied for the gig and after multiple auditions and interviews in mid-December 1988, the ABC offered me the job. I thought of it as a worthwhile short-term detour on my way to being a barrister, and I reckoned somewhat cynically that it might improve my prospects of getting established more quickly once I did go to the Bar. I had no idea of the variety of work the ABC actually offered and had no intentions of embarking on a career as a broadcaster. I certainly could not foresee that a probably short stint working for the ABC would circuitously lead me back to the Mighty Apollo and his sister, Thelma Hawks of Top Springs, via of all the improbable characters the irrepressible Frank Hardy, yarn spinner, notorious activist and author of *Power without Glory*.

Even after finalising the estate of Thelma Hawks, I had occasionally stayed in touch with Apollo, visiting the gym and listening to more of his stories over a mug of tea. He was always friendly and gave me regular updates on how his three sons were progressing in life. He was getting old, talking even more slowly in his distinctive, clipped manner, sometimes losing his thoughts and even the entire thread of conversation, always worrying why there were fewer and fewer customers in the gym. The machines dotted around the top floor of Hawke Street were usually idle and now so old it was almost a museum of fitness equipment rather than a working gym. Apollo lamented that he could not afford any of the newer and fancier gadgets that were standard in the booming personal fitness business. He knew that time had passed him by, but had no mechanism for letting go. He was not the first older person to experience that and will not be the last either. But for someone so proud and so invested in his self-image it was doubly cruel.

* * *

The ABC was like an utterly foreign world. As part of a massive bureaucracy now, I was expected to cover legal issues and events that occurred not just across Australia but anywhere around the world and to be an instant expert on any law news that broke.

Jan was heavily pregnant when I started my new gig on *The Law Report,* and in March 1989 our second son, Jack, was born. My parents gradually embraced my blended family, overcoming their disappointment that I had strayed from choosing a Jewish partner. What had been important to them until then became less and less significant as grandchildren arrived.

The new ABC job meant that I was required to constantly travel, but was always feeling guilty about being away. I loved working nationally though and quickly realised that the ABC would approve a request for travel for any genuine program-related reason. In no time at all I was darting from capital city to capital city, attending conferences and recording interviews with senior judges, academics, Law Society presidents and CEOs, industry regulators, activists and people far more senior than me, all of whom were delighted to have the chance to extract leverage courtesy of the megaphone of the national broadcaster. It was a constant adrenaline rush and I loved it.

The office and ABC studios were in Lonsdale Street, Melbourne, directly opposite the courts, which was perfect for a law reporter. All I had to do to find a story was step out the front door and start chatting to any of the many people I knew wandering around the precinct. My skill set expanded to include cut editing of reel-to-reel recording tape using a razor blade and a chinagraph pencil. Splicing and sticking the gems of somebody's recorded words together removed all the flab from longwinded interviews and reduced it to piles of slippery discarded tape coiled on the floor. I was taught to script tightly, to pronounce properly and to edit mercilessly. It took years but I slowly became a broadcaster.

Rubbing shoulders with some of the stars of radio was thrilling and I marvelled at how I shared a kettle with the legendary Terry Lane and the top-rating 'Drive' host Doug Aiton. Their work in daily live radio seemed so much more thrilling than the more serious prerecorded documentary-style show that I was employed to make, and I particularly enjoyed doing a weekly law segment with the brilliant and feisty Ramona Koval. I developed links with ABC shows in Adelaide, Brisbane, Canberra, Hobart and Perth and did cross-promotional spots with someone somewhere in the nation most days.

Every day there would be some important court case or major legal issue in the news. I was on call to jump into a studio to explain, analyse, answer talkback questions or just to provide contacts for specific topic experts. The Aboriginal Deaths in Custody Royal Commission handed down its report in April 1991, a topic of vital significance around Australia. Although Nigel had extended family members who were caught in the criminal justice system, I knew none of their details – it was another world, which I was not invited to visit. At the same time, the empires of Alan Bond and other white-collar tycoons seemed to be collapsing left, right and centre, raising complex issues of corporate responsibility that left the public fuming. How can someone owe a bank a billion dollars? The sensational Russell Street bomber's trials and appeals demanded daily scrutiny.

The High Court decision in the landmark test case by Eddie Mabo was delivered in June 1992. Early in my stint on *The Law Report* I had flown to Brisbane and watched for a half day as the Melbourne barristers Ron Castan QC and Bryan Keon-Cohen argued their 'lost cause' at the trial stage, long before it went to the

High Court. I had reported on it before it made headlines and was as astonished as anyone when the verdict was delivered. No other court decision has had the same impact, dividing the nation and triggering an appalling racist scare campaign. Senior politicians from the conservative side of politics delivered astonishingly ill-informed and frankly mischievous commentary, needlessly alarming property owners by predicting the imminent loss of farms and suburban backyards. I found myself in vigorous debates with senior reporters, politicians and commentators, people with vastly higher profiles than me and decades of experience, but who had not followed the case nor read the actual words of the judges. Confident declarations that the Parliament needed to override the decision before there was a revolution simply had to be countered and there were few people available or prepared to do it. Going against the tide is never easy, but as one of few people who had actually bothered to study both the facts and the law, I got angrier and angrier with the undermining campaign, led by people with vested interests in farming and mining. Occasionally, I found myself emotional, angry even, at the blatant prejudice emerging when a declaration of nothing more threatening than equality so frightened the establishment. I never disclosed that my own stepson was Aboriginal and that I was emotionally invested.

My disposition was not improved by a family tragedy just months before. Nigel's father, Ted, whom I had never met, was killed in April 1992 in a terrible 'good Samaritan' conflict, shot dead when he intervened to protect a woman being attacked in a neighbourhood family violence dispute. The shocking trauma that is part of the fabric of daily life for Aboriginal Australia was not just of academic interest to me – it was shaping my family.

The death of any teenager's parent becomes the defining moment of their lives, and upon Ted's death it was even more important than before to provide support and stability for Jan, Nigel and Jack. The repercussions of that one event have been incalculable in the lives of Ted's extended family, but I do not have their permission to tell those stories.

* * *

As each year progressed, around September I had to turn my mind to providing some content to fill my time slot during the summer holidays. I was expected to prepare a series of eight radio shows distinctly different to the regular weekly fare, not date or time-sensitive and suitable for a more relaxed holiday sensibility. The usually irreverent, hilarious after-dinner speeches from elderly and long-retired judges inspired the idea, nurtured by a Sydney QC Dr Greg James and the broadcaster Tim Bowden, to record oral history interviews with old lawyers. Oral history and radio go hand in glove. A generation of great raconteurs of the bench and Bar was fast disappearing, and the idea was to simply record their battle stories and make them available to a wider audience than that found at a legal function. Funding was secured from the profession in each state to cover my travel and, when packaged as a *Law Report* summer series called 'Taken On Oath', the interviews were edited together and broadcast over January and February 1991, later transcribed and published in a book of the same name.

I had set out to find the oldest lawyers in each state and to get them to tell stories about their career and to describe how the law had changed in their time. One of those who had to be included was the legendary Sir John Starke QC, long retired from the Supreme Court of Victoria. He was the embodiment of an establishment figure, the son of a legendary High Court judge himself, and a crusty old bugger with a reputation for having no filter. I approached him expecting to be told to stop wasting his leisure time. Quite to the contrary, I was invited to visit his Mount Eliza mansion and recorded hours of sometimes hilarious tall tales ranging from why he was expelled from Trinity College at Melbourne University (he was drunk) and why articled clerks are 'bloody useless', to how he ended up being the reluctant judge who had to sentence to death Ronald Ryan – the last man in Australia sent to the gallows.

Mid-interview, I asked him about one of his most famous victories – how it came about that he was junior defence counsel in the criminal libel trial of Frank Hardy after the 1950 publication of the scandalous *Power without Glory*. A committed communist, Hardy had written a thinly fictionalised account of corruption and political influence-peddling in the 1920s and 1930s involving the wealthy, bent and powerful character John West, readily identifiable as leading Melbourne corporate and sporting figure and multi-millionaire John Wren. No established company would dare publish the book so it was printed and distributed guerrilla-style off the back of trucks. Shortly after, for his trouble, Hardy had been charged with the rarely seen crime of criminal libel. A typical civil defamation claim is for damage to reputation for which the remedy is the payment of money. Hardy had no money at all, so that claim would be futile. For criminal (or seditious) libel, involving malice, instead of paying money, the outcome can be a prison term for the author as well as the more important remedy of a court order banning circulation of the offending material. The prosecution intended to shut Hardy up rather than further enrich the already very wealthy Wren family.

The resultant court case was front page national news for months in the early 1950s, at exactly the same time as the Menzies Government was trying to criminalise communism. Hardy's prosecution became a cause célèbre and was politicised from day one – the devoutly Catholic business figure trying to hide his shady past by suing the communist agitator who was shining a spotlight onto it. The sub-plot – that a communist author had targeted prominent figures in the Catholic Church, while the Church was using any technique available to stop the influence of communism – was not lost on anyone.

Settled deep into his plush armchair at home in Mount Eliza, Starke told how he had been chosen by Don Campbell KC to be junior counsel and that they knew their fees each day were being paid by the deeply unpopular and under surveillance Communist Party. He recounted that, as the trial ended, they thought Hardy likely to go to prison and warned him on the day of the verdict to 'bring a toothbrush'. But the jury acquitted Hardy, the rabble-rousing communist. Starke revealed to my microphone an encounter that took place years after the trial: '*I met the foreman* [of the jury] *at the races and I had a talk to him and I said "Why did you acquit him?" "Well," he said, "old Wren had been a bloody scandal all his life and the first time he's hurt by anything he rushes to the law for protection and we thought 'to hell with him'".*'

The interview with Sir John Starke, when broadcast to a fair amount of media interest, also attracted the immediate attention of none other than Frank Hardy himself. He wrote to me at the ABC asking to listen to the unedited version of what Starke said, not just the extracts that were put to air, to which I readily agreed. I got to meet one of my literary heroes – I had strong memories of reading *Power without Glory* during my Barker Harty commutes and regarded it as a masterpiece.

Hardy came to the ABC in Lonsdale Street at the now demolished 'Broadcast House'. I was beyond excited but tried to disguise my anxiety as I sauntered into the lobby to collect him. He was pacing around, slim and shorter than I had expected, signature hat tilted jauntily across his head. His eyes worked as hard as his mouth – neither kept still for a moment. He radiated an energy that is rarely encountered and as we walked down the corridor between radio studios going live to air it would not have surprised me if he had just walked in and gatecrashed a random program. He had that air of unpredictability, that edge that some find exciting and others terrifying. To me it was intoxicating, and I pinched myself that I was sitting knee to knee with the author of not just *Power without Glory* but also *The Outcasts of Foolgarah*, one of the funniest and most irreverent books I had ever read. Here was the unbeaten winner of the Darwin 'Yarn Spinning' contest for the last twenty years, the bloke who had beaten 'Tall Tales Tyrell', undefeated as the best bullshit artist in a land that boasted plenty of them.

Hardy fidgeted as I laced up the unedited reel-to-reel tape on the battered machine in the tiny sound booth. We played it through twice. He wanted to know more than my questions had revealed, so he asked to meet with Starke to fill in some of his own gaps in understanding what had transpired when he was put on trial forty years earlier. He was determined to find out who behind the scenes had initiated his prosecution, convinced that Starke could help him sort out the mystery. He openly speculated that some sort of Catholic mafia in the police or government had been out to scapegoat him and to use the case to further demonise communists as a danger to civil society generally. He expressed remorse about the impact it all had on the lives of the Wrens, who had been as much caught up in those controversial times as he had.

To my surprise, Sir John Starke readily agreed to a reunion with Hardy, and both were happy for their meeting to be recorded for broadcast on *The Law Report*. Early in the morning of 26 November 1992 I pulled up outside Frank Hardy's Carlton home in an ABC station wagon to chauffeur him the hour and a half to Mount Eliza. Sprightly for his seventy-five years, Hardy climbed into the government Commodore and before we had even driven one block, lit up his omnipresent pipe. I politely and deferentially explained that smoking was not allowed in ABC vehicles. Hardy grinned, asked me whether I wanted him to do the interview or not, and said *'either I smoke in the car or I get out … if you want me to do this then I'm smoking my pipe … or you can drop me at the next pub'*. I wound down the windows and kept driving.

Sir John Starke was one of the most garrulous people I had ever met. Tall, stooped in old age but with a fierce gaze from his heavily bagged eyes, his voice still carried the authority of his many years sitting in judgement of his fellow citizens. Yet after Hardy barrelled into his living room, Starke could barely get a word in. Later in the morning we paused the recording to refresh the batteries – in both the recording equipment and in ourselves. Out in his kitchen, watching the kettle boil, Starke leant on his walking stick and out the corner of his mouth said, 'Geez, he can't half talk, eh?' which coming from Starke was seriously funny. After we finished and a newspaper photographer took photos of the two shaking hands, Hardy and I headed back to the city. As I dropped Hardy home, I asked him to sign my battered copy of

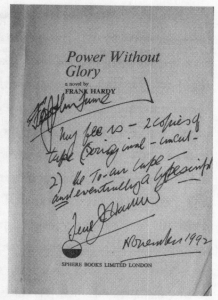

Frank Hardy negotiated when signing my copy of *Power Without Glory*, November 1992.

Power without Glory. The scrawl on the title page tells much about Hardy. *He* had asked *me* to arrange the interview with Starke, but according to his penned note on the title page:

> *To Jon Faine*
> *1) my fee is 2 copies of tape, original, uncut*
> *2) the to-air tape and eventually a transcript*
> *Frank Hardy, November 1992*

The subsequent radio program attracted even more media attention and Hardy was pleased to be back in the spotlight. He would call me every few weeks for a chat, still determined – obsessively – to unravel what lay behind his prosecution.

The Law Report on Radio National had kept me more than busy for four years, and gradually the ABC started using me as a fill-in host on talkback radio during the holidays. I was regularly popping up on 3LO, the local Melbourne station, and the adrenaline of live-to-air interviews became utterly seductive. There was a sense that every day made a difference, every show had an impact, every interview could move the dial on the issues of the day. I got more feedback from friends and colleagues when I was filling in on 3LO than I ever got from *The Law Report*. Typically, the producers would prepare and type an introduction for an interview for the host to read, and some suggested questions to get the interview started, but where an interview went next depended on the skill of the host. As I accumulated more 'flying hours' behind the microphone, and became less self-conscious on air, I would depart more frequently from the scripts and trust my instincts instead. One day as fill-in host, just as the ABC news bulletin was finishing to signal the start of the top-rating 'Drive' shift in the late afternoon, Louise Cooper, one of two producers, asked if she could check that my pile of scripts were in the correct order. I handed them over and as the opening theme started, she calmly walked out with all my scripts in her hand. In absolute panic, I glanced at the screen where senior producer Kate Latimer had typed: *just talk*. At the end of the show, I was soaked in perspiration and my head was throbbing from concentrated effort. Louise and Kate laughed and said, 'See, you got through – you don't need scripts' and I never used a scripted intro or list of questions ever again.

After four years of *The Law Report*, just as I was contemplating moving back to being a real lawyer, someone deep in the mysterious cave inhabited by that wise breed of ABC managers decided to offer me a permanent change, to move me away from specialist prerecorded programs, and I was offered one of the coveted weekday shifts on 3LO. Apart from the constant buzz and prestige, the new gig offered more money and a welcome respite from the constant interstate travel. The novelty of flying had long ago worn off and instead I wanted to be at home more. Jan's work meant she was always busy; Nigel was a teenager and Jack was soon to start school. It was a good time to make the change.

Daily radio is as much fun as it is possible to have while working. I got to ask anyone anything and clown around with the audience every day as well. Having initially snobbishly dismissed talkback as lowbrow chatter, I discovered not just how much fun it could be but how important and useful it was to interact on the stories of the day with a wider audience. What was said on the radio really mattered, was capable of helping shift people's views of the news, and it was a privilege to be part of it.

Quite out of the blue, Frank Hardy rang one day and told me he had gone back into his archives and identified the actual policeman who had signed his summons back in the 1950s. As a favour to Frank, and through the retired police association, I eventually located the old copper on the NSW south coast. Over the phone he remembered little of the minutiae of the events of so long ago but agreed to meet up with Hardy, who was confident that he could squeeze more relevant details from him if given the chance. We tried to schedule a visit for mid-1993 but our new contact was having some surgery and asked if we would put it off a while. I was flat out anyway so deferred the visit, telling Frank that we should plan to make the trip together in March or April 1994.

Just after I got back to work after the holidays in late January 1994 I was stunned to learn from the radio news bulletin that Frank Hardy had suddenly died. I had relished our encounters, found him endlessly fascinating with a bottomless pit of usually hilarious and occasionally true stories and had looked forward to more collaboration with someone who was such an important part of literary history. I had briefly met his partner, Jenny Barrington, during the sessions sitting with Frank over bottomless cups of tea in Carlton – listening to him yarning, despite regular interruptions by the races blaring out on his transistor. I bought some flowers for Jenny and took them around, knocking tentatively at the door, not wanting to intrude. Frank's entire family were gathered there, and Jenny thanked me tearfully as I beat a hasty retreat. I thought no more of it until a few days later when I got a call from Alan Hardy, Frank's son. He asked if the ABC would record Frank's memorial service and celebration of his extraordinary life, which meant that I became the Master of Ceremonies.

I expected a few family members and some literary colleagues would make a speech in a pub somewhere, but never in my wildest imagination did I expect it would turn into such a big event. Within a week the family had booked the Collingwood Town Hall and I had persuaded the ABC we ought to broadcast the memorial service live over the radio. I found myself introducing a stooped Gough Whitlam, among others, to a crowd of over one thousand people overflowing from the Town Hall and all the way out to Punt Road beyond. The service was brilliant – quite fitting for a great larrikin, with back-to-back storytellers from his family through to various co-conspirators in the great game that was the life of Frank Hardy. There were plenty of laughs, and Gough, though clearly aging and walking slowly with a stick, still filled the space with his charisma and commanding presence. With that unique Whitlam oratory, he recounted how Hardy, more than anyone, had opened his eyes to the desperate plight of Aboriginal Australians, through his adoption of the Gurindji struggle at Wave Hill in the 1960s and his writing that stemmed from it. Gough spoke passionately, his sincerity reinforced by genuine tears as he finished his eulogy. I moved across the stage to assist him to negotiate the steep steps but instead he turned towards me and as he rested his head on my shoulder, sobbing, the Town Hall crowd rose in a prolonged ovation as their political hero eventually negotiated his way down from the stage and resumed his front-row seat.

The next speaker was Mick Rangiari from Wave Hill, one of the last surviving petitioners from the Gurindji walk-off. 'Hoppy' had rushed first to Darwin then flew to Melbourne to pay respect to Hardy, whom he aptly described as 'this great man'. He too was showing advancing years as he slowly ascended the stairs and, in a suddenly hushed hall, spoke in English mixed with Gurindji to tell how Frank Hardy had taken their quiet protest at Wave Hill and took their story to the nation. Without him they may never have succeeded. He was followed by 'the young fella', Michael Paddy, who read a message from the entire community at Daguragu. They were thanked with sustained applause.

The 1968 bestseller *The Unlucky Australians* was that compelling story, Hardy opening the nation's eyes to something that until then Australia was reluctant to see. It was deeply moving to hear the Gurindji language being spoken and to know it was being listened to by not just the crowded Collingwood Town Hall but hundreds of thousands tuning in on the live national broadcast. The crowd rose for another standing ovation as Hoppy and his son made their way down from the stage. The service concluded with a rousing chorus of the communist anthem 'The Internationale' and I was embarrassed to be stranded up on stage while not knowing the words.

> *Arise ye workers from your slumbers*
> *Arise ye prisoners of want*
> *For reason in revolt now thunders*
> *And at last ends the age of cant.*
> *Away with all your superstitions*
> *Servile masses arise, arise*
> *We'll change henceforth the old tradition*
> *And spurn the dust to win the prize.*

At least I knew some of the words to the chorus ...

> *So comrades, come rally*
> *And the last fight let us face*
> *The Internationale ... unites ... the ... human race.*

As the crowd slowly departed the Collingwood Town Hall the family invited me to join them with some other guests at Frank's local pub in Carlton, the Great Northern. Unsurprisingly about half the crowd from the service turned up and it became a raucous, lengthy but fitting wake for a great yarn teller and drinker. When Gough arrived, he was literally mobbed – and enjoyed every moment of adoration. His stoop seemed to straighten, although we soon made sure he had a chair and some fresh air. He lingered long into the afternoon and enjoyed multiple toasts to various Hardy memories. If only someone had been there to film or record it – which I ought to have anticipated but to my eternal shame did not.

The Gurindji walk-off at Wave Hill was Australia's most famous assertion of an Indigenous claim to land until Eddie Mabo went to the High Court – and lost. It is an obscure but sad detail that Mabo's claim failed although the case he led succeeded. His co-plaintiffs, the claimants James Rice and Dave Passi, were recognised by the courts as having the requisite continuous connection to identifiable land. But Eddie Mabo was not. The principle of 'terra nullius' – an empty land – was forever removed from Australian law in 1992. Recognition of native title is Eddie Mabo's true legacy, despite his personal claim failing, but it could never have happened without the various struggles that came before, especially that of the Gurindji.

Most Australians know the Gurindji story through the iconic Kev Carmody and Paul Kelly song 'From Little Things, Big Things Grow', released in 1991, more than twenty years after the strike happened. Standing to the side of the Collingwood Town Hall stage at Hardy's memorial service, listening to Hoppy deliver his eulogy in language, I was transported back to Top Springs. Wave Hill is just down the road from Thelma's pub, and the Gurindji walk-off, that most celebrated of Indigenous

Frank Hardy's *The Unlucky Australians* is his first-hand account of the historic Gurindji walk-off. [Nelson/Estate of Frank Hardy]

protests, had all taken place while Ma Hawks was running the nearest pub. In a genuine lightning bolt moment, it was obvious that Frank Hardy – never one to go past a drink in a bar – must have had more than the occasional beer at Thelma's pub. I had to find out if their paths crossed. The first step was to plug a gaping hole in my education by reading *The Unlucky Australians,* and that same evening on my way home I went to a second-hand bookshop and grabbed a hardback first edition. I wished I could reach into the grave and get Hardy to sign that one too.

CHAPTER 12
SID HAWKS

The daily 3LO show rolled on through 1994. The conservative Kennett Government had been elected in Victoria and the political climate changed overnight. Kennett promised a more exuberant and dynamic brand of leadership, and he loved live radio – but not the ABC. Although my gig was not one of the key shifts – 'Mornings' with the well-connected and influential Ranald Macdonald and the top rating 'Drive' show with the uncannily insightful Doug Aiton did the heavy lifting – I still got to cover some of the big news of the day and even occasionally joust with the premier and his ministers.

The station manager – the six-foot-plus mercurial veteran Brian Hugo, nickname Lurch – spent his day sitting behind an enormous desk pushed up close to the Victorian-era window that opened like a door onto a balcony. He overcame the 'No Smoking' edict by stretching his long arm so he could dangle his ever-present cigarette just outside, while still in his desk chair working. He challenged me to grow the middle of the day audience and to deliver listeners to the 'Drive' program which followed it. I started a joke of the day competition, where straight after the news bulletin, which always attracted peak listener numbers, a listener told a joke on air. The challenge was to keep the audience from turning off after the news finished. A caller would tell a joke on each of Monday through to Thursday and then on Friday we invited a celebrity judge to listen back as we reviewed and critiqued all four joke tellers and their jokes. It was risky – live radio always is, but a joke-telling competition is asking for trouble. The celebrity judge – as well as having a long chat – got to award a prize for the best joke of the week. In no time it became hugely popular and the Friday segment to be the judge was in demand. We moved from inviting comedians as the judge to authors, TV and film actors – anyone interesting – and their longer interview became a feature. When the premier invited himself to judge the joke of the week, we knew we had made an impression. I thought radio was both fun and useful, that broadcasting was now my future, and I stopped thinking of myself as a barrister-in-waiting.

In August 1994, in at the office early for the daily routine of leafing through the newspapers looking for inspiration and story ideas, I got a terrible shock. Flicking past the obituaries in *The Age*, I cried out loud as I read that Paul Anderson, known as the Mighty Apollo, had died. I shed a tear while telling my producers about this amazing man. Surprisingly, the obituary said that Apollo had been an Olympic gold medallist, hardly a small detail that the ever-boastful Apollo would have left out of his storytelling. It also claimed he had performed in the USA, which he had never talked about. There were other lesser achievements in the obituary that did not connect with what I already knew about him, but overall it covered many of his extraordinary feats of strength and acknowledged the passing of a performer the likes of which the world would not see again.

After my show, I rang the only number I had for contacting the family – at the gym. I hoped Paul, Mark or Bruce, or all three, might answer the phone so I could pay my respects. After only a few rings, I nearly fell off my chair when the recently deceased Apollo answered in his unmistakeable throaty voice.

'Hello ... Mighty Apollo Gym and Combat Centre ... How can I help?'

I was lost for words, looking at his obituary in the newspaper while talking to him. 'Paul? It's Jon Faine ... Good to hear your voice ... um ... ah ... How are you?' was about all I could muster under the circumstances.

'Not bad, Jon, not bad, getting by ... How about you?' he said without the slightest hint of stress. Clearly, he was not dead. What followed was some inane chitchat while I gathered my thoughts.

'Apollo – have you seen today's newspaper?'

'No, I don't get the papers anymore ... Why? Am I in it?' was his immediate response.

I promised to visit straight away and bring the newspaper with me. When I arrived and read him his obituary he was agitated, then angry. I must admit I had never had to read someone their obituary before, so I am not sure what other reaction might be possible.

'Gee, it's not good is it Jon ... People will think I didn't do any of my feats of strength ... that I was an imposter.... there was an American guy, a weightlifter, who had the same name as me ... he was also Paul Anderson ... And they've got us muddled up. He was a

Apollo surrounded himself with memorabilia.

An aging Apollo dressed up for a profile story in 1992.

gold medallist here at the Melbourne Olympic games, not me, but then they say that he did the things I did ... they will think he did them all. This is terrible, is there anything I can do about this ... Can you help me?' as he looked up pleadingly, knees wide apart, shuffling the newspaper and frowning.

I called *The Age* to try to get it sorted. In an at times farcical conversation, I explained to the person in charge of obituaries that Paul Anderson – the Mighty Apollo – was definitely not dead, explained the mix-up and asked for a correction to be published. After quite an argument, which I thought was absurd and said so, he reluctantly agreed but a few days later only two lines were printed. There was nothing about Apollo's theatrical feats of strength being his alone, no explanation that the Olympian Anderson's conventional weightlifting career had been incomparably different and the narrative in the obituary attributing Apollo's showbiz career to someone else was in error. I had to explain to Apollo that I could not compel them to print anything else and we had to accept the unfairness of it all. He contemplated suing them for defamation but the cost would almost certainly have outweighed any likely gain.

Not long after, on my birthday in September 1994, towards the end of what I thought was a successful second year on 3LO, I was called into the new boss's office for what I assumed was to be a pep talk. Brian Hugo had recently retired and the new boss was the much younger, less experienced and less friendly Steve Ahern. He bluntly told me I was being dropped as a host for 1995. There had been no problems, no warning, no complaints and the ratings were healthy. He coldly told me the decision had been made at head office in Sydney by Barry Chapman, the Director of Radio, whom I had never met or even spoken to on the phone. Not only was I losing my own show, but there was no other work for me and I was being made redundant. I would be required to leave the ABC entirely at the end of the year, even though ABC TV had just auditioned me for a regular gig on *The Investigators*, a popular consumer show. I was shell-shocked, but when I left Ahern's office I found the direct number for Barry Chapman and rang him to seek an explanation. He was clearly rattled, caught out by my ambush, and struggled to get a clear sentence out. Eventually he said, 'Whatever the future holds for you, Jon, it's clearly not broadcasting … your future lies elsewhere; we don't think you ought persist with a career in the media.'

On what had become the most miserable birthday of my life, I found myself in my mid-thirties, with a young family and facing the unpleasant double of public embarrassment and unemployment by the end of the year. Being sacked is always awful for anyone, but when you are in the public eye it is doubly difficult. The heavy cloud of failure lingers in people's minds forever. My world had been up-ended and I struggled to explain it to Jan. One minute we thought everything was going swimmingly – the next it was derailed. Not only was my pride wounded, but it shook my confidence. I thought I was doing a great job, but maybe my grip on the world was clouded by arrogance and hubris. Maybe others did not see me the way I saw myself. I was not used to self-doubt, and that was the hardest part.

To add insult to injury, I had to stay upbeat on air every day for the next few months without telling anyone, not even my producers. Only Jan was privy to the secret and I simply had to tough it out. But all media thrives on gossip and at the ABC it was like blood running through its veins; without gossip the entire place would grind to a stop and rumour mills always ran hot. The mood change within my small team was obvious, and if I was to make it through to the end of the year, I needed to clear my head and get away. There was some unused leave which would not be part of any payout, so in order to squeeze every bit of value from my contract, distract myself and to get away from the scene of the crime, I took two weeks off in October. I needed to totally unwind, to find something to immerse myself in to stop self-pity engulfing me. I planned a trip to the Territory.

* * *

Darwin offered a complete escape, friends to catch up with and the faint prospect of chasing tales about Ma Hawks, in case one day I might be able to tell her story. Despite dealing with Apollo and his sons for so long, I had never really got to know much about Thelma. What was she really like? Could I find people who knew her well enough to learn more about Top Springs? For all the deliberate self-aggrandising that characterised Apollo's showbiz career, Thelma's decades flogging grog at Toppie had the hallmark of wilful obscurity.

John Flynn was as welcoming as ever. Apart from hosting a classic Darwin beer, prawns, beer, steak, beer and beer barbeque, he put me in touch with Thelma's ex-husband, Sid Hawks, and several other old-timers who knew Thelma back in her prime, including Norm Douglas, who was now retired from his marathon drink-a-thon at Top Springs and settled comfortably in Katherine living on the pension. Sid readily invited me to visit him and his Indonesian-born wife, Thien, and young son, James, on the Bagot Road, opposite Darwin Airport. Although he and Thelma had split in 1960, more than thirty years before, Sid was happy to reminisce. Norm agreed to a chat if I could make it down to Katherine.

Sid was eighty-seven years old and welcomed me to his home with a strong handshake and a steady gaze. We settled in on his typically wide Darwin verandah, with a slow fan on the ceiling and a big jug of iced water. He was a natural storyteller with the remnants of an English accent just detectable. His long face bore the trademark sun scars of a life outdoors in the deep north. Skinny knees poked out from baggy shorts, spare folds of skin hinting at the legacy of muscles long since aged away. He warmed to the challenge of recounting his story from the beginning and generously answered all my questions, occasionally getting distracted and wandering sideways. I had no idea about any of his life except what Apollo and Flynn had told me – that he had married Thelma during World War II, had later gone with her in a war surplus truck to the Territory and established the general store at Top Springs. The store at some point transformed from being a sly grog shop to a proper licensed pub, he and Thelma had fallen out at some stage and he had moved on to a new life in Darwin. His promise that he had much more to tell did not disappoint.

Cedric James Charles Hawks, known to everyone as Sid, was born in Belfast, Ireland, in 1907, but as he joked: *'I didn't know much about that, did I, and you didn't want anyone in Belfast to know you as Cedric, did you?'* His father was in the British military and the family sailed to China when he was small but then came back to live with his grandmother during World War I. He lived in Birmingham, then with an uncle in Norfolk, and was sent to Naval College in Portsmouth. After nearly a year he was thrown out *'because I disgraced myself with the gardener's daughter ... I got a dishonourable discharge and was sent to work for an uncle who was a naval draughtsman in Belfast for a six-year apprenticeship'*. The naval dockyards, like the entire city, were full of sectarian violence between Catholics and Protestants, and because he had a Catholic girlfriend he was given *'a belting'*. He couldn't stand the conflict, and at age twenty-one quit his apprenticeship and sailed to Sydney. He was immediately employed as a fitter and turner on the road machines but soon got better work as crew on the migrant ships bringing 1800 people at a time from England. By the late 1930s, with war on the horizon, he started pilot training at Kingsford Smith Airfield – he thought the Navy was too harsh. His tuition started on Tiger Moths for one pound an hour, but *'I soon realised I would not cut it as a pilot but I joined the RAAF anyway and became an aircraft fitter. We spent most of our time learning to march – it was a bloody terrible waste of time'*. Sid regaled me with more tales of his unexceptional war service, including being marked as 'a militant type' for disagreeing with a superior officer. He chuckled and clearly wore that label as proudly as any medal. Posted to Laverton in Melbourne to work on Lockheed Hudson bombers, he went to watch adagio dancing featuring 'The Young Apollo' and met Thelma Anderson. They were soon a couple, spending more and more time together, sometimes with her brother as well.

Sid was characteristically frank about the man who became his brother-in-law. *'I didn't like him – he was very arrogant, although very able with his self-defence and everything. I once saw him throw*

Thelma Anderson and a uniformed Sid Hawks courting, 1943.

a man – a sailor – over a wall; I thought he had killed him. We were walking along the beach at St Kilda, I was in my RAAF uniform and he was in this chocolate-coloured jacket, bright green trousers and Oxford brogue shoes with flaps down the front. He was a snappy dresser, and these blokes started to chiack him over his clothes. He just picked one of them up and threw him over the seawall. I thought he'd be dead. His mate ran away. He was a good performer though and I think he made a lot of money eventually.' I looked forward to reporting all this back to Apollo in Melbourne – he would be highly amused.

Bizarrely, Sid claimed that Apollo and Thelma spent *'a year and a half touring in Germany and performed for Hitler and Goering'.* I had scoured Apollo's scrapbooks on my various gym visits, and knowing his vanity, there was zero prospect that he would have kept a secret of that significance, nor was there an unexplained absence of any prolonged duration. Like the muddled obituary, the Apollo legend had grown a life of its own.

Sid and Thelma spent their courtship in the inner-city slums of Collingwood and Carlton – which despite coming from strife-torn Belfast, Sid described as a *'rough area. A fella jumped me once in Drummond Street where she lived, but he didn't get far. I could look after myself alright. We married in Brisbane, I had to be quick … there were other fellas after her. She was a very pretty woman'.*

As the Japanese were being slowly pushed back across the Western Pacific, Sid was injured in a minor plane crash and sent to Sydney for rehabilitation. He learned to repair sewing machines and after the war, the newly married Hawks settled in Brisbane. Drawing on the skills taught by Thelma's mother, they established an embroidery and satin stitching business, supplying church altar cloths, regalia for the Freemasons, sports clubs and the like. They employed several women, but after the war ended *'these Hungarian Jews came from Europe and worked for less money and we couldn't keep going'.* They sold all the machines and bought an almost new army surplus Chevrolet truck with only 800 miles on the clock for a couple of hundred pounds. Sid made up a cabin with bunks and a fold-down counter, and they loaded all the leftover rolls of material and headed north. *'We did thousands of miles with that truck, selling materials and clothes off the back to all the small towns and remote stations. I made a measuring stick from brass that was just a bit too long, and some old duck where we stopped off in the main street in Camooweal said "Your measuring stick is short" in front of everyone. I challenged her and said, "Madam, do you think I would rob a lovely lady like you?" and invited her to measure it herself and she went all red in the face. Word got out that we were fair and we did a good trade. Those rolls of material would have been worth nothing in Brisbane.'*

Sid Hawks selling to locals from his hawker's truck, 1949.

Although there was plenty of money to be made, Thelma and Sid soon decided the travelling life was not a long-term proposition. *'There was a lot of humiliation in travelling around ... you'd get called a bloody so-and-so and a dago bastard and all sorts of things and I've met some nice dagos, but it wasn't right so we got out of it.'* To be dismissively labelled as a 'dago bastard' meant more than just a bit of lip and abuse. It meant exclusion. Why this was directed at the Englishman Sid and his Collingwood born-and-bred wife (who had none of Apollo's dark looks) is hard to explain – unless it was the assumption that anyone living the life of a travelling hawker was best kept on the margins of society.

Postwar, the north of Australia was undergoing dramatic change. Darwin in particular, a small outpost until the Japanese bombing, had become a major city. Almost overnight the population went from a few to 25,000 at the peak of the conflict.

There was an expectation in many minds that it would stay that big. On one of his outback trading expeditions, Sid chanced upon an old mate who tipped him off on what he claimed was the official postwar plan for the Territory. *'Colonel Rose told me, and I believed him, that Darwin would soon be as big as Brisbane, and the government was determined that the defence of Australia depended on building up Darwin and finishing the railway all the way through from Alice. He had heard there was going to be a spur line built to get all the cattle from the stations where the Vestey mob were and whoever got to set up there would be sitting pretty when the railway came through.'*

Sid and Thelma were caught up in the excitement and speculation. They took a detour on their outback trading route and went to explore the Victoria River district for themselves. *'It was just after the wet; green grass and palm trees, water in the rivers, the waterholes had fish in them and the birds were incredible. So we chose the best spot, put up some water tanks and pulled dead cattle out*

Sid and Thelma's hawker's truck in the outback, 1949.

of the Armstrong River to make the water OK to pump for drinking.' No permits were sought or required – the site was so remote, they simply squatted for the time being. Later, a special purpose lease was sought from the NT administration.

Towards the end of 1949 and into 1950 Sid frequented the war surplus auctions to equip their new home at Top Springs. He sourced sawmill machinery from Brisbane, an almost new Case tractor in Darwin, the decommissioned refrigeration plant from the Catalina flying boat base in East Arm in Darwin, a crane truck – all picked up for a song. It was essential to be self-sufficient when living so remotely, and his training at the Belfast dockyards and during the war made him a proficient mechanic.

Settling at Toppie, isolated as it was, offered an escape from condescension and being patronised. But critical to their success was the rapid transformation of a trading post to a general store, then to a hotel with a liquor licence – the only pub for hours

Newly married, Thelma and Sid took to the outback in their hawker's truck.

Sid and Thelma's hawker's truck with the original Top Springs bark hut store, early 1950s.

around. '*People were complaining there was no booze but we ran a general store, post office and a banking agency. I started carting beer in bottles packed in straw and no-one cared, but then it got so popular we had to get a permit. There was a family that broke down near Yellow Waters, they had nearly run out of water and would have died. I had a big A frame on my six-wheel-drive truck, and a winch on the front and a winch on the back. There are 208 creek crossings between Top Springs and Katherine but there was no bog-hole that I couldn't get out of. I rescued them, Thelma nursed them, saved their lives really, and we got our pictures into* Pix. *It put us in a good light in Darwin. We got the liquor licence and it was a gold mine. One season we had seventy-eight huge mob of cattle go through. The waterhole was the best one around and each drover can spend a couple of thousand on booze, tobacco, saddles, hats and boots, the trucks need tyres and fuel — everything; we had whatever they needed. I'd take a truck and trailer across to Brisbane and load it up for supplies, loaded to the knocker*

The first store at Top Springs was little more than a humpy. Thelma with dogs, 1950.

The rough original store at Top Springs. Thelma with unknown man, 1953.

it was.' It was easier to get from Top Springs to Brisbane rather than Adelaide, as back in the 1940s, the road to Queensland had been sealed whereas the road south did not get bitumen until the 1980s. Even though the distance between Top Springs and Brisbane is longer, the trip east was much quicker.

Needless to say, the rules and conventions of commerce out bush are totally different to those that apply elsewhere in a city or even major rural towns. Being isolated from everything meant that Thelma and Sid were a law unto themselves. *'We gave a lot of credit – you had to trust. I only ever got stiffed once ... we put dud cheques on the wall behind the bar to embarrass people and make them eventually pay – which they almost always did, because they needed us. There was one time this bloke, half cooked, tried to jump the bar to get his cheque off the wall and Thelma had her pistol that she kept under the cash drawer and she stuck the pistol into his ribs and he jumped back as quick as he jumped over and everybody was roaring laughing at him as he cursed her ... she would have shot him if he tried anything.'*

The Redex Round Australia trials held during the 1950s saw hundreds of cars compete to prove their ability to conquer the outback. Attracting enormous attention, the rallies made superstars of the drivers and supercars of the vehicles. Cinesound newsreels and the magic of radio meant that a travelling event could be covered in a way that had never been possible before. Redex sold oil additives and, as a growing number of Australian families could afford a car, reliability in the outback was a marketing dream – success on the rally was reflected in the salesroom. Jack Davey was already a star, having for many years been a top-rating radio host in Sydney and the voice artist for Fox Movietone News. His celebrity participation in the rally was a major drawcard, but according to Sid, his fame meant nothing to Thelma. *'Jack Davey thought he was pretty flash and asked if he could use our gear to talk to someone down south on the radio. The radio set was behind the counter and Thelma told him that she was the official operator. But he thought he was pretty flash and could do whatever he liked so he jumps the bar. Next thing she gets the pistol and shows him and says you do what you're told. He jumps back and she says, "Mr Davey, you walk around when I say you can" and he got all shirty, said he'd make a complaint and report her and everything and he did but it came to nothing and didn't do us any harm.*

'There was the time when some tourists complained about the price we charged for fuel. With the old petrol pumps, you had to work a lever to pump the petrol into a glass header bowl and then let it down by gravity into the car. A lady got me to hand pump a load of fuel and then asked how much we charged and when I told her she said, "Forget it, I'm not paying that much, we can wait ... where is the next fuel?" so I dropped the fuel back into our tank and told her the next fuel is a hundred miles away at Wave Hill. Then she asks how much is their fuel and it was half as much again, and she said then we will buy it here and she tells me to pump it back up again. I told her forget it, we only pump it once and walked off and she said she'd complain to the oil company about me – but they just laughed at her.'

Sid told of policemen poking their noses in when not welcome, and feuds with rival truck drivers in the early days of hauling huge loads of cattle with what became road trains. Top Springs General Store had become a favourite stopover on the fabled Murranji Track for the drovers, and for a few years they sold more Akubra hats and boots than any other store in the entire nation. Their advertising boasted:

C J Hawks & Co

Top Springs N.T.

General Storekeepers

Specialising in Saddlery, Stockmen's Clothing and Rifles

Agents for Dodge, De Soto, Morris Trucks, Howard and Nuffield Tractors, Q.E.C. Electrical Equipment, Vacuum Oil Co Depot, Crammond Radios.

The Store in the Back of Beyond that Keeps the Outback Supplied

As the droving game dwindled and trucks became more reliable and capable, old-school horse mustering became uncompetitive. The era of the road train had begun, huge trucks with at first two, then three and even four trailers of double-deck loads of bellowing cattle heading off to distant abattoirs and markets.

Securing the Vacuum Oil agency for a huge part of the NT was a coup. Sid covered the NT all the way to the border with WA, and ran truckloads of fuel drums on a succession of bigger and faster trucks seven days a week. It was physically demanding, loading and unloading hundreds of heavy fuel barrels as well as hours of driving primitive machines. *'Vacuum became Mobil a few years later, and I was mates with the boss in Darwin. You had to have a good truck and I kept buying new ones so I would be reliable. I was in their depot one time and they were getting a new truck for themselves and he asked me what their old truck was worth and just joking I said a couple of hundred bucks and quick as a flash he said, "It's yours" and I had bought myself another truck.'*

The airstrip was cleared – partly by 'borrowing' the government grader and partly by hand – in 1955 and there was

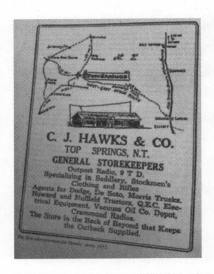

LEFT: Sid Hawks advertised the store in the rural press, 1955.

BELOW: Top Springs, 1956, signs to Katherine and Wave Hill Station.

an attempt to use Connellan Air freight planes to fly cattle to market. *'He was pretty fussy old Eddie Connellan. The airstrip had to be smooth as a table, no stones bigger than a small glass – we got a whole bunch of Aborigines to clear it with wheelbarrows and we gave them a killer* [cow] *and some tucker and we kept going until it was done. My wife felt sorry for them; they had come in from the desert with nothing.'* As the roads improved, the weekly cattle flights soon became uneconomic and the road trains took over, but the airstrip remained, mostly used by the Flying Doctor. *'Did I tell you that Thelma's mother Margaret is buried at the airstrip? She had cancer and came to stay with us but she only lasted about a year. I had to dig her grave and say the words and then the policeman said he had to check on her. We left her with a sheet of iron over the top until the policeman could come. And then I had to bury her deeper and fill it in.'*

He bore no great ill will towards Thelma despite scandal at the time of their split which was all to do with money. The rot started when Sid wanted to try his hand at the lucrative business of fattening cattle for market. He tried to buy some land at Yellow Waters but, when he visited the bank manager in Darwin to arrange finance was told that he could not afford it. As he was constantly on the road, with lucrative contracts for carting to the uranium mines and even as far away as Borroloola in the Gulf country, Sid assumed that there would be plenty of money in the bank when he needed it.

'I started snooping around. I found a bank book for an account in the name of Jack Tye, that had money transferred to it. But Jack Tye had died a few years before in a big accident; maybe his ghost was still doing his banking. I knew straight away Thelma had put a whole lot

of money into this account – she ran the post office and the bank agency so she could do all this without anyone knowing anything. I thought she was sending money down to her brother in Melbourne who was trying to buy a city building for his business.'

Sid also found that a lot of bills had not been paid and money was owing to many people and the tax department. He went to see their accountant Alec Toy, who confirmed that no tax returns had been lodged for several years. Sid was puzzled, as Thelma had asked him to sign tax cheques for thousands of pounds.

'The penny dropped that she was taking the money and sticking it into these secret accounts. It was obvious we were going to have to split the blanket and there was going to be a big stink. One night I snuck into the office and got hold of her briefcase with all the papers in it, and using a torch I read everything and worked out what was going on. Soon after, the bubble broke. A flash new Holden station wagon was parked over at the stock inspector's house, locked but loaded up with water, jerry cans and chairs, ready for a long trip. I saw the arse part of my green deed box poking out from under the seat – it was normally hidden at home. I asked Thelma, "Whose car is that?" and she told me she didn't know and to mind my own business.'

It happened that the Wave Hill policeman was visiting Toppie at the time, doing vehicle checks and shooting dogs, and had to intervene as Sid and Thelma argued. Thelma denied that the car was hers and said she didn't have the keys so Sid broke in, retrieved his deed box and drove back to the store. Sid found the keys to the box at the same time as Thelma turned up with the car keys and claimed the box was hers. As Sid had the key, he opened it to discover it was full of cash. 'It's mine now,' he declared and locked it again.

'She was going to do a runner and take all our cash and leave me with all the unpaid bills and nothing in the bank. She must have been planning it for ages. We had these big heavy glass insulators for the power lines and they were on the shelf behind the bar and she threw one at me and it just missed my head. It would have done me in but it hit my shoulder instead and didn't hurt me much. Then she ran into the bedroom where there was a .22 under the bed. She came out of the bedroom and pointed the gun at me, so I hit it and she cried out and then fainted. I said to the policeman that there had been an assault, but he said, "You realise I'd have to arrest her ..." and I said forget about it, I've had worse and I'm over all the talking.'

Thelma accused Sid of squiring a beautiful redhead around Darwin. Sid explained, 'I did know a beautiful redhead, she was married to a friend and worked in our accountant's office. I was not having an affair but I would have liked to – Heather she was – tall with a good figure and well spoken, really beautiful, and Thelma got on fire over this. Just as well we'd never had children; she was healthy enough and I was alright as I proved later on'.

Sid had just bought a new Leyland truck and it was a fair split that he kept the trucks and Thelma kept the store. Years later, I met Nerolie Withnall who had practised family law in Darwin back in the wild days. I asked if she knew Sid or Thelma Hawks from Top Springs and she astonished me by saying she had acted for Sid in their divorce. 'It was very straightforward, we just had to do paperwork because they had already worked the property split out. I won't breach confidentiality even after all these years except to say she was a cranky old "b" and I remember him fondly. It was always awkward back in those days when you had to tell petitioners that the law required them to disclose their adultery ...' Despite my pleas to

Nerolie, and my exhortation that both Sid and Thelma were long dead, she declined to reveal any more out of respect for Sid's family.

Our chat on the verandah overlooking the busy traffic along Bagot Road, punctuated by the occasional plane overhead, was interrupted by sandwiches brought to us by Sid's wife, Thien. Many years younger than Sid, she had met him in Kupang on the western tip of Timor when he was ferrying cargo after Cyclone Tracy. She worked in the Indonesian Consulate in Darwin. As he reflected on his time at Toppie with Thelma, there was a long pause, and a rare flicker of emotion crossed Sid's eyes. *'She was a good person in herself. She was a morally good person, but she was enamoured by money, just could not leave it alone, whether it was mine or anybody else's. And she was too hard on the customers. I was away on the road all the time but people talked. She would put the prices up and it was bad for public relations. She knew she had them over a barrel, that was her version, but I didn't approve; I liked to be friends with my customers. The drovers would get pretty wild and it wasn't good to annoy them. Maybe she was vindictive towards me because I was away on the transports so much and she thought I was having an affair ... Yeah, I was away all the time on the road and she was left all alone.'* I left the silence for a prolonged pause, hoping that Sid might reflect further on his relationship with the ferocious Thelma, but he just stared, eyes slightly watering, and then changed the subject, lamenting the series of fires that saw the pub rebuilt. He claimed no inside information about the rumours of serial arson.

Top Springs pub was originally a few miles from where it is now sited. There is 'old' Top Springs and 'new' Top Springs. The reason for relocation tells us much about Thelma. *'There was a surveyor working out where to put the bridge across the Armstrong*

River. The road was being upgraded to all-weather. He was staying at the pub, and she insulted him or had a blue, wouldn't serve him or something. So, he sent the road the other way instead of past her pub, four miles away from the waterhole in a barren and open place in the middle of nowhere to get his revenge. She had to rebuild, which is why the pub burned down. She was like that — she thought she didn't need anyone.' His story about a major road being diverted as a personal grudge, as a reaction to an insult, is improbable in any other context, but for the NT it is utterly believable.

Not long before visiting Sid in Darwin I had been on stage at Frank Hardy's memorial service back in Collingwood. Sid was coy about his contact with local Aboriginal people, and claimed only passing contact with the Gurindji during their long and historic strike. *'I knew they were on tight rations there ... Vesteys paid them skinflint money and were notorious for being hard on them. They got a rough spin. If a drover overslept, they wouldn't wake him, they just put a cheque in his boots and left him behind. There was unrest because Vesteys were too mean and if they'd been more liberal there would have been no big storm. I met young Lord Vestey, the heir apparent. I was asked to take him out to Wave Hill. He was a smart looking, well-spoken fellow, mid-twenties, and we camped in the bush, lit a fire and cooked a feed. Then he gets up and asks me where the toilet is — and we are hundreds of miles from the nearest house. No idea, these fellas. He asked me to keep quiet about who he was when we got to Wave Hill, so they wouldn't treat him differently. He wanted to see it like an outsider, he said, "This could do me some good," so I did.'* Later in life, Lord Vestey lived on an estate in Suffolk and was driven in to the head office of the family's global company three days a week in his Rolls-Royce, but to impress upon his staff that he was not ostentatious with his wealth, he kept an Austin 1800 in a garage outside the city and swapped over just before arriving at the office. His home was staffed by a housemaid, cook, butler, secretary, chauffeur, gamekeepers and gardeners. Nothing ostentatious at all.

'That communist Frank Hardy was right, things had to change. The place was run like a military camp. The boss before Tom Fisher was ex-military and ended up getting charged with raping five lubras. Judge Wells heard the trial and Tiger Lyons was lawyer for the accused. The first witness, Nelly, said she took him in a cup of tea and he pushed her onto the bed and put his hand up her dress and she bit him but he kept going and he was too strong. When he finished, he still had his cup of tea. He was cleared in court but he had to leave anyway. I was out of Toppie when Hardy came and I was friends with lots of Aboriginals. One time I had a big load on and was heading back near Number 4 bore and the load shifted and a rope got loose on one side. I climbed up to tighten it and got my foot caught and fell from the top to the ground and copped a great big cut on my head from the sunglasses. I was out cold for hours until Pat Quirk and his missus came along. They found me with meat ants up my nose. I'd been out cold all day and the ants had started to eat my face, and Pat and his missus took me to their humpy and washed me down and swabbed me clean. I drove back the next day to Top Springs and the Flying Doctor came and I had to have my septum removed. If Pat and his lubra had not saved me in time the meat ants would have eaten me alive and I would have been as dead as a sun-grilled maggot on a midday rock.' Not often am I stuck for words, but at this stage I just sat in my chair and stared at this amazing old man opposite me. I have never looked at an ant nest quite the same way since.

We had been talking for hours and Sid was starting to tire. I promised that next time I was in Darwin, I would visit again. Although he lived another ten years, I did not keep my promise and am the poorer for my failure. In concentrating on stories of Thelma and his earlier life, Sid did not reveal anything about his vital role in one of the most significant historic events of the time. Sid made no mention of ferrying Kerry Packer, Australia's richest man, and a *60 Minutes* TV crew to Dili in 1975 at the height of the Indonesian invasion. I was oblivious to his involvement until I stumbled upon his name mentioned in *Compulsive Viewing*, the memoir of legendary TV reporter Gerald Stone, published in 2000.

With the world distracted by the end of the Vietnam War, in August 1975, the Indonesians occupied the eastern half of the island of Timor, until then a Portuguese colony. The Portuguese left rival local militias fighting for control, which gave the Indonesians the rationale to masquerade as 'peacekeepers' and invade. The conflict was kept secret from the world through a media blackout imposed by the Indonesians. The Whitlam Government adopted a policy of non-intervention and banned Australians from going to Timor. Short-wave radio reports told of widespread violence, atrocities and Indonesian brutality. As Gerald Stone recounts – '*forbidden stories are all the better for the telling*' – so he put together a proposal to smuggle a crew from *60 Minutes*, the leading Channel 9 TV current affairs show, into Timor to tell the world what was happening. His boss, Kerry Packer, agreed to pay for the trip with one condition: '*Fine, as long as I go with you.*'

The *60 Minutes* team asked around Darwin for a ship and crew to take them to Timor. They were sent to Sid Hawks, who regularly went to Dili and had recently salvaged the *Konpira Maru*, a 100-foot former Japanese trawler grounded during Cyclone Tracy eight months before. Commercial terms were agreed to – $6000 up front for a six-day charter – and the team set off, led by former Vietnam War correspondent Gerald Stone, with Brian Peters (later killed by Indonesians at Balibo) and a volunteer, Dr John Whitehall. Packer treated it like a safari. Bored on the two-day sea voyage, Packer ordered the crew to throw their empty beer cans off the back of the trawler where he would use them as targets for shooting practice. Stone was worried that Kerry Packer's guns might alarm any trigger-happy Indonesians and undermine their false claim to be a humanitarian aid ship. Arriving in embattled Dili, and with no authorisation whatsoever, Sid controversially displayed a huge homemade Red Cross flag over the side as cover. After being sized-up by the

Top Springs pub, 1959, Sid's fuel haulage truck in foreground.

Indonesians, they were escorted in by a speedboat piloted by an Australian hotelier resident in Dili, Frank Favaro, who acted as intermediary and maintained their cover story. Sid berthed at the almost destroyed dock and the ship was immediately besieged by desperate locals looking to escape.

The TV crew spent a few days ashore and gathered world-scoop footage as fast as they could, while the doctor and ship's crew – and Kerry Packer – administered whatever assistance they could to injured civilians and pregnant women. Sid cautioned the TV reporters about their clothing – army surplus gear from Australia – and worried that the reporters might be mistaken as combatants. 'You put that on, you become a target,' he forewarned. Packer handed out Australian cash as he walked the streets of Dili with his Portuguese ex-commando bodyguard, visibly distressed by the plight of children in particular. After a few frightening and dangerous days' filming, the *Konpira Maru* headed off to the safe enclave of Atauro, where flights still operating to Australia allowed Packer, Stone and his precious film footage, together with some locals with medical emergencies, to fly back to Darwin.

Sid Hawks sailed back to Dili to see if injured, ill, pregnant or emergency patients could be evacuated back to Darwin. As his ship was ready to depart, crowds surged through the feeble security and almost swamped the trawler. Sid and crew tried to prioritise the passage of women and children, and had some robust physical encounters with local businessmen in particular offering cash bribes to escape. Some of the more insistent men were forced off at the point of a bayonet. The trawler took on as many women and children as was safe and headed back to

Australia. A baby was born at sea, and almost two hundred Timorese refugees arrived safely in Darwin. Then there was the inevitable argument between Kerry Packer and Sid Hawks about money. Sid claimed he was owed extra because the trip took longer than was originally agreed, and Kerry Packer refused to pay. Kerry told Sid that he had access to 'the best QCs in the land and you won't win' so instead Sid helped himself to a portable generator, some inflatable rubber zodiacs and an outboard motor.

I was totally unaware of this extraordinary saga when we chatted. It was a sign of Sid's lack of ego that he did not think to tell me about his personal close encounter with Kerry Packer, the richest and most powerful man in the nation. He did not aggrandise his role in the humanitarian rescue of ill and pregnant women, nor the role he played in getting the truth about the atrocities happening in East Timor out in the global media.

Sid did tell me how he recovered financially from his split with Thelma and went on to any number of adventures with a bewildering succession of ships and businesses around the Territory and into South-East Asia. I reluctantly left Sid still sipping his ice water in the shade. Although we had talked about Top Springs for hours, I felt that I had not got to know Thelma much more than when I started. In typical fashion for someone of his age and gender, Sid told me what they did, but not how he felt. I would need to dig deeper to get to know Thelma better. Thien waved goodbye from the verandah as I counted myself lucky to have spent so much time with a genuine pioneer of the outback.

CHAPTER 13

NORM DOUGLAS

As a change of pace after my visit with Sid Hawks, I wandered off into the Darwin humidity. Most tourists would visit the crocodiles or maybe the excellent art gallery, but it was my habit when in Darwin – in fact, wherever I was on holidays – to watch the typically absurd theatre of the local courts, scenes which hardly meshed with the reality of life outside on the streets of Australia's most multiracial city.

Most of the court list stems from violence fuelled by grog, and sadly too much of that impacts on the First Nations communities. In surrounds of wood-panelled, air-conditioned calm, life in remote communities is exhumed and examined in forensic detail. Events that happened thousands of kilometres away – and often in the most remote corners of the Territory and likely several years ago – are reimagined in Darwin for a jury who are somehow expected to magically piece together the truth from the fragments offered up in court.

The judges and lawyers are as acutely aware as anyone of the artifice of it all, but inertia is hard to stop – the system, the conveyor belt, just keeps on rolling. It is heartbreaking for

Norman Douglas at Top Springs, around 1960.

the participants and just as bewildering for those who watch. After court, I dined with Melbourne legal aid mates relocated to the Territory, none of them under any illusion about the shortcomings of the very system they work in and maintain. Their work seemed miles from where my career path had taken me and I recoiled at their war stories of incompetent magistrates and ruthless police prosecutors. Still in shock over the prospect of losing my radio gig at the ABC, I contemplated asking Jan to relocate to Darwin. Would I find a niche here, returning to the law, but in a dramatically different environment?

Sid was never far from my mind as we ate, drank and dissected the failings of 'bush justice' Territory style. I was trying to reconcile his account of life with Thelma at Toppie with the occasionally conflicting information from Apollo. Thelma giving Apollo money to buy a property for his gym? Apollo owning a building in central Melbourne? Absurd. I knew he never owned any real estate other than an uninhabitable beach block in the sand dunes at Venus Bay he'd been conned into buying. Does that make the rest of Sid's story unreliable? I thought not, but it did make me a little wary of taking it all at face value.

The next morning, I took to the Stuart Highway and drove three hours south to Katherine. Other than the regular historic wartime airstrips dotted beside the track, the road looked unfamiliar to me, even though it was the same route taken back in 1982 with Flynn. It may as well never have happened, that pub crawl twelve years earlier.

Norm's tidy and unremarkable Katherine home was on the unkerbed road winding along the riverbank and, somewhat anxiously, I knocked on the door. This was, after all, the man I had negotiated against, the claimant who was the sticking point in the Estate of T C Hawks for such a long time. Back when we finally settled his claim, I had been warned that it needed to be done expeditiously as he was in poor health. How would he be now, a decade later? Or was that only bluff and bluster from his lawyers to secure a settlement? I expected to find a shell of the man I had met at Top Springs.

A cheerful Norm shuffled to the door and ushered me into his modest, sparsely furnished home. He immediately offered me a seat at the wooden kitchen table and went around the breakfast bar to put the kettle on. No trace of rancour or anger was detectable, and he was clearly pleased to have a visitor – even me. He was a slightly built man, with huge ears and almost no hair, stooped and bow-legged now, dependent on his walking stick. His sun-scarred forearms had the remnants of ancient tattoos, from some other era in Norm's life. Some photos on his mantlepiece, either side of a 1940s wind-up chiming clock in a walnut case, showed a younger and strikingly strong version of the same man, patting dogs or standing beside a heavily laden truck at what almost surely was the early incarnation of the Top Springs store. His strong English accent belied the decades spent in the Australian bush, and he gladly told his story.

Born in Cumberland in 1925, Norm joined the army during World War II. He served in the Italian Alps, where he worked with mules, the only way of getting weapons, ammunition and supplies to some of the more remote mountain outposts. After the war, demobbed and back at home, he called on that experience and worked with racehorses but leapt at the chance to emigrate as he had no money and wanted to try something different. In Australia, he quickly got farm work, then he went to Narrabri and worked his way across Queensland to the Northern Territory. He'd worked with croc shooters on the Roper River, *'but I did no good because I didn't have the right gear. When I was in the Katherine I was introduced to the Vandeleurs and I got a job doing fencing for the muster at Camfield'.*

These were all names familiar to me – Camfield was one of the giant cattle stations in the district around Top Springs and the Vandeleurs were well-established local pioneering station managers.

'When that finished I was in at the mechanic at Katherine and that's where I met Sid Hawks. He said I could put in some time at Top Springs and I got there in '54. There was plenty to do because the black boys had pulled out as there was trouble on the Murranji Track. Sid was still going around with the hawker's van while Thelma was setting up the store. It was just a tin shed, a wooden shack with rough bush timber posts and a tin roof. They sold clothing and whatever anyone needed. Tobacco, car parts, truck tyres, fuel, whatever anyone wanted. Sid was travelling so he could bring things back whenever he went into town. It was a good place for a store – the roads went off in every direction; the main stock route from WA and to Dunmarra and Victoria River Downs and all the cattle used to come past. I stopped there much longer than I thought.' I had to suppress a chuckle – by the time he left, Norm had been at Top Springs for most of his adult life.

He drifted off a bit, told long-winded stories about how to install fence posts so that they did not fail, and how the walls of the original store were constructed to be ant proof. To regain our focus, I asked specifically what Thelma was like – both as a boss and presumably as a friend. *'Well … it is a bit difficult to*

Norm Douglas crouching with dog, Chattering Charlie by his side, and unknown man, Top Springs.

say ...' and then there was a long pause, almost as if he was self-censoring, but then his internal battle was over: *'Bloody hell, it was tough out there. It was a battle and she was a woman all alone ... She was about 5'2" and nuggety, solid and pretty even in her forties when I arrived. She could be soft and caring; but really, she was a businesswoman, and it was rough being the only woman in the place among all the males, always battling to make the place pay. A lot of people owed her money, some of them millionaires, but they never wanted to pay their bills – big money, station money. Sid always said that they fell out over money, but when he left he seemed to take his share. He didn't suddenly go; it wasn't like that. They did argue, but he used a lot of their money to buy a new truck and a big trailer and he went cattle carting and Thelma didn't want him to. But after they split up, he went his way and she just kept going with the store. They must have worked it out between them'.*

He echoed the refrain I had heard the day before in Darwin from Sid himself – how Sid was constantly away 'doing transport' and left her to run things. *'She was tough – she had to be. If there was something she didn't like, oh gawd, she'd tell you pretty quick. She carried a gun but – not in all those years – I never saw her use it. There was always trouble, usually with natives. When they drink, they want you to give them things and not pay for it or they promise to pay you later and if you say no there would be fights, usually between themselves.'*

Norm kept birds in cages – budgerigars – and for whatever reason they chose this exact moment to burst into vivid song. He introduced me to his caged friends one by one and made another cuppa. The awkward topic of multiple suspicious fires that struck Top Springs during Thelma's time had to be addressed.

'Well, I don't know too much. There are people who say Mrs H started them for insurance, but she would have got nothing out of it from what I know. The second one – we all had to go to court in Darwin and the insurance company said she had claimed for things that were not destroyed.' I pressed him for clarification, but he simply repeated: *'I don't really know what happened, because I had to wait outside the court because I was a witness, so I don't really know any details … and she never talked much about it.'* He was remarkably ignorant of the biggest events that happened in his decades at this tiny remote outpost and I was frustrated that he was lacking the sort of curiosity and nosiness that most of us would naturally pursue. Was it a legacy of the times, of being a Territorian, that you knew your place, minded your own business and did not query things?

He gave a full account of what happened on the morning in 1981 when he went upstairs to Thelma's flat and found her body and how traumatic it was for him after working so closely with her for nearly thirty years. We chuckled over the story of the frog and the policeman stealing the money. For Norm, though, the main memory was *'the shock of it ... I guess it's like family ...'* and I felt a momentary twang of guilt for the years of haggling on behalf of the Andersons, whittling down his payout, but said nothing to him. Best not to open up that entire line of conversation, I wisely decided.

He recounted how, over the years, Thelma frequently suffered from asthma, and the seasonal pollens, spear grass and dust from trucks and cattle in the old days triggered it. *'She went down south and had an operation at some point which left her with a little scar on the tip of her nose. She was quite vain about it, but you could tell it was there. When the asthma got really bad she would stay upstairs and do bookwork instead of coming down to the pub. I used to just get up, do my work, go to bed, get up do my work and go to bed. There wasn't much conversation, and we never had meals together; not ever, not at all.'*

Norm offered to show pictures of Thelma and the pub from his earliest years there. He went across his living room, remarkable for the almost total absence of any decoration or adornment, and retrieved the framed photos sitting on the mantlepiece. With brief commentary, they were offered for closer scrutiny, and then Norm produced a few more dog-eared black-and-white photos from a shoebox, insisting that I keep them as no-one else seemed the slightest bit interested in his story.

He gave me a slightly creased snap of an elderly Aboriginal man, tall and well dressed in trousers and hat. *'That fella, "Poor* bugger" we called him, Mrs Hawks and I, because he had two wives that sat down at Top Springs with that old boy. Although the old girls used to do some work around the place for Mrs Hawks he just sat around all day. Sometimes he painted himself but he was a funny fellow.'

Triumphantly, Norm found a black-and-white photo of the original Top Springs store – a bark roof across a large shed with walls made from empty fuel tins, flattened and affixed to cover the bark beneath. 'This here is where we had a small lock-up area and if you went in this door there was a counter to the left and a kitchen to the right. Sid and Mrs H lived off to the left, but this was before we had the licence; it was just a store. Over there is the LandRover and that's me there with more hair, crouching patting the dog. The fella next to me – his name was Chattering Charlie because he never stopped talking. Mrs H had three dogs and behind them you can see the old hawker's van parked out front. I think it's probably still sitting there at Top Springs. When Sid got a new one he just left it sitting there and when I left it was still right where he left it. Probably still there?'

I admitted it was some years since I had been to Toppie so I was unable to answer his question. I asked him why he always referred to Thelma as Mrs Hawks or Mrs H. 'No-one did call her Thelma. Not in nearly thirty years did I know anyone to call her Thelma except Sid. Some people called her Ma Hawks but I never did. It wasn't strange to us; women were always given respect and you didn't call them by their Christian name. All the station managers and owners' wives were always Mrs This and Mrs That.'

I quipped back to him, 'I bet she didn't call you Mr Douglas, did she?' and he laughed and said, 'No, never ... that is how it was out bush. It was different. In twenty-nine years, I hardly left the place. I only went into Darwin the one time for that court thing I told you *about, and most of the time I only went to Katherine a few times a year ... one time I had not been anywhere for three years; it seemed normal back then. It was a lonely life.'*

We chatted some more about other old-timers but he did not have any phone numbers or addresses for where they may be. He had lost touch, he apologised, and it was clear that his life was somewhat diminished. He had always been the quiet, unquestioning sidekick – first to Sid, then later to Thelma – who kept to himself, drank too much, did what was asked of him and kept out of the way. The huge change since he had left the pub, remarkably, was that there was no sign in his home whatsoever of any alcohol. I was too polite to ask, but it would seem that moving to Katherine and getting away from being surrounded by grog had done Norm Douglas, the notorious pisspot, a world of good.

I gratefully filed away the photos he insisted I take and thanked him. As I took my leave I wondered if his life was any less lonely in Katherine than it had been in Top Springs. I was grateful he had been prepared to talk to me at all, given the nature of our earlier meetings as we disputed Thelma's invalid will. Seeing Norm took me right back to his solid, undemanding presence at Toppie and it pleased me enormously to see him looking so well. If he had inherited the Wanda Inn after Thelma's sudden death – another alcoholic trying to run a remote Territory pub – I doubt he'd still be alive to chat over tea and tend to his feathered friends. Maybe it was all for the best.

CHAPTER 14

THELMA

All sorts of bizarre second- and third-hand accounts of Thelma's skulduggery had been recounted over the years. Did Thelma carry a pearl-handled revolver? Had she nicked the takings from a sozzled bookie at the Top Springs picnic races? Did Thelma have a fling with the manager of a nearby station? What about the description of Thelma's accounting being 'as creative as Hollywood', charging people for food, grog and fuel they had never bought? There was the yarn about a drum of diesel charged to a drover who did not own a truck and only rode a horse. The time when she offered kids a few lollies from a jar but then the parents were charged for an entire box of sweets. Her reputation grew and the stories were embellished.

Although Sid and Norm had been generous in sharing their recollections of Thelma, they were both protective of her memory and emotionally connected. If I was to get to know her any better and to separate fact from fiction, I had to cast my net further. Luckily, there were plenty of old Territorian yarn spinners with stories about Thelma and Top Springs.

June Tapp is a Territory legend. Her family have owned cattle stations in and around Top Springs since the 1950s and she embodies the unique and distinctive cattle station culture. She knows where all the bodies are buried and enjoys exhuming them. June is garrulous and hilarious, with the capacity to greet you for even the first time as if you are a long-lost friend. We sat down in Katherine as she was still reeling from the latest round in a protracted legal battle with the banks that cost her family their fortune. It was therapeutic for her to be distracted from those troubles and instead tell stories about Thelma.

'Thelma? She was a short, dumpy woman with fat legs. When I first met her she kept her greying hair coiled up on her head in a bun, but it went down as far as her waist. She didn't particularly care about her appearance although people often said she was vain. She thought she was special, better than everyone else. Did you know she used to be a performer?'

I revealed that I knew quite a bit about Thelma's early career on stage with her brother 'The Young Apollo' and gave her the edited highlights.

'I always thought that stuff was bullshit; seemed far-fetched, but there you go,' she responded with a shrug of the shoulders. We were sitting in comfy chairs on her wide deck in 'The Kath-er-yne', as she insisted on calling her town, making it rhyme with 'mine'. She flicked her hair from around her eyes, as well as a beetle from the crisp white cotton work shirt she wore, sleeves rolled up, like the station worker she had been since a teenager.

'Has anyone told you about those shorts? Sometimes I'd see her up a ladder, hair falling free, tight shorts – very tight short shorts, with the rim of her backside poking through, which you'd have to say is

A youthful Thelma
Anderson before she
married Sid Hawks.

*very unusual for a woman in her sixties ... she was a bit of a tease,
I suppose, but I can't imagine any man ...'* and then she giggled
and corrected herself. *'We shouldn't be talking about her in this way.
You never really know someone, but she was pretty amazing to be
a solo woman running that pub out there all those years.'* There is
some personal projection here, as June Tapp also has survived the
rough and tumble of a very masculine world, running the family
cattle empire since the death of her husband Bill just a few years
before our chat. June was just getting warmed up.

'*She had a terrible reputation about money ... some people said she
was generous and would do you a favour but my impression was she
was mean and greedy and always just looking out for herself. There were
blokes from Killarney, our station, who would throw their cheque at her*

and reckoned that when they booked stuff up with her she would count things twice and double up on them. That was her general reputation: that she was money hungry. There was always a question mark about her arithmetic, but there wasn't exactly another shop across the road you could go to instead, was there? Unusually, I never saw her drink, not ever, which as you know is pretty rare around these parts. Sid did and Norm certainly did, so she must have been very disciplined.'

Publicans in the NT of old fall into two categories – those who were famous drunks and those who never touched the stuff, ever. I am no expert on the drinking habits of the other members of the small club of women publicans in the NT – legendary figures like Mayse Young from Pine Creek and the notorious Fannie Haynes who had the Federation Hotel in Brocks Creek – but there was no doubt that teetotal Thelma was a rarity in her line of work.

June Tapp had seen different sides to Thelma during her many years crossing paths and trading with her, even attempts at socialising. *'There was this time when she wanted to show me some new pyjamas she had bought ... all frilly and lacy things, and there we were, two women looking at pyjamas in this rough pub in the middle of the bush, and then she said that she wanted to give me something. I was quite touched because it is not like she was a woman's woman or anything, so I thought how sweet of her. She led me behind the counter and into the storeroom and plucked a packet of desiccated coconut off the shelf. It was yellow it was so old, and she said "I want you to have this". I didn't know what to say it was so strange. It was like she wanted to be friends but didn't know how,'* she chuckled.

June stared off into the greenery, sipped from the ice water in front of her and turned back, laughing again. *'I've always been a bit of a talker but with Thelma there wasn't much chitchat.'*

June knew some of what happened when fire destroyed the original Top Springs buildings in the 1960s, shortly after Sid had left. Years earlier, John Flynn had told me that *'Thelma hired Gus Partridge to burn the pub down, but when she didn't pay him the money, he dobbed her in'*. Sid and Norm had both denied knowing what happened and even denied knowing whether Thelma had been prosecuted for arson. June Tapp laughed and expanded on Flynn's scant account.

'Well ...' and she drew a deep breath and said with a twinkle in her eye: *'People used to think that Gus Partridge was her boyfriend. He had a bit of a reputation and was a pretty good-looking kind of guy, well presented for around here'* – this from one of the only women who had been in and around these parts as long as Thelma. Gus Partridge – or Angus Ian Noble Partridge to give him full weight in the naming stakes – was a notorious crook, a con man, known by police all around Australia as he moved around the country looking for a quick buck. He was the last man sentenced to a flogging at Fannie Bay Gaol, in the early 1960s, although the barbaric punishment was never carried out.

'Just after the big fire, he came over to us at Killarney Station with a black girl called Olive and they were both full as boots. Olive had a husband on the grog at Toppie and Gus and Olive shot through out bush for a few days together. But they weren't too sure how they could just reappear back at the pub; it's not like you can hide – there's only this one bloody big building. How can two people reappear as if nothing happened while you were off for a sneaky for thirty-six hours? It was pretty obvious from what Gus was saying to us that he helped Thelma burn down the pub for the insurance. It was a scam, but I'm sure she was charged – not with arson but with trying to defraud the

insurance. She claimed to have lost a whole lot of stock but it was all stashed down the creek bank. Gus gave evidence against Thelma at the trial but the judge said he didn't believe a word of it and she got off.'

We gradually pieced our theories together, the two of us playing amateur Sherlock Holmes. June reckoned Thelma and Gus were having an affair when they hatched the plot to finance a new pub by collecting insurance from a fire. Shortly after, Gus went bush for a few days on a tryst with Olive. Thelma felt betrayed, and refused to pay him the agreed arsonist fee. When questioned about the fire, she tried to save her own skin and get her revenge by blaming Gus. When the police questioned Gus, he volunteered that Thelma was supposed to pay him, hadn't kept her word and was falsely claiming insurance for lost stock. Just this one time the con man may have actually told the truth! The investigators confirmed the fire was deliberately lit but could not prove who had done it. The evidence of insurance fraud was clearer and led to Thelma being charged. When giving evidence in Darwin, Partridge was dismissed as an unreliable witness and Thelma was acquitted. Norm Douglas was called to give evidence, but true to form claimed he knew nothing. The insurance company was obliged to pay Thelma as neither the arson nor the fraud could be proven. What an outcome. June was roaring, rocking back and forwards in her chair at the absurdity and audacity of it all.

We walked together around the corner to visit June's close friends Paul and Betty Vandeleur, local cattle station pioneers but retired from station life and living in town. Within a few minutes we were teasing out loose threads of local history, Paul's mind as sharp as his eyes despite his advancing years.

'*I remember Sid and Thelma when they were still hawking around in that truck. Sid was a perfectionist with machinery, very fussy and very capable. He wasn't a taker at all, always helping people out of trouble, and you have to remember he was working on some of the roughest roads in Australia. He had a war surplus GMC, then later a six-wheel-drive thing – I think it was a Leyland Hippo. They stopped off at Top Springs and set up the first rough store there by the Armstrong River. That was before the first fire and of course as June was saying, everyone thought the fires were, what do we say, suspicious; they weren't accidents. Do I remember Gus Partridge? Yes, I do but I'm not going to comment on that … well, OK, he may have been paid to do it.*' He folded his hands with a triumphant air, as if he had just broken news, and glanced towards Betty and June for back-up. They laughed at his short-lived attempt at discretion.

'*She had a lot of admirers, did Ma Hawks, old drovers and the like who all thought she was a pretty good old stick, not bad looking and everyone assumed she was loaded, and pretty good at looking after money. Once we were waiting on a load of stores for Camfield and quite a bit of it had fallen off the truck; they were always overloaded. I went back a few days later to see if any of it had been picked up. She swore black and blue that none of it had ever turned up. I went around the side where there was an open mesh wire storage area and I could see all these cartons marked Camfield and I said, "Well, how do you account for that?" Although we eventually got it all back she just said she didn't know how they got there.*' Paul chuckled at the memories and warmed to the task.

'*At the picnic races in September 1960 – the only race meeting we ever had at Top Springs – we took along seven or eight of our best horses and won quite a few prizes. We were supposed to get a tartan cooler as a prize, which Betty thought was a pretty smart piece of kit for those days, but when it came to handing out the prizes, Thelma had decided that there had been a mix-up in allocating the prizes to different races and said the committee had decided to change things. She was the committee, of course, and she ended up with the cooler and we got nothing; all we went away with was the experience.'* He laughed some more as June and Betty joined in. But the story of the races got better, and shed new light on what Sid had told me about the end of their marriage.

'Later that night everyone got half charged and Sid and Thelma got into a blue; Sid took off to Darwin in his new truck and I don't think he ever got back. I remember him saying to Thelma "money is your god" and Mrs H fainted on the steps and the policeman had to calm them down. She had taken all the race club money and tucked it into a bag in her new car, and Sid thought she was doing a runner. The policeman had to ask her if it was her car and why did she have all this money in it, and do you mind if we search your vehicle. With that she just collapsed.' Paul's account puts flesh on the bones of the story Sid had told – his version involving a deed box – but the precise details are recorded in the NT archives.

The Timber Creek Police Station Journal is the daily record of all police activities for these remote outposts. The entry for 29 September 1960 records (all spelling verbatim and speech transcribed):

'Const Gordon and Tracker Smiler departed 1:30pm to attend Top Springs races. Arrived Top Springs 8pm. On duty around store until 11pm. A number of drunken men around store – several drunks on premises – the place in a filthy condition. Const advised the licensee

Mrs Hawks to comply with provisions of Licensing Ordinance or she would be prosecuted.'

The next day: *'Patrol around store and various camps until 12 m/ night. All in order with exception of usual drunks who were moved on and advised to go to their camps.'*

The journal entry for Monday 3 October 1960 expands with detail about the rest of Paul Vandeleur's story of the race meeting fallout:

'Const Gordon and O'Brien on duty at Top Springs. At 1030am Mrs Hawkes storekeeper reported that 3,500 in ten-pound notes had been taken from a brief case in her wardrobe and that she was sure that her husband C J Hawkes had taken it. Mr and Mrs Hawkes have been fighting over the last three years and apparently things came to a head during the weekend. Const advised her that her husband would be as much entitled to the money as she would and that it was not the policy of the Police to get mixed up in domestic arguments. She stated that a certain amount of race club money was included in the 3,500. Const visited Syd Hawkes and questioned him and he denied taking any money. He stated that his wife had her car packed ready to leave for Darwin and that she no doubt had the money. Const Gordon then went to the stock inspectors house where Mrs Hawkes was staying. He requested her to drive her car back to the store and have it searched. She was very reluctant and kept telling Const Gordon to go and search her husband. Const insisted on searching her car and she fainted. Const then searched Ivor Hall's car. Mr Hall was going to visit Darwin with Mrs Hawkes. Mrs Hawkes later came out and requested Const to call the whole thing off as she didn't want other people involved. Const advised her that was impossible. Const then searched Mrs Hawkes car and found £2,000 odd in cheques and about £1,300 in notes. The two

constables and Mrs Hawkes then visited the store and searched same. All particulars of money found was taken by Const O'Brien. The 3,500 in ten-pound notes was not found, and it is doubtful whether it even existed. It is felt that Mrs Hawkes was trying to use the Police as a weapon against her husband. One Norman Douglas an employee on the place was questioned and his room searched but without result. Ivor Hall was questioned and his belongings searched without result. Mrs Hawkes was horrified to see the Police searching and questioning innocent people (including herself). She obviously thought the Police were only going to question and search her husband. Mrs Hawkes has the reputation in the country of being a rogue as far as money is concerned. According to her husband she has been double crossing him for several years and it is only recently he has discovered it. She has handled all the book work and he has done all the outside work. Full report on the matter will be submitted by Const O'Brien at Wave Hill. Next day attended and shot 40 dogs in native camp ...'

Sid's account of this same story departed on details but was roughly aligned with the police account. His reflections on their relationship and the reasons for its failure have a ring of truth to them. Not unusual for the times, as he conceded, he was often absent from the pub, working – perhaps at the expense of their marriage. But what was unusual for the times was that Thelma was no stay-at-home wife, nor were they living in the suburbs.

I found a new respect for Thelma, albeit staying a tad wary. Her reputation may have preceded her, but it seemed clearer that before the split with Sid she was looking for a way out of the unhappy marriage, but never found it – her escape was blocked. After the confusing race day events Sid got out first. Left on her own, Thelma remained, maybe feeling trapped financially, at the pub and ran it solo until her death. She may have been tight, incredibly focused and even shady, but she was, as Norm Douglas explained, in the roughest and toughest environment imaginable, and in true Darwinian fashion – in both senses – it was survival of the fittest. If nought else, a survivor she was.

The deferential treatment the police gave Sid on the night of their confrontation, matched to the assumptions Constable Gordon from Timber Creek made about Thelma, are also typical of the times, when it was simply assumed that a woman in any relationship was subservient to her husband. Seen through a contemporary lens, the episode could be seen entirely differently.

Paul Vandeleur asked if I had spoken to Norm Douglas and then cast new light on Norm's life story too. *'Norm came out here after the war. His best friend ran off with his girlfriend while he was away in the army and he was heartbroken, so he came out here and just wandered around until he settled at Toppie.'*

Norm had just spent half a day telling me his entire life story without mentioning his prewar girlfriend. He would not be the first nor the last man to head out bush to seek a cure for a broken heart, and this tidbit of information slotted into his narrative perfectly. It does go some way to explaining the lonely figure he cut, self-exiled to the outback, escaping his emotions. Paul was not surprised that Norm skirted around that detail and explained: *'He worked for me for a while but then ended up at Top Springs for years; very protective of Thelma he was. He had a sort of mother-son relationship with Thelma and would never have a bad word to say about her. He felt obligated to stay and help her after Sid shot through and he would do anything for her.'*

271

Paul seemed to be the only person who took the liberty of calling Ma Hawks 'Thelma', although he then explained, '*I always called her Thellie actually, she didn't mind, but she did have other names you probably know ...*'

I was aware that, somewhat coarsely, Thelma was widely called 'old leather-tits' behind her back. June exploded from across the room.

'*That's disgusting, you can't say that; it's not fair ...*' she yelled at Paul and me together.

'*But that is what they called her! Come on, June, you know that is what it was ...*' said Paul, glancing guiltily at me, hoping for masculine solidarity and support, and he chuckled like a naughty school boy. '*Well, she was a pretty tough old bird. She thought she brought a bit of glamour to the bush; she had tickets on herself from her old performing days. She showed me photos of those times, the tent shows with her brother ... she was a pretty attractive bird,*' he remarked almost wistfully.

The rumours were that Thelma always carried a pearl-handled pistol. '*There was a time when I know she used one. Jack Bithnell and a few of the boys got stuck into the rum one night and were chasing a few gins down the creek and she squirted a few shots down onto the rocks to bring them to their senses and they took off. They thought up to that time that she was only joking, but she looked after herself pretty well, she needed to. When you think of the truckloads of grog that went through there — it was a licence to print money out in the bush in those days and there was no regulation about how much she was selling. It was the dearest grog in Australia, at least a 100 per cent mark-up, but it depended on who you were. She'd see you coming, and she'd size you up. I remember when John Renfree, a cattle buyer from Queensland, called in and he said, "You can't charge this much, these prices are too hot" and she just said, "No, that is the price out here, you can take it or leave it."'*

June chimed in: *'And then there's extra for a cold one ...'* she laughed. As several raconteurs had said, you couldn't exactly take your business elsewhere out there at Top Springs.

'Yes, that's right,' said Paul as our conversation was winding up, *'it was threepence extra in the early days if you wanted it cold ... but once she got to know you, she charged correct weight and didn't put the touch on you anymore. She never drank any herself – it was as if she had seen what was on the other side of the bar and said to herself: "Well, I'm not going to end up like that".'*

Thelma notoriously worked with three different prices – one price for white locals, a higher price for white travellers and then the highest and most extortionate price reserved for takeaway grog for 'blackfellas'. Both June and Paul nodded uncomfortably in confirmation, but clammed up as so often happened in these conversations as soon as discrimination against Aboriginal Australians was offered up for comment. On that front I had only just touched the surface and as I drove back up the track and returned to traffic lights and bitumen in Darwin, it nagged away deep inside me. I had spoken to countless Territorians over the years, in and around Darwin, Katherine, Alice Springs, into Arnhem Land and the Victoria River District, people of all races and backgrounds. The clear, unambiguous, evidence of racism was everywhere, but white Australians never wanted to talk about it, or in most cases even acknowledge it. Was it too hard? Too painful? Too confronting? Too much guilt?

* * *

Peter Dermotty was the architect Thelma hired for the early 1970s rebuild of Wanda Inn after the destructive fire. When I caught up with him he was midway through recommissioning an old yacht at Darwin Yacht Club, so we chatted on the deck as it sat up on hard stands in the yard. Surrounded by spars and clinking rigging, we were interrupted by noises from sanders and grinders, making for a stop-start conversation.

'Thelma hired us to do this huge solid building at Top Springs, which was ridiculous if you think about it – it was so out of scale, massive, much more than was justified. She insisted that she wanted to build something in brick and permanent, no matter what it cost. There were always rumours about the road being upgraded, that the government would seal the road to Jasper Gorge, and the Buchanan Highway would be good all the way to Timber Creek, but they were only ever rumours. It was impossible to get blokes to go down there to work, and the types that would go were all either alcoholics or the sort who would plant some dope seeds out in the bush and tell you how fabulous it was going to be when they came good. They always ended up being tomatoes though; hopeless. Everything cost a fortune and I think she spent over $300,000 all up; it was astounding. I have no idea where the money came from but she was very good at finding a reason not to pay people.'

This had become the defining theme, the recurring and primary recollection of everyone who dealt with Thelma. Why was she so tight, living in an environment where everyone depended on each other? In such a tiny close-knit community, where everyday survival required give and take, it seemed strange behaviour. Mutual assistance was the key to relationships in the bush. Were the rules different if you were running the only pub –

Thelma Hawks at Top Springs feeding an orphaned joey.

an essential service – for miles around? Could you become a law unto yourself? Was she greedy, opportunistic or just thrifty?

'You would not want to cross her, she was that tough. I remember that she did some crazy deal for a generator – she needed about 10Kva but she found some plant that was 70Kva and was big enough to run all of Katherine. It turned up on a truck and we had to build a special shed for it. Once it was up and running, she contrived a reason – like a loose screw or something trivial – to not make the final payment. Because it was a two-day round trip to go and front her about anything, you had to decide if you could be bothered. She knew that and counted on it. She had this "poor deserted woman" routine after Sid left – mind you after a while I could work out why he left,' he said laughing, but quickly qualified the insult and reflected positively about his former customer.

'We used to have dinner when she came in to Darwin. I thought of her as a friend eventually, and she was always very proper, would take

tea in a cup with a saucer and all the airs and graces. She was much more educated than most of the people down there and I suppose she was a bit of a snob. She thought nothing of charging $25 for a cask of wine for blackfellas who came in from Hooker Creek when you could buy a cask in Katherine for $4, and her bottles of rum were $95 – extortion really. She had her fans; it was like she was the Queen of Top Springs. Norm was always around but I don't think there was any hanky-panky – Norm was such a pisspot he wouldn't have been up to it anyway.'

Peter's assessment of Norm's platonic relationship with Thelma chimes with June and Paul's views from the day before – it was never a romantic connection, but employer and employee, albeit an astoundingly loyal one. Before thanking Peter and climbing down the wobbly ladder from his half-repainted yacht, I had to ask him about her nickname. *'No, she didn't like being called "Old Ma Hawks" ... she didn't like the "old" tag. She thought she was pretty trim. And "leather-tits?"'* he guffawed, *'I don't think anyone would have been game to say that within earshot!'*

Between visiting old Darwin hands, I retreated to the sanctuary of Darwin's iconic Roma Bar. Occupying a strategic spot opposite both the ABC studios and the Law Courts, it offered a casual meeting place for lawyers, journos and pretty much anyone else who wanted to eat without going to either a proper restaurant, a pub or a pokies venue. Cafe culture, Top End style. Established years ago by a Victorian duo from Fitzroy's trendy pub scene, it is a home away from home for all the southern do-gooders who take a Darwin detour in their careers. It is often quipped that most newcomers to the NT are one of the 'three M's' – mercenaries, missionaries or misfits. For some, you could tick all three boxes at once. Typically, I bumped into a few former colleagues from either the law or Auntie's studios across the road, caught up with some gossip, traded a bit of my own and downed a few lemon, lime and bitters with my favourite yuppie toastie (cheese and avocado).

Soon I would have to go back home to Melbourne, to confront some uncomfortable truths. I was facing the humiliation of a public sacking from my ABC radio gig and not looking forward to it. But I was missing Jan, Nigel and Jack, and needed to squeeze as much from my Darwin expedition as I could. I headed out into Darwin's suburbs again.

My last house call was to Ernie Rayner who was the stock inspector at Top Springs for a few years from 1964. He welcomed me to his leafy home and settled me down with a mug of tea. He still stood tall, showing few of the telltale scars of Territory hard living, and, with a welcoming twinkle in his eye as he trawled through the past, he remembered vividly the time he and wife Pauline spent at Top Springs as a newly married young couple.

'Thelma ran a tight ship. It was good to be sent down there and I enjoyed it. It was just a store, a Sidney Williams-style corrugated iron and angled iron frame, a bit of a verandah out front, a dunny built over a big crevice in the rocks ... a flaming fury if you like. The stock inspectors had a good house with a verandah on two sides. Thelma was friendly and really looked after Pauline, as I was often away on work doing blood tests and inoculating and stuff. She was well groomed, quite attractive for a woman in her fifties, hair always up in that bun ... pretty happy she was, and she should have been — it was a gold mine, she had the game sewn up really. I remember there was a bit of a rumble when some fella had been droving the Murranji Track and came back and there was a drum of petrol on his *bill from Thelma but he didn't even have a truck or a car ...'* While being supportive of Thelma, Ernie confirmed the 'charged like a wounded bull' tendency so many people had consistently said about her.

'Beer was three or four times the price in town but you'd drink it anyway ... there was no alternative. She had a green fridge and if you wanted your beer from the green fridge it was threepence extra, because it was run off a petrol generator and she said she had to pay for the fuel to keep anything cold. Even if she only put it in there for one minute you still had to pay the fridge price.'

Ernie was just warming up, the memories tripping over each other as he revisited his younger self. *'I wouldn't be surprised if she carried a gun – most people kept a squirter just in case; you never knew what might happen. I never saw her use one, but she had a reputation. Norm was always around, he lived out the back on the verandah and just had a camp bed really. Sometimes I would get back home at two in the morning and Norm would be asleep in the bar, and I ratted that place so many times; it was easy. If he was asleep behind the bar I would wake him and put him to bed and slide the cash tin in under him. He'd always have several bottles on the go – a beer going at the bar, and another in the fridge, and another out the back and he'd just sip on them all as he went about his work and as he cleaned up at the end of the day he'd finish them all off. That was Norm, by the end, every single day he would be well and truly pissed.'* Ernie welcomed my news that Norm was now healthy and living sober in Katherine. Territorians have a grudging respect for anyone who manages to get off the grog.

Ernie remembered another story illustrating how tough life was and how tight Thelma was. *'Mick Crowson was out the back of somewhere with a truckload of beer and the load shifted and he had to* unload all this grog. Before he could reload it he needed more ropes to stop it falling off, so he arrived at my place and said how about we go and get all this piss and reload the truck. We went and stocked up the LandRover and got stuck into it all, lucky no-one else had come along, but we loaded all this grog and stores on the six-ton truck and worked like navvies to get it done. We were just about cooked. I thought, sure she'll toss me a carton or something decent, but nah, when we got it all done she said, "Thank you Ernie, I should buy you two a beer". I was filthy, but after she went upstairs Mick, shouted me a carton and I got a decent drink for my troubles.'

Ernie's tenure as the stock inspector coincided exactly with the Gurindji walk-off. His work required him to spend a lot of his time with the Vesteys managers and the Gurindji stockmen at Wave Hill. The entire nation had been closely scrutinising the tumultuous events going on in his patch and I expected he would have some insights into race relations at the time and the historic events.

'Well, even though I went out to do work at Wave Hill, I didn't have anything to do with the walk-off, I kept my distance from all that. Thelma wouldn't have blackfellas drinking in the bar. Mick Daly was the first white bloke legally allowed to marry a gin. Gladys Namilglu was her name. They were camped out there, and Mick was always in the bar and she'd get on the grog and come in to the bar and he would tell her to go away. Thelma would too, and she was half cooked — or full cooked — and she says to him real loud: "Mick Daly, you rotten stinking fuck, you white cunt". So he quietly puts down his beer and slow as you like strolls out … he's a soft-spoken bloke, never raises his voice … and he came back with a fucking rope and grabbed her and flogged her with it. There was no interfering, not by *anyone, I am sorry to say. Then he runs this rope around her legs and even though there is gravel he drags her down to the camp, dress up around her shoulders, and then he just came back and sat down at the bar again, picked up his beer and said, "I don't think she'll be back". Incredible.'* I am chilled by the recital of such violence, horrified and struggling to hold my tongue, but Ernie does not flinch in the telling. I pressed him on more details about the walk-off, but am left unconvinced by his claims not to be able to contribute to the history. If he does not want to reflect on it, I have to respect his decision to keep his memories to himself.

'*I was out at Toppie for four years, but after, if I was passing through, I'd go in and say hello. She was always friendly and pleased to see you. When I started, they only had hurricane lamps in the store, and then later they got electricity from a tiny gennie around the back that broke down all the time. Gee, it changed ... I guess that place now – it is like a monument to Ma Hawks really.'*

I enquired if any of his friendships with stockmen from Kalkarindji/Wave Hill had endured and he sighed. '*It was never like that, good blokes most of them and all, but you were never friends.'* He recommended some more of his old public service mates that I should talk to, and my list of Thelma storytellers kept getting longer even as I crossed names off the top.

Over the phone, I filled in some gaps with Gavin McDonald, who had followed Ernie as the stock inspector at Top Springs from 1968 until 1979. He only met Sid once, as Sid had already split with Thelma, but '*if anyone mentioned anything about Sid then Mrs H would go and hide. But he said she fleeced him*'. Needless to say, Sid would not be the first bloke to claim to have come out of a divorce with the rough end of the stick.

'She was such a serious person – on a scale of personality from 1 to 10 she was a 1. No small talk at all – just "What do you want: fuel, food or beer?" The only time I saw her animated about anything was when she had the plans for the new building laid out on the bar and wanted to know what you thought, brick by bloody brick; the first time it was interesting but after that … She always finished a sentence with a sniff, as if to emphasise everything, but when I heard she had asthma that all made sense.' When I told him the details of Thelma's death he was not in any way surprised that asthma was accepted by the coroner as the cause of her death.

'They were all alcos, all of them, and they were a pretty rough bunch. Bill Crowson's brother Mick was supposed to be her truck driver and go back and forth to Darwin but there was a hell of a lot of drinking between trips. He'd be there all day sipping steadily and mostly got paid in grog. Norm never got paid, he just got pocket money. She ran a book system, where you'd settle up at the end of the month, and if you'd bought a carton of beer she'd put you down for two; she was famous for it, so I started to pay as I went to avoid any arguments.' Thelma's unique bookkeeping skills and innovative accounting were now well and truly beyond dispute. Her reputation was well deserved and he told me another nickname: the 'Armstrong River Vampire'.

'The Department of Agriculture had a house up the road and one time there was a fridge and some stuff that disappeared. I went and asked her if she knew what happened – nothing happened without her knowing – and she denied knowing anything about it. But I could see it sticking out from under the tarp. She was incredible. She did NOT like other women, and there was never any ladies' chat, and if my girlfriend Cookie was with me, Thelma would be different and *stay away. You couldn't get a decent meal – she turned it on as far as a tin of bully beef and some Sao biscuits with tomato sauce or a tin of baked beans or something; she made no effort to make it nice. Cobwebs everywhere, no ornaments or pictures, no effort at all, she just wouldn't spend any money. We'd prefer to light a fire and cook for ourselves. We used to eat with the Aboriginal stockmen if they were working with us, but they weren't welcome at the pub. She wouldn't let them in, but she'd sell them grog twenty cartons at a time. Some of the white drovers would stop off there after a muster, sometimes for two or three weeks and just drink and drink … "Wanda Inn and stagger out" we used to say.'* I cracked up laughing, as in all the years I had been yarning about Thelma and Top Springs, that was the first I had heard of the Wanda Inn being a punchline to a joke.

'One fella, Tom Turner, was so sick they had to call the Flying Doctor and take him off; she just fed him grog till he nearly died. Norm was that sick with the grog that he'd shake when he tried to put the bowser nozzle into your Toyota. I visited Norm years later where he was living in Riverside Drive and he was all dried out and healthy and it was a pleasure to see him away from the grog. She never even gave him a room, you know, he just had a swag on an old bed out in the verandah and a bit of tin in case it rained. "Hooley dooley" was his greeting, in his Pommy accent. Despite the grog, there weren't many fights at Toppie. In Katherine there were fights all the time but not at Toppie. Funny, eh, because there were no police there either. If you went to Elliott, Newcastle Waters, Timber Creek, Mataranka – there were always fights but we just left them alone. It was always the grog.'

For all the bravado that Territorians carry on with, for all their legendary drinking culture, the damage grog has done to so many lives is incalculable. So many of the old Territorians reflect critically on their youth, but there never seems to be a matching resolve by anyone to tackle the problem in any meaningful way. The celebration of drinking as an integral component of the lifestyle is rarely questioned and when it is queried, it is readily dismissed as wowserism at best or more commonly 'un-Territorian'. Any politician at local, territory or federal level who ventured to try the obviously necessary changes would be out of office in a flash. The archives are full of reports condemning the culture and suggestions on what needs to change, but fundamentally, the people who live there love it the way it is.

Everyone I had spoken to had colourful memories of Thelma, readily summonsed for the telling. June was quite wistful in her recollections of Old Ma Hawks, and she'd had the most to do with her. A picture emerged, fleshed out by her friends Paul and Betty, of a somewhat lonely and solitary figure, treating each day as another battle. A woman who found herself stranded in an inhospitable male world, unsure how to navigate beyond the day-to-day business of selling petrol and grog. She relied on her wits to survive. Those who had less to do with her only saw the public face of Thelma Hawks, and the former stock inspectors Gavin and Ernie all thought she was just a rogue trader ripping off everyone whenever she got the chance.

But Peter Dermotty, who had a genuine friendship with her, and a mutual respect that endured over a longer time, left me wondering if Thelma was performing at Toppie just as she had at the Tivoli with her brother. Instead of adagio dancing, she was dancing to the tune of the cash register, keeping the audience guessing, just like her famous brother.

And what of the rumoured spur line to Top Springs, the original tip-off that led to Sid and Thelma settling there in the late 1940s? A railway survey from 1928 showed plans to join Alice Springs to Darwin and then gradually develop an entire network of railway lines to service the northern cattle industry. But with the postwar evolution of road trains, it instead became cheaper and more effective to build roads which were useful for more than just transporting cattle.

After the bombing of Darwin by the Japanese, there was talk of moving the capital inland, to Elliott (about three hours south-east of Toppie), to make the administration of the rapidly developing northern frontier safer. The various administrations decided Elliott was not viable as there was little room for expansion, and Darwin had the major benefit of a port. The proposal did go as far as surveyors preparing a town plan for Elliott, at around the time Sid was tipped off about the long-term prospects of a town being established at Top Springs. The grand plan was abandoned, as have so many in the Top End.

Sid and Thelma may have banked on their inside information when deciding to establish their store at Toppie, and there was always a chance they would have cashed in. Events did not unfold the way they were hoping.

The railway line between Darwin and Alice Springs was finally completed in 2003, fifty years after Sid and Thelma gambled on its construction. The spur line from Katherine to Top Springs has never been built and never will be.

CHAPTER 15
APOLLO'S DEATH

Back in Melbourne, washing the Territory sweat off my shirts and re-introducing my feet to shoes, I had the unenviable ordeal of still having to perform on air, pretending to be cheerful, grinding out a program until the end of 1994, knowing the news of my sacking could become public any day. When it was finally announced, before the Christmas break-up, it embarrassingly featured on the front page of *The Age*. I went to air that day dreading the reaction, but the audience were wonderfully supportive and heartening and my colleagues even more so. There were letters to the newspaper, talk of a petition to protest my removal and any number of angry letters and cards sent from lovely listeners – none of which made the slightest impression on the decision-makers who sacked me.

As my final show approached, a Friday in mid-December, a rumour swept the ABC offices that I was going to use my last few minutes on-air to give the managers a spray. Several wise older hands around the radio station – Sue Howard and Doug Aiton in particular – generously and sensibly cautioned me against using the farewell to settle scores with the bosses. 'Don't burn your bridges. If you trash the joint on the way out the door there is no coming back' was how it was put to me. I did not start those rumours, but I confess I was happy to fuel them in order to trigger a few anxious moments in the hearts of those I felt had done me a great wrong. Instead, I ended the show by thanking my producers and the entire team, the extended family of regular guests, the audience, especially paid a teary tribute to Jan and the kids, and then closed by saying … 'And finally – yes, there is something important I want to say to the ABC managers … [long pause] Merry Christmas'. And that was it, I cleared my desk, handed in my staff pass and was no longer an employee of the ABC.

Bizarrely, at the exact same time as I was being sacked from ABC Radio, I was being recruited by ABC TV. The long-running weekly consumer advice show *The Investigators* hired me as a contractor for the new year to present a weekly segment that typically was about something to do with the law. With a remarkably patient film crew, I would explain consumer law, or tenants' rights, or how to negotiate a better deal with a bank and also did my share of chasing a shonky builder down a laneway or some similar tale of woe. I also made a pilot for an ABC show exploring ethics, and was asked by a private production company to front a pilot about cars and motoring.

Then the ABC developed a wild and sometimes unruly teenage-focused TV show called *Wize Up*, best described as a juvenile version of *Q&A*. Using the famed *Countdown* studio in the ABC TV complex in Ripponlea, I would wrangle a mob of teen panellists who would tackle thorny issues with expert guests on a set full of carefully curated junk designed to look like a graffitied rubbish tip. Each episode, the diverse bunch of about twenty from private and public schools, youth homeless refuges, migrant backgrounds – even a few from happy homes – would grill a guest who might be a family court judge, or a top cop or a school principal – over why the world was so unfair to teenagers. We filmed two series and although hectic, it was fun. At least I still had work, although I missed the buzz of daily radio. Somewhat satisfyingly, the ratings in my old slot slowly dropped after I left.

Visiting Apollo was high on my list of things to do, and I was looking forward to telling him some of the stories that I had heard up north about his sister Thelma. Sadly, around this time he endured another major health crisis and never fully recovered. His reliance on and belief in psycho-astro wave lengths did not help when he had to go to hospital with a heart condition, fluid on the lungs, a blockage in his carotid artery, followed by

One of the last photos of Apollo in his gym in Hawke St, West Melbourne.

another mental health crisis. As his body was slowly letting him down, the decline triggered a collapse in the very self-belief that had served him so well throughout his career. His mind and body were unravelling together. As next of kin, eldest son Paul reluctantly consented to multiple courses of electroshock therapy for his father.

For several months, he was confined to a locked ward in a psychiatric hospital, sedated and non-responsive. Paul was heartbroken to see his lion of a father reduced to a zombie-like state. *'But at least it worked a bit – they re-set his brain, and he could leave the hospital. When he went in he thought that vitamins were poison, but later he just sat and stared and it was horrible to see. He said "I'm no longer the Mighty Apollo, just call me Paul" – it was ghastly.'* After leaving hospital, he could not return to his home at the gym. He went to Queensland for a while to stay with Bruce, came back in a wheelchair and, for a while, could not even get up the stairs to the gym unaided. *'He had to live in a nursing home. He made it up the steps to the gym one last time. He was walking around touching the equipment, almost caressing his trophies. It was like he was saying goodbye, and I guess that was what was happening although I didn't know it at the time,'* recounts Paul.

I visited him once in his Essendon nursing home around this time, for what turned out to be our last chat. He was pale, gaunt, his eyes retreating into his head and his hair uncut and a little wild, most uncharacteristic for a man who was so vain and – for ample reason – proud of how he appeared in public. He was beyond looking after himself. He did recognise me, thankfully, and we chatted for a little while, mostly just small talk, but he was so diminished in spirit and mind that he had little conversation left. In response to any news about Thelma gleaned from the visit north, he had no commentary at all. It no longer mattered to him, and maybe my visit reminded him of what he could no longer do, and what he could no longer be. All he had left were vague memories and a nagging concern for his sons, whose wellbeing was always front of mind. It was distressing to see Apollo unable to maintain the usual barrage of stories from his stellar past, the meticulous recital and word-perfect retelling of the intricate details of his many record-breaking feats.

Nursing homes are sad places at the best of times and, with typically limited budgets, make for unpleasant surrounds to see out final days. Back in West Melbourne, his private space at the back of the Mighty Apollo Gym and Combat Centre was spartan, but at least it was his own. Although the Anderson sons looked for the best option for their father, Apollo's accommodation was shabby and basic, the common areas dominated by the omnipresent TV, blaring inane daytime soap operas or quiz shows, and residents wandering around in their confusion. Depressing enough on a short visit and grim to inhabit.

Paul took Apollo out for lunch the day before he died. After a bite to eat and a chat, he dropped his dad back at the nursing home. *'He asked me if I wanted to come in for a cup of tea. I said no, I'm in a hurry, see you next week. Next morning, they rang me to say he had died overnight in his sleep. It was a heart attack in the end. I had to tell my brothers, and then organise a funeral. It was ghastly; we didn't get to say goodbye, and I was lost for a while.'*

On an overcast weekday morning in February 1995, at a small church in Essendon, around fifty people gathered and prayed to God for the soul of a man who had an unconventional relationship with that very God. He had frequently invoked his religious beliefs to explain his 'God-given' ability to do things no human being ought to have been able to do, but mixed it with a contradictory cocktail of mysticism and mumbo-jumbo that diluted his connection to any one line of Christian or other religious teachings. For all the talk of God, Apollo was not a member of any congregation, was not known to pray, did not connect to any specific school of Christianity and seemed to call on Buddhist and other mystical teachings as much as the Christian tradition. He mixed and matched as he liked.

At his funeral, the small congregation heard but a smattering of stories from the remarkable life of Alexander McPherson Anderson. Every mourner in the church knew him as Apollo, some may have thought he was really Paul, but none knew him as Alex. The pews were populated by a colourful assembly of characters from the colliding worlds of circus, showbiz, weightlifting and his gym. There were almost no women and no family other than his sons. He had long ago lost touch with his other Anderson siblings except Thelma; and no cousins, nephews, nieces or other relatives featured in his adult life nor his death. Rondahe was not mentioned. The funeral concentrated on the remarkable and unbelievable acts he had done, his prowess as a showie, a strongman, a performer on stages large and small. His world records, his feats of strength and his daring successes were recited but there was little to reflect on about Apollo as a human being. His work was his life.

Paul, Mark and Bruce, with Apollo's oldest mate Ron Taylor and some friends, carried his coffin from the church to the hearse. The sombre crowd lingered in the car park for a while, in that awkward post-funeral mingling where no-one quite knows what to say or do, but everyone I spoke to agreed it was the end of an era. I negotiated my way through the small gathering and made my way to the rear of the hearse to pay my respects to each of Paul, Mark and Bruce. With his characteristic grin, Paul greeted me and reintroduced me to his brothers, who I had not seen for so many years. I felt suddenly old, observing these young men from the sidelines after such a long interval.

Apollo's embroidered track suit declares him 'Official International Champion of Champions' and Worlds Records Holder.

Remarkably, only one of the three brothers had a partner at the church. They seemed as solitary as their father, possibly a legacy of their traumatic early years thrown into institutional care.

I hung around the car park to see if there was anything that seemed like a wake, but if there was, I was not invited. As the mourners dispersed, so did the opportunity to hear more stories about the Mighty Apollo, the last of his breed. Just as he juggled three names, he juggled three action-packed lives: the world record–breaking weightlifter, the circus strongman, and, most significant to him, the dedicated but distant father to three beloved sons.

The week after Apollo's funeral, *The Age* refused my offer of an obituary. 'We've already run that; we can't do it again,' said the same section editor I had argued with months before when the American Olympic wrestler Anderson was mistakenly credited with much of Apollo's career. It would though have been the perfect tribute – the Mighty Apollo, the only person to have two differing obituaries, ample confirmation that his career was beyond being adequately described with just one.

CHAPTER 16
BENDIGO SWAP MEET

Newly underemployed, only occupied part-time with *The Investigators* and *Wize Up* on ABC TV, I pretended I could make documentaries and precociously put a few ideas to Film Australia. Relationships forged over the years were invaluable in opening their door, and I presented some ideas for scrutiny. The outlines were approved for development into scripts. One project of the three suggested was about 'bush courts', and in mid-1995 it took me back to Darwin.

Ian Gray, the Chief Magistrate of the Northern Territory, had a stressful and complex job, but I had known him years before, when he was a lawyer at the Victorian Aboriginal Legal Service up the road from Fitzroy Legal Service. He was a bit older, a much more accomplished lawyer than me, and some years before had moved north to run the NT's legal aid office. Later, he had been appointed as a magistrate and then promoted to Chief Magistrate. I entertained the faint hope he might be amenable to the highly unusual and controversial step of having his court filmed while on circuit.

My interest was in telling the story of the bush courts, an under-resourced parody of the Australian criminal justice system. Although the professionals involved did the best that they could, they were working in a system that was far removed from basic civil liberties and human rights. A 'fly-on-the-wall' documentary about remote circuit courts, highlighting the absurd constraints they operated under, might help make their case in the ceaseless bid for more money. He rapidly agreed, given the overwhelming workload and vital role of the service.

At its simplest, a bush court is a mobile court, wherein magistrates regularly go bush to hear mostly criminal prosecutions in remote towns in Queensland, WA and the NT. The court would travel to the community instead of the other way around. Some Arnhem Land and desert communities were only accessible by air for half the year, during the 'wet', when access roads are flooded. Other communities could only be reached after long dirt-road drives through the bush. Not unlike when the circus came to town, the police, prosecutors, legal aid lawyers and Aboriginal community liaison staff, as well as the court personnel, would travel as a group. Typically, the judge would sit at a trestle table under a tree or in a health centre, a single legal aid lawyer would try to achieve the impossible and represent everyone – sometimes twenty or thirty people – while the police would slam through as many cases as possible. After a typically exhaustingly long day, there would often be a shared meal – despite people being on opposing sides – and then everybody would get back onto a small plane and fly on to the next community and do it all again.

I clearly remember my shock when I realised that some of those accused did not speak English fluently or at all, and there were never qualified interpreters available. It was not at all unusual for someone to be sentenced to a term of imprisonment with no clue as to why. It was rough as guts, and Ian was keen for me to show the rest of Australia about this utterly appalling version of justice. No other Australian citizens would ever be subjected to such a scandalous departure from fundamental legal rights. Imagine if someone in a major city had to attend court and in many instances be sentenced to prison without an interpreter explaining to them what was happening – it is inconceivable. But it was standard procedure out bush.

I eagerly grabbed the chance to 'go bush' with Ian on a typical circuit and had everyone's permission – usually strictly forbidden – to snap away with my camera while court was sitting. The plan was to prepare a story board, a filming plan, to guess a budget and to assist logistics for when I would come back in a few months with a full film crew. We flew first to Alyangula on Groote Eylandt, where the court sat all day with a massive schedule, and then to Gove, where another full list was waiting, those accused mostly from the nearby Aboriginal communities of Yirrkala and Nhulunbuy. It was promising to be a compelling film, and when I got back home from scouting the locations, I excitedly busied myself creating the story outline.

Shortly after submitting the expanded proposal together with a modest budget and story board for commissioning, the Howard Government was elected in a landslide in March 1996. One of the first things they did was to announce a funding freeze and review of Film Australia. I didn't take it personally, but it was devastating and was the end of my career as a documentary filmmaker. Months of work was wasted, more significantly an important story would remain untold, and I slipped into a quagmire of bitter and negative moods. I retreated to the shed and tried to replace productive work with mechanical tinkering. Cheaper than a shrink. Just.

Unemployed and anxious about making a living, deskilled as a lawyer after six years at the ABC, reluctant to return to working in a city law firm after nearly a dozen years away, not confident that I could secure enough work to succeed at the Bar, I talked through the options with Jan. We decided it best if I looked for a small office to rent in the inner city to start my own legal practice. Vain enough to think I could make a living, I wanted to run my own race and start from scratch. The last few years of professional disappointments left bruises, so I opted for self-reliance and independence, deciding that at least I would have no-one but myself to blame if things didn't work out. The sooner I got started the better.

Midway through inspecting a shopfront for lease in Gertrude Street, Fitzroy, my new 'brick' mobile phone rang and the estate agent's pitch was interrupted by Sue Howard. Previously a broadcaster colleague at ABC Radio, she had abandoned on-air radio stardom and moved into ABC management, where she climbed rapidly due to her radio smarts and her gentle but firm people skills. She asked me if I would consider returning to 3LO for 1997 to host the key morning slot, but with extended hours. There had always been two separate shows splitting the morning between them. I had just been through the depressing cancellation of *The Investigators* and the documentary projects, and I had reconciled myself to leaving behind the adrenaline surge of both TV and daily radio, slowly finding comfort with the notion of working as a lawyer again. Lots of our friends were wondering why I kept chasing the media instead of turning back to lawyering, and my disapproving parents added their two bobs' worth too. Sue Howard's quick conversation and the ABC's about-face left me totally confused, but the broadcasting drug is powerfully addictive. She offered me some fill-in slots as auditions during the school holidays in late 1996 and straight after, when she offered me a permanent gig, I stipulated the ABC must agree to a two-year contract, to give me a decent run. She agreed and I started as the new 'Mornings' host in January 1997, on air from 8.30 until noon. My aim was to survive for four years.

Making a three-and-a-half-hour daily current affairs radio show was not a job – it was a lifestyle. I was perpetually exhausted, always low on sleep from getting up at 4.15 am. By Friday afternoon, I would crawl home, curl up in a corner and howl at the moon. Well, not quite. Jan sold her old home in Brisbane which meant we could pay out the mortgage on our home and put a deposit on a house at Point Lonsdale, a sleepy coastal hamlet an hour and a half from Melbourne. We tried to get there with the kids every second weekend, year round, with the warmer months being dedicated to the beach and the winter visits being more about blustery walks with the dogs. It was like having a long weekend each fortnight. Nigel was working in construction, playing a lot of sport and did not often want to be with us on a weekend. Jack had no choice.

My first two years back on air in the crucial and highly pressurised 'Mornings' shift were excruciating and an incredible slog. The ratings were slow to improve, the competition from other established broadcasters intense. The state government under Jeff Kennett barely acknowledged the ABC and when it did, it was to treat us as second-class citizens. Ministers would routinely decline our requests for interviews on the big news stories and instead constantly provide our commercial rivals with exclusive access to new government information and developments. The Murdoch owned *Herald-Sun* newspaper was merciless in its criticism of everything we did, delighting in poking fun at the ABC and characterising us as endlessly biased. It was a thankless task trying to stay well informed when it was state government practice to freeze us out and preference the rivals. The premier once told me the only reason he spoke to me at all was because we had considerable clout in regional Victoria as our transmitter carried our signal across the entire state. The radio signal of his preferred commercial spruikers could not be heard at all outside Melbourne.

Remarkably, the Howard Federal Government had the opposite attitude and was far more mature and nuanced in its use of the ABC and talk radio in general. John Howard loved being on the radio and became more familiar to voters accordingly. He popped up in a radio studio wherever he was around the nation several times a week, rarely missing any chance to engage with the public. He believed that taking talkback offered a great barometer of public opinion, and he was not wrong. He also happened to have an extraordinary capacity to rely on his memory for the most obscure details. Most ministers would arrive for an interview laden with pages of notes covered in little multi-coloured 'post it' notes, but John Howard would come into the studio without any briefing notes or prompts at all.

My stretch on air each weekday included a statewide self-contained hour from eleven o'clock called the 'Conversation Hour' which became a showcase for the arts and longer interviews with mostly creative types. A rotating roster of well-known and loved-members of what was really an extended family on the radio were roped in as co-hosts and helped create a relaxed 'fireside chat' on-air ambience that was a marked contrast to the faster pace and more searching approach used for news and current affairs earlier in the morning. I loved the opportunity to really lock horns with a guest and get into a deeper conversation than the typical seven-minute exchange. The featured 'Conversation Hour' became sought after by publicists and publishers as the perfect medium for flogging their authors, actors, comedians and visiting celebrities. When Hugh Grant and Kylie Minogue were both in the studio on the same day, I felt we had at last established a presence. The 'Mornings' show start to fulfil the brief and my two-year contract was renewed and then renewed again.

My third year on air, in 1999, was a Victorian state election year and it was the view of most of the print and electronic media that the imperious and combative conservative Premier Jeff Kennett was guaranteed to be returned for a third term. His antagonistic and personal attacks on me continued, with regular abuse and suggestions from him, live to air, that I stop asking what he regarded as intrusive questions about what his government was doing and instead 'do something positive for a change'. It was appallingly rude on his part, and I was thoroughly sick of his boorish, patronising bullying. We clashed over my continued questioning of the decision to locate the F1 Grand Prix in public parkland, necessitating its closure for a third of the year. The scale and ownership of the new Melbourne casino that had just opened was another point of abrasion, as were his government's continuing closure of public schools, selling off of public assets and privatisation of infrastructure and services. Of deep concern was the premier's undermining of the independence of the Director of Public Prosecutions and the Auditor-General. For daring to question him about these topics, I was regularly berated and humiliated on my own show live to air and described by him as being 'un-Victorian'. In contrast, his weekly comfortable chat with the commercial rival was sickeningly matey.

In the final week of the campaign, as always, I offered both the opposition leader and the premier the showcase first half hour of airtime. The ALP leader Steve Bracks was fairly new and an unknown quantity, but he was first and agreed to be interviewed on the final Wednesday. According to opinion polls, an unusually high percentage of Victorians said they were 'undecided' in the last week, and my theory was that everyone had made up their mind about Kennett – a divisive character – but they had not yet made up their minds about the new young alternative. The next morning, the Thursday before the poll, Jeff Kennett was my studio guest. In what has been dubbed the 'cup of tea' interview he had a complete meltdown. The spark for his extraordinary behaviour was my question about some material published online by a disgruntled former Kennett ministerial press secretary, Stephen Mayne, who had created a website called Jeffed.com. Mayne compiled what he claimed were accounts of serious irregularities and conflicts of interest within several ministries that had passed unchecked. Although Jeffed.com was well read by journalists and political junkies, not a single interviewer had dared ask Kennett about any of it. I figured that it was a requirement of my job to be fearless, and that if I was going to let myself be intimidated by an interviewee then I did not deserve to be in the chair. If I didn't

Jeff Kennett mid-insult in the infamous 'cup of tea' interview, 3LO studio, 1999. [ABC News camera tape]

ask, I ought to resign; and if I did ask, I was toast, as Kennett was renowned for being vengeful and would probably never do an interview with me again. I would be no use to the ABC if the state premier refused to come onto my show – so I would likely be out of a job.

I decided to ask about Jeffed.com, whatever the consequences. Instead of directly asking if the scurrilous allegations were true, I framed my question somewhat laterally and asked Kennett why he had not addressed the allegations or sued Mayne for defamation over their publication. He exploded live to air, arrogantly dared me to outline any specific details – and fell headfirst into my trap by doing so. It enabled me to recite all the allegations on Jeffed.com, which I then did. Subsequently, he just refused to answer my questions. Kennett snarled: 'You're pathetic, just pathetic; go on, I'll just sit here and drink my tea' while ostentatiously and loudly slurping into the microphone and refusing repeated requests to respond. He mocked and scolded me. As the nine o'clock news bulletin approached, I wished him luck for the Saturday poll. His reply was, 'I don't know why I waste my time coming here to talk to you … if the people decide they don't want me, at least I won't have to come and talk to you again'.

Two days later, on voting day, it was the unanimous prediction of the commentariat that Kennett would easily win. The real interest in the result, they said, would be how large a majority he would secure. I had a quiet wager with one leading psephologist, Nick Economou from Monash University, that Kennett was in for a shock, but it was a lonely position to hold; I sensed there was deep anger in the electorate. The tragic death of the member for Frankston East, Peter McLellan, on polling day meant that the vote there was declared void and another vote would be needed. Nobody expected it would have any bearing on the outcome – until the results started to show a substantial anti-Kennett swing. By the time counting finished, the parties were neck and neck and the outstanding bayside seat would be decisive. It took weeks to arrange the supplementary election, which was won by the ALP, still in opposition, while Kennett was a caretaker premier. Neither party had a clear majority and the balance of power rested with three rural independents, already being duchessed by both Kennett and Bracks. After weeks of deliberating while the Frankston East re-run campaign was underway, the independents announced that as Kennett had been dismissive of their requests for reform, but Bracks had been receptive, they were supporting a change of government. Tumultuous times. The 'cup of tea' interview was credited with being one of the turning points, and instead of being isolated and frozen out of the state politics equation, the new Premier Bracks was very happy to appear regularly on my show. Liberal Party powerbroker Michael Kroger told me that interview was played to prospective Liberal candidates for many years as a training module on what not to do.

Not long after, John Howard taught me one of the most important lessons of my broadcasting career. In 1999, the ABC TV program *Media Watch* had revealed that Sydney 'shock jocks' Alan Jones and John Laws, as well as a few others, were being secretly paid significant amounts of money to soften their criticism of the big banks. In August 2000, the Australian Broadcasting Authority delivered its findings from an inquiry into what by then was called 'Cash for Comment'. Days after, John Howard was a guest in my studio. As well as covering all the other hot topics, I asked him if, after the release of the ABA report into 'Cash for Comment', and the finding that Alan Jones and John Laws had been in effect corrupt and unethical, he would continue to appear on their programs.

The prime minister smiled slightly and then skewered me. *'When I come into your studio, you probably think I am here to talk to you. But I'm not – I'm really here talking to your audience, and as long as those gentlemen have an audience I will talk to them too.'* Game, set, match John Howard. He understood what I did better than I did myself.

A year later, the terrorist attacks on the twin towers in New York changed our world and the continuous coverage demanded enormous reserves of emotional stamina. So many talkback callers were in shock, and even those of us with no personal

Prime Minister John Howard on air, 774 ABC Melbourne studio, 2004.
[John Woudstra, *The Age*]

or immediate connection to New York and the dead and injured were still in many ways bereaved. Several days into the emergency, I cried on air and was asked if I needed a break. 'Not at all – it is authentic and what everyone is doing – so why is it a problem if I do too' was my response to the boss.

State and federal elections came and went, Mel Brooks and Jane Fonda dropped by for a chat as did Randy Newman, Joan Sutherland, Lou Reed, Steve Waugh, Cathy Freeman, Barry Humphries, Frank McCourt, James Taylor, Arundhati Roy, Noel Pearson, Joan Baez, Jackson Browne and any number of other superstars from entertainment, sport and showbiz. I cajoled Malcolm Fraser and Gough Whitlam to sit down together and talk through the dismissal, sat in awe as Sir Peter Ustinov told stories from his astonishing career, and marvelled at the intellectual command shown by Melvyn Bragg, later Lord Bragg. I pinch myself when I look back at it all. I never got used to it –

but as John Howard had taught me, they were not really coming in for me, but to talk to the audience.

Some time late in 2004, the energetic reformist Attorney-General of Victoria, Rob Hulls, asked if I would come to see him in his office. I had never met any government minister in their private offices, and it was most unusual. I accepted the invitation but as he greeted me I sensed what he was about to say and cautioned that if he was about to offer me a government job, then I had to immediately – the next day – absent myself from the airwaves. It would be totally unethical to stay on air pretending to hold the state government to account while negotiating with them for a job. He took the cue and told me obliquely that he was wondering if I could assist him by suggesting anyone who may be suitable as the next Legal Services Commissioner, the statutory officer who investigates complaints against lawyers. I told him I would contemplate who I could recommend and after calling Jan went straight back to the ABC to tell Sue Howard I was about to be offered a job. I told her it was tempting, as it came with a five-year term, a significant pay rise and a government car. On the spot, she matched the salary, and after some speedy negotiations, I also secured a six-month break after I finished three years of a four-year contract. I had to apologise to the A-G and assure him I was not playing him off against the ABC, and he graciously replied that he thought I had made the correct decision. The eventual long-service leave, in 2008, was spent on an extended overland trip with Jack, who was on a gap year. Together, we drove for six months from our front gate in Melbourne to London. Our book *From Here to There* told the story.

Within weeks of my return, while I was still getting back into the groove behind the microphone, Victoria was engulfed by the worst bushfires in the state's recorded history. Our role as emergency broadcaster meant I was totally consumed by work, day and night, for weeks. My exotic indulgent trip was suddenly forgotten. The crisis extended for not just months but over several years, right through the slow extended recovery. Being on air throughout that dreadful evening and night of Saturday 7 February 2009, when more than 170 people were killed as flames engulfed their homes and towns, is without doubt the hardest broadcasting I have ever done and tested me beyond what I thought were my limits. Some of the people who called us in desperation looking for help or just guidance did not survive. The subsequent days were harrowing and deeply emotional. The entire team at the radio station were extraordinary, selfless, totally committed and dedicated to the often distressing task. It was a privilege to be able to help individuals and communities, to assist the bereaved, smooth the recovery, to amplify the call of those struggling to be heard. I spent countless hours, even days, negotiating and sometimes threatening insurance companies, cajoling bureaucrats and politicians and smoothing the waters with the police and the coroner. We learned that families could not access their loved ones' remains for funerals – strict mass-death disaster protocols dictated that no remains were released until all remains had been identified. Funerals were delayed, trauma prolonged. The distress was heartbreaking. We ran appeals to assist those who were left with nothing but the clothes they were wearing when they fled, and etched into my memory was a talkback call from one community asking for donations of men's suits. When I suggested that overalls would be more practical for the clean-up, it was explained that suits were needed by mourners for funerals.

As the impact of the fires was slowly absorbed, broadcasting returned to a more normal pace. Opening the mail at work one morning in 2010, in between all the press releases, sample books and irate letters of complaint about my pronunciation, I gasped as a slick shiny brochure fell out of a manila envelope. The three-storey warehouse where Apollo's gym had been, in Hawke Street, West Melbourne, had been sold and was in the gleeful hands of property developers. Gentrified and converted to studio spaces and up-market residences, the Mighty Apollo Apartments incorporated his story into their marketing pitch. The familiar staircase and industrial doors, the exposed beam roof, the stunning wide wooden floorboards – all were lovingly retained and repurposed in keeping with the building's history. I chuckled to myself and wondered how Apollo would have felt with his meagre and shabby living quarters now preened and primped for yuppies. Alongside the new building, the Melbourne City Council renamed the bluestone laneway Mighty Apollo Lane, to cement his footprint on the site.

My hobby of tinkering with old cars and motorbikes continued. I had spent years accumulating a shed full of old BMW motorbikes dating from the 1950s through to the '70s, but as Jan became more and more reluctant to go pillion it became selfish to persist, and I sold them all and bought an old car. It was my main escape from stress but I never expected that my hobby would lead me back to The Mighty Apollo.

Each November, the annual Bendigo Swap Meet attracts around thirty thousand like-minded old car and motorbike afflicted idiots looking for nuggets of mechanical gold. A bunch of us have made the annual pilgrimage for decades, sifting through other people's rusty junk in the forlorn hope of finding some small car or bike part that is actually useful. The ritual is as deeply comforting as it is pointless.

The 2011 swap meet had a Mighty Apollo surprise. Although predominantly about car and motorbike bits, it is a popular event for antique and second-hand dealers as well. Trying to keep the dust and hayfever at bay, and rifling through some old wooden fruit boxes filled with cuckoo clock carcasses, out of the corner of my eye I spotted a Mighty Apollo display board. Instantly recognisable as one of the old gym decorations, I supressed an urge to excitedly pounce and instead, a model of restraint, calmly asked the stallholder lounging on his deck chair what he knew about it. Showing too much excitement about any object at a swap meet just sends the possible purchase price soaring. The tactic is to pretend to be just curious, not actually interested in buying.

'Well, *it's a bit of a story ...*' he said, as everything at a swap meet always is. '*Do you know anything about him?*' he asked. I admitted that I had met him and that he was quite a character. Brendon – the stallholder – continued, just as eager to find out more from me as I was to find out more from him. '*When they were cleaning out the old gym in West Melbourne they threw all his stuff into a skip. Before it went to the tip my mate grabbed it all and took it home. I bought a whole lot of stuff from him. There's his bed of nails, sledgehammers, A frames, a whole lot of old hand-painted signs ... all sorts of stuff.'* My performance of indifference was painfully slipping by this stage and I was seriously excited.

Further enquiries involved finding out what it would cost to relieve Brendon of his entire hoard of Apollo memorabilia. *'It owes me a couple of thousand dollars. It takes up a lot of space and it is all cluttering up my shed. I'd quite like to find someone who wants it to give it all a home.'* I could not believe what I was hearing and seeing, so I assured Brendon that I would find a home for his collection of Apollo memorabilia, feverishly took down his number, wondering whether the Anderson 'boys' (now well and truly men) would be interested, or where else it could all go. I had not been in touch with them at all since Apollo's funeral, fifteen years before. Whatever else, I knew it ought not stay in Brendon's garage. Swap meets can trigger the most serendipitous of meetings.

A few days later, I called the Mighty Apollo Gym and was relieved it was still in the hands of Paul Anderson. *'How has life treated you, Paul? It's been years since we have spoken'*, and he brought me up to speed on the family. I told him what I had found at Bendigo and asked if he or his brothers were interested. I hoped they weren't, as I quite fancied being able to mount a display of Apollo relics at home. A historic bed of nails does not come along every day after all.

Paul nearly climbed through the phone and may have shed a tear. *'I cannot believe this stuff has turned up, Jon. When Dad died, I was lost and didn't know what I was doing. Mark and Bruce went back to Queensland after the funeral, and I just wanted to clean all the old gym stuff out. I needed to get rid of all the ancient machines, no-one wanted to come near the place while it was cluttered up with all these creaky useless pieces of equipment. It had become a sort of museum of gym equipment and I hated it. I knew I couldn't get any customers in unless I modernised everything. I thought it went to the tip,'* he explained.

Paul continued: *'I got some blokes to help me and when we started tossing stuff ... I don't know what came over me but we just started throwing everything away. I was a bit out of it, a bit crazy, and I didn't really think about what I was doing. And now when I look at what I kept and I know what got tossed, I just can't believe what I did. I would love to get it all back – that would be fantastic. I don't even care what it costs – it is priceless to me.'* I admit to being slightly peeved, but there was no hesitation in my mind that all the relics were going to where they belonged. Brendon's number was passed on, and Paul immediately called and bought everything he had. I felt that I had done my good deed, but now Apollo and Thelma were back in my head. Paul and I stayed in touch and a while later I dropped in for a visit.

The Apollo Gym had relocated to Footscray, and Paul was still very much in harness. He was still getting value from paying homage to and using his father's image and reputation to augment his own. There would not be many gyms that can claim a father-son lineage and history. Paul had become a mountain of a man since I last saw him at his father's funeral. He was, simply, huge – muscles on muscles and he had that amazing walk that some athletes have where they walk on the balls of their feet, thighs pumping and shoulders rolling with each step. He wore the tightest of T-shirts and skin-tight leggings with a pair of short shorts over the top, and, together with his shaven shiny head, he looked like the sort of bloke to avoid in the unlikely event that I was out late at night.

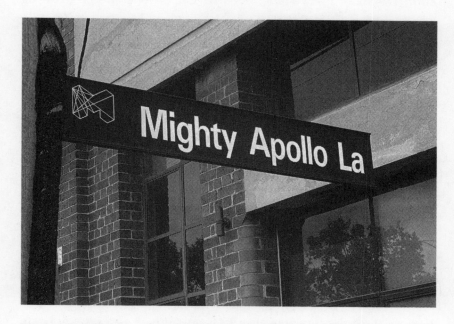

Mighty Apollo Lane off Hawke Street, West Melbourne ... Apollo
immortalised.

Paul proudly showed me the Apollo collection that formed a feature wall for the business, displaying many of the relics that had popped up from the chance encounter at the Bendigo swap. His gym was busy and he was clearly doing well, with flash shiny machines everywhere, not that I knew one end of a rowing machine from another. There were several customers sweating their way through routines and Paul made sure they were feeling loved while at the same time showing me through his Apollo collection.

'I am so grateful to get back that stuff. I can't believe I let it go. It's incredible if you think about it,' he said with genuine emotion.

At last, there was a shrine, albeit a small and private one, for 'Paul' Alexander McPherson Anderson, the small lad from the mean streets of Collingwood who had lifted himself from poverty to go on to be the world's strongest man.

Paul had been consulted about the apartments at the site of the old gym in West Melbourne and had provided the developers with some of the imagery for their marketing. He showed me a replica street sign 'Mighty Apollo Lane' and explained that as it kept getting souvenired in situ, the council had made a new batch and he bought one in memory of his father.

Apollo *'would be fucking rapt, it's like a tribute to him. And he would love it that the sign keeps getting knocked off,'* said Paul, puffing up with pride.

Apollo would indeed be delighted that a street was named in his memory. He would also chuckle to know that his old building was renovated for people who would never have dared enter when he was there.

CHAPTER 17
TRUTH TELLING

Nigel, our eldest, headed north years ago, looking for adventure as well as work. Denials that his fishing obsession lured him first to the Kimberley, then to the Territory, rang hollow. By far his best catch has been his partner, Rachel, and with their daughter, Rose, they settled in Darwin after years working around Arnhem Land and the Tiwi Islands. The capital's most appealing feature has always been its multiculturalism, although it is only a romantic who ignores the problems. But Darwin celebrates Indigenous culture like no other Australian city, and it has never failed to send a little shiver down my spine every time I wander around the streets and shops. Even in multiracial Darwin, Nigel still finds himself on the receiving end of subtle discrimination, but nothing like what he faced in his daily lived experience in Melbourne or anywhere else he has been.

On one of our now regular visits, in 2016, a welcoming John Flynn told me a few new Thelma and Top Springs stories as we tucked into dumplings over lunch. My curiosity was piqued afresh, and, with a few spare days during this trip, it was not hard to persuade Stuart, a Darwin-based friend, to go on a road trip down to Toppie to see what the pub was like now; as well as making a visit to Wave Hill (now known as Kalkarindji), together with the adjacent community of Daguragu, formerly known as Wattie Creek.

Stuart and I set off from Darwin and hit 'the Track' as the Stuart Highway is universally known, cracking lame dad jokes all the way to Katherine and then on to the Victoria Highway heading west. The turn-off to Top Springs, where the Buntine Highway diverts south, appeared as we rounded a sweeping bend, and although there were no signs at all years ago, there has since been installed a huge billboard-sized road sign. 'Wave Hill Heritage Region: Top Springs 165 km; Kalkaringi [as the sign spells it] 335 km; Halls Creek 736 km'. The bitumen ribbon down the centre of the highway got thinner at the same time as the roadside verge of soft gravel and red dirt got wider. There was just room for two vehicles to pass, but whenever a hulking road train and its attendant stones and dust bore down on us, we took the cautious approach and got off the bitumen and slowed right down to wait for the air to clear before moving on. There are few things more dangerous than braking suddenly when your car has tyres on one side firmly gripping bitumen but the other two slipping on soft red dirt. The outback is notorious for rollovers, and the rusting shells of wrecks, stripped of anything useful, are just left as reminders to the passing traffic.

The land was dry and barren – the same horizon to horizon expanse, the vast void populated by little more than ant nests and the occasional cluster of stray cattle. Cattle grids rumbled the tyres and shook the car as we ploughed on towards Top Springs.

When the unmistakeable silhouette of Wanda Inn finally appeared, shimmering in the distance like a mirage, it was as if Toppie was pulling us towards it.

My expectations were low – I remembered an almost oasis-like cluster of trees and a rough-as-guts brick pub, no glass in the windows, a concrete floor, next to no furniture and just a petrol bowser on the forecourt outside. Surely the

Wanda Inn, Top Springs, 2016.

pub would not be the same bare and bleak structure as thirty-five years before. It had changed hands multiple times since then and had been in some hot water at the Licensing Commission over the huge amounts of grog being sold to the communities of Kalkarindji, Lajamanu and Yarralin.

In 1993 the Licensing Commission heard that around $100,000 a week was being withdrawn from the ATM in Kalkarindji, but only 25 per cent of it was spent at the adjacent store. The local police said that the remainder was going on grog runs to Top Springs. One police interception of a young local behind the wheel of a dangerously overladen car revealed twenty cases of beer ferried on one trip. Although these are dry communities, it was quite normal for the drinkers to congregate just outside the town boundaries to demolish the smuggled grog, leaving a mountain of cans and bottles as their marker. Determined drinkers have little trouble circumventing the rules.

On approach, there were more trees around the pub than I remembered, and the clutter and junk had been cleared. The awning over the twin petrol pumps seemed higher, and one bowser was laced in plastic safety tape and a rough homemade cardboard 'out of order' sign. The entire complex was still as absurdly out of scale as it ever was. Thelma wanted to build something permanent and she most certainly did; the fifty years that had passed since it was built had not diminished the footprint and presence of Wanda Inn whatsoever.

We parked on the dusty forecourt, the concrete apron baking in the sun, ever-present and persistent flies the only welcoming party. The screen door banged as we entered the gloom. The bar had thankfully had a makeover and seemed almost hospitable: chairs where there used to be none, and the walls sporting huge photos and detailed coloured maps of the Victoria River district. Waist-high timber panelling changed the entire complexion of the pub, and the bare concrete floor of old was covered in brown ceramic tiles. Positively civilised, but the windows, doors and all the fridges still carried heavy steel-mesh protection. An ignored but noisy satellite-connected flat-screen TV up high above the fridge showed golf somewhere green and leafy, and a coin-operated pool table sat amidships waiting for players. The overall impression was entirely different to the ambience – if it could be called that – from the Ma Hawks era.

There was no-one around. We wandered through some optimistically installed plastic fly-deterrent ribbons on the back doors and into a dining room where three or four steel tables with plastic tablecloths and salt and pepper dispensers waited in hope. A table in the corner promised cereal ready for the morning, and an urn suggested hot water for the tea bags and instant coffee in glass jars sitting next to it. What used to be a bare, rough dirt and gravel car park was instead dotted with palm trees, patchy grass and shrubs in pots, a few benches and tables inviting outside drinking. It would be embellishment to call it a beer garden, but that is what it aspired to be. The sleep-out where I stayed all those years ago was locked, the windows covered with filthy curtains.

A middle-aged blonde woman with shoulder-length hair eventually appeared from around the side, wiping her hands on a tea towel, welcomed us, and bluntly asked if we wanted 'a beer, a room, a meal, fuel or all of them'. I explained that we were just heading through to Kalkarindji but suggested we might stop off that night or the next depending on how we travelled. 'Is there food available if we do?' She shrugged and said they could do 'a burger, chips, a steak sandwich, that sort of thing'. She quickly summed us up as a waste of her time and lost interest. I offered her some history. 'I was here in the early 1980s shortly after Ma Hawks died ... do you know about her?' seemed adequate as an opener, not sure if she would even know who Ma Hawks was. She could not have cared less, shut down attempts at conversation and disappeared back into the kitchen, leaving us to wander around.

On a shelf above the bar was propped a Slim Dusty vinyl record, *Country Way of Life*, complete with cover photo of Slim himself leaning on a gum tree with his customary hat flopping down at just the right angle. Hardly unusual in any remote Australian pub, but this one had a special twist. Track 10 is 'Top Springs', recorded by the legendary country singer in 1995, and in his trademark laconic way he celebrated a brawl at Top

Springs pub. The chorus delights that 'they never saw a blue' that matched the one at Toppie, and how the travelling shows were never going back to Top Springs, instead taking a detour to avoid it and the inevitable fights. There are four verses altogether. Slim Dusty had a pretty good handle on Top Springs, but sadly no mention of Thelma.

Out the back, only a few people were around, including a woman who introduced herself as a remote area nurse. She was sitting with a cuppa reading a book and was curious about these new arrivals, had all the time in the world for a chat, and explained she had stopped off for the night in the 'dongers', as construction huts are known. With air conditioning and a basic ensuite, the dongers provided caravan park–style accommodation, compared to the dingy rooms where I stayed with Flynn back in the '80s. We chatted about her work in Aboriginal communities, walked around some more, then fuelled up and drove on. I am not sure what I was expecting, certainly not a red carpet, but it was disappointing and deflating. Other than the occasional flash of recognition of some aspect of the buildings, there just was no connection, emotional or other. Sometimes it is better to leave memories undisturbed.

It was another ninety minutes to get to Kalkarindji and we wearily pulled up on the forecourt of the community-run general store. There were cabins to hire in the leafy tree-sprinkled camping ground alongside, and a young woman who served us behind the cash register slipped some keys off a hook and walked us across. She explained that unfortunately there was no water for the showers or toilets because just the day before a tractor broke the pipe to the pump, but we were welcome to stay for a suitably discounted fee. We unpacked our overnight bags and then wandered over to the community club for a beer.

A large metal notice over the sparse steel-and-brick bar in the Warnkurr Club laid out strict rules. 'No person on bail for an alcohol-related matter will be permitted entry. People deemed to be intoxicated will not be served alcohol.' And there followed fifteen more reasons why someone could be banned from the club for between one month and life, as well as a general prohibition on humbugging, as begging or nagging is known throughout Indigenous Australia. The club was incredibly neat and quiet, small groups of mostly men sitting around watching football on the TV or smoking and talking. We chatted with Calvin and Peter, inquisitive and friendly young men who were curious about us but guarded about their own community, and they in turn introduced us to some older men, closer to our age, who sensed a free beer might be in the offering. We did not disappoint.

Next morning, Viv Downes, the long-serving manager of the community centre, showed us through the art and craft studio and the historic archival collection documenting the Gurindji walk-off. A replica of the iconic petition to Lord Casey, the then governor-general, date stamped 19 April 1967, is the centrepiece, pleading for the return of tribal lands. The Gurindji *beg of you to hear our voices seeking that the land marked on the map be returned to the Gurindji people ...*' and actually offers '*to pay for our land the same annual rental that Vesteys now pay*'. The elders argued that they did not want an Aboriginal reserve but instead enough land to form a functioning and sustainable cattle station. They concluded: '*In August last year we walked away from the Wave Hill Cattle Station. It was said that we did this because wages were very poor (only six dollars per week), living conditions fit only for dogs, and rations consisting mainly of salt beef and bread. True enough. But we walked away for other reasons as well. To protect our women and our tribe, to try to stand on our own feet. We will never go back there.'*

The words *'to protect our women'* leapt off the page. It resonated with what I already knew of the 'frontier wars', which violently split the outback between the traditional owners and white settlers while the rest of the nation turned a blind eye. The Gurindji had something akin to a 'me too' moment in 1967.

The letter to the governor-general from the Gurindji elders (whose families gave permission for their names to be used) states *'these are our wishes, which have been written down for us by*

Frank Hardy at Kalkarindji with the famous Gurindji sign, 1968. From *The Unlucky Australians*. [Nelson/Estate of Frank Hardy]

our undersigned white friends as we have had no opportunity to learn to write English' and under the fingerprints of Vincent Lingiari, Pincher Manguari, Gerry Ngalgardji and Long-Johnny Kitgnaari are the signatures of Frank Hardy and J W Jeffrey, the Wave Hill Native Welfare Officer who defied his bosses in Darwin and Canberra and collaborated with Hardy to support the strikers.

Spread across the remaining wall space were replicas of Hardy's pencil and ink sketches of the major players from the walk-off story. The illustrations are reproduced in most editions of his book *The Unlucky Australians* and capture the very essence of the stockmen, the drovers, the union organiser Dexter Daniels and other participants. The details are exquisite and elevate the story.

The display was deeply moving. So much that has happened since and still happens now can be traced back to this very spot. The ambition and the sheer scale of enterprise harnessed in that letter was astonishing, but I saw it in the depressing context of the continued impoverishment of the adjoining communities of Daguragu and Kalkarindji. It was and still is distressing that so little of that vision has been achieved, so little of the optimism has borne fruit. I thought I had a good handle on the story of the walk-off, but my obvious ignorance of much of the detail, the sequence of events, the gravitas of this local history irritated me. It was over twenty years since Hardy's funeral and my first reading of *The Unlucky Australians* and I committed to reading it again and filling in the gaps as soon as I got back to Melbourne.

Viv introduced us to Jimmy Wavehill, one of the original strikers, an Elder (whose family gave permission for his name to be used) acknowledged as the last holder of the walk-off story, who died not long after our visit. Jimmy readily agreed to take us on a tour and be our guide, and we agreed to pay whatever his fee turned out to be. We were honoured to be escorted by a great man, a living champion of the nation's history, and it was like stepping into a time machine. He was tall and straight-backed, snowy-haired under an enormous wide-brimmed white cowboy hat and naturally gregarious. He jumped into the front seat of Stuart's car and pointed us in the direction of Daguragu, across Wattie Creek bridge and around to the historic site where the iconic moment, the pouring of sand from Gough Whitlam's fist to Vincent Lingiari's open palm, took place. The spot was marked with a plaque on a huge boulder, set on the edge of a sports ground. Jimmy talked us through the day, told how unfamiliar the strikers were with whitefella ways and the protocols and etiquettes of a prime ministerial visit, the attendant media and all the fuss that descended that day on their quiet town. He told how proud the Gurindji are of their place cemented in Australian history and, just like grandparents everywhere, he lamented that the current generation of kids were not learning enough about their culture.

After a guided tour of the town and the few remaining old buildings, Jimmy directed us back up the road for about 20 kilometres to 'old Wave Hill', yarning all the way. Little remained, mostly just debris and scrappy traces of the ruins of timber-and-iron buildings along with remnants of rotting and collapsing fencing. Guided by Jimmy, we strolled across what was left of the muster yards, the station manager's house, where the drovers' dormitories were, the laundry and workshops. He animated the ruins with his tales of life before the strike, back

Jimmy Wavehill and the plaque commemorating the Gurindji hand-over, Daguragu, 2016.

before everything changed. The Gurindji had been refugees on their own land – surviving, subsisting, dwelling there but not welcome. His depiction of how harsh this part of the Vestey empire had been still shocked us, even though we already knew that grim background.

The Vestey dynasty first invested in cattle operations in Australia in the 1930s, sensing an opportunity to secure huge tracts of cheap land and even cheaper labour. Well-connected both in England and here, they confirmed their reputation as highly litigious by contesting a claim against the Australian Tax Office all the way to the High Court, famously managing to persuade their Honours that although based in the UK and without a single family member present on this continent, they ought to be regarded as 'resident' for taxation purposes. For decades, Vesteys paid zero tax in Australia despite massive profits. Aboriginal workers were paid no wages at all, only provided with basic food and 'lodgings' which consisted of humpies, described by one government welfare inspector as '*little better than dog kennels, providing not even the most rudimentary provision for educating the children as the company argues that educating the children will only make then "cunning and cheeky" … the trouble is that they become enlightened and as a result dissatisfied with their conditions*'.

The noted anthropologists Dr Ronald and Catherine Berndt, authorities on Indigenous affairs throughout the outback, observed that they were '*appalled at an inspection* [of Wave Hill] *and could hardly believe what* [they] *saw. The Aborigines lived in crudely built shacks of old bagging and iron. These were rarely waterproof and would disintegrate in a strong wind. Sanitation and rubbish disposal was virtually non-existent. There was scarcely any access to potable water. On one station night soil was dumped in an area used to catch water in the wet season. Although the white men's drinking water was filtered or came from tank rainwater, the Aborigines were refused permission to use the station garden hose to replenish their own supplies. The hours of work were unlimited, child mortality was huge, food was often but a hunk of dry bread, a piece of cooked beef, a pannikin of sweetened tea, mouldy jam or weevilly porridge that was thrown out of the company store as not fit for Europeans. Girls as young as seven have been seen taken into traffic ostensibly to assist Europeans to avoid venereal disease. Beatings and chaining natives to trees was observed, and the*

[Vestey] *company resents any interference with "their" Natives and their attitude is "you have got to keep the n****rs in their place".* This was recorded in 1948.

Walking a while along the actual track taken by the strikers and their families as they abandoned Wave Hill and defiantly settled themselves instead at Kalkarindji is a spiritual journey. Years ago, for one of the anniversary years, it had been formalised as a walking trail and widened, graded, gravelled and signposted with glorious and elaborate historical markers. A series of tall interpretive storyboards told the history going back to before Vesteys and during their tenure, and told the bare bones of the walk-off tale. It was brilliantly done, all the more impressive for being out in the middle of nowhere.

We picnicked on egg and cheese white-bread sandwiches and lemonade from the community store as Jimmy recited his well-practised memories. We were just the latest audience in his oft-performed theatrical production, as good a show as anything you might see on any formal stage. He wanted us to understand how brave the mob were, and emphasised that from the Gurindji perspective, the walk-off had not crystallised overnight. Its origins went back long before the eventual eruption and was about far more than just wages. I was fresh from reading the remarkable book *Yijarni*, the landmark chronicle which recorded all the walk-off survivors' stories and captured them for eternity. Compiled about five years earlier, it brilliantly combined oral history with stunning photo essays depicting the very scenes we were walking through. Covering the background and build up to the walk-off, it was the ideal companion volume to Hardy's contemporary account and had the advantage of being able to look back in time. It was as if both books came alive that day.

Australia is built on racism, and we were never taught the true history of our earliest years – the birth of white settlement and the true toll it took on those who already lived here. It is at last emerging out of academia and into the mainstream after generations of embarrassing suppression. My Jewish heritage meant I was no stranger to how trauma is readily passed from generation to generation. The first lesson at synagogue Sunday School was that Jews were persecuted through history, and preservation of the culture is an act of defiance, an undoing of Hitler's holocaust, the Tsarist pogroms of the 1880s and all that preceded them for thousands of years. The startling parallels with Aboriginal trauma, as I saw through the experiences of my own son and our extended Indigenous family, sensitised me to what otherwise was usually dismissed as irrelevant or ancient history. It is neither. What is known of Australia's colonial history is but a fragment of what happened but is so shocking it hurts to read. Our obligation today is to stop looking away, to stop pretending, to stop the cover-up. It can no longer be ignored or just brushed aside as irrelevant. History is never irrelevant.

The dismissal of Aboriginal Australians began with the first white explorers, who described them as savages and the most miserable people on earth. 'Smoothing the pillow of a dying race' was the rationale behind the policy of successive colonial administrations from 1839, when the decision was made in London to appoint Matthew Moorhouse as South Australia's first Chief Protector of Aborigines. The Adelaide administration had authority until 1911 over what later became the Northern

Territory. Moorhouse was directed to instruct Aboriginal people *'in the arts of civilisation'* and *'the fundamental truths of Christianity and the habits of useful industry'*. Despite his title as 'Protector', Moorhouse was personally in charge of a raiding party that massacred an estimated thirty to fifty Barkindji people at Rufus River near Lake Victoria in 1841 after violence stemmed from white men raping Aboriginal women.

The earliest white settlers arrived around Kalkarindji in the mid-1850s, and the same pattern of conflict erupted in the Victoria River district as had happened wherever white settlers tried to occupy Aboriginal land. The rapes and murders began, with unspeakable savagery.

Around the Victoria River district by the 1890s, the notorious Constable William Willshire killed Aboriginal people in circumstances that were so appalling he was sensationally sent to trial for murder – but to the acclaim and relief of the white settlers, he was acquitted.

The pattern of degradation and murder was not unique to any single colony. The first Protector in Far North Queensland was Walter E Roth, who staged a photo of a naked Aboriginal couple 'in coitus'. His claim it was 'for purely scientific purposes' did not save him from dismissal, and he was moved to the West Indies. In Southern Queensland, Archibald Meston was appointed Protector in 1898, a position he held until 1903. His commitment to those in his care extended to having a sexual relationship with a domestic servant. In Tasmania, a genocide was underway too.

The default reaction to the slightest conflict with Aboriginal people was to 'teach them a lesson' by authorising a shooting party. Lt Colonel Boyle Travers Finniss, a former British Army officer, was appointed Government Resident in 1864 at the only white settlement in the north, at the mouth of the Adelaide River. One of Finniss's first 'parties' saw sixteen men form a posse to shoot Aboriginal men randomly on sight. Finniss was recalled, not because of the massacres but for the sins of wasting time, money and labour.

In 1885 near Daly River, four *'respected and industrious pioneers'* were murdered by *'bloodthirsty savages'*. It transpired they were in fact responsible for *'outraging Aboriginal women'*. Territory settler spokesman Alfred Giles scoffed at suggestions of *'violation of the chastity and purity of women whose chasteness was unknown. The very idea of chastity for black women is preposterous'* he declared. Shortly after, the South Australian Select Committee wrote: *'If you put rams in with ewes what do you expect ... Men are in a position where they do not see a white woman for years ... if a lot of flash young lubras are about you can hardly expect men not to touch them.'*

Sporadic killings continued: *'if not by Martini Henry rifle then by poisoned water holes ... Miners and pastoralists were shooting Aborigines like crows'* according to testimony given to another inquiry in 1898.

Tom Liddy was condemned for massacring Aboriginal people and then rasping the soles of the feet of survivors to stop them running away. Policeman Gordon Scott was found to have shaved the feet of a boy with a rasp and chained him to a tree to stop him escaping punishment for spearing a cow. Scott's behaviour became too much even for the NT police, and he was recognised as a serial basher of Aboriginal people and a drunk and was sacked.

Lutheran missionaries in South Australia introduced 'civilisation' by force if necessary, trying to replace the intact Indigenous culture with the Bible. Sympathetic early traveller Charles Priest insightfully observed how the preachers dismissed '*natives as savages because they believed in spirits. Those same priests believed in angels, immaculate conception, heaven and hell*', just substituting one set of mystical beliefs for another.

'Miscegenation' means the undesirable interbreeding of different races. A letter to the *Northern Territory Times* in Darwin in 1913 bemoaned the '*public scandal*' of babies of all colours on the breasts of Aboriginal women. '*Unless we wish the territory to go to hell altogether the government should step in and impose a heavy penalty on any white man offending in this regard. If a man is too lazy, drunken or too mean to get a wife of his own, then he should not be allowed to create a breed which is a menace to society.*'

The NT Children's Court maintained a Register of Wards, nicknamed 'The Stud Book', which registered and categorised every Aboriginal and mixed-race child into full-blood, half caste, quadroon and even octoroon. Legendary singer, gargler, early welfare officer and later Administrator of the NT Ted Egan explains, '*Aborigines were classified as town blacks, mission blacks, station blacks and bush blacks. Dreadful white overseers were just called "cheeky old buggers" rather than cruel vicious torturers*'.

People alive today remember their grandparents telling of being put into chains and being hunted. It is not ancient history. The last eyewitness to the 1928 Coniston Massacre only died in 1984.

Did Sid or Thelma know about Coniston? The last documented mass killing of Aboriginal people, it ought to be called the Coniston Massacres, plural, and occurred only twenty years before Sid and Thelma arrived at Top Springs. A white dingo trapper, Fred Brooks, was found buried a few hours' drive south-east of Top Springs, at Yukurru (Brooks Soak), down the Tanami Track. A posse of police and civilians was assembled in Alice Springs and went on to kill an unknown number of men, women and children over several sites over several months. Months. Not hours, nor days. Months. Officially, thirty-one people were killed. Recent research suggests a death toll closer to two hundred people.

Local missionaries 'made a fuss' on behalf of survivors, who explained that Brooks was killed by a man who was taking revenge for the rape of his wife. Already bewildered that fences were being built on land freely roamed for generations, and crucial waterholes were being damaged by cattle, the locals became militant when white settlers raped black women. A 'Board of Inquiry Concerning the Killing of Natives in Central Australia by Police Parties and Others' reported in January 1929. Presided over by a police magistrate from Queensland, the inquiry panel of three included Mr J C Cawood, the Government Resident – who was the official who authorised the hunting party. The obvious problem that the person responsible for the manhunt was being asked to independently investigate the manhunt was overlooked. The inquiry heard only white witnesses. They concluded that *'no provocation has been given which could reasonably account for the depredations by the Aborigines and their attacks on white men in Central Australia'.*

Despite that, in a novel development, and after a noisy campaign by local missionaries, two members of the Brooks hunting party, one a policeman, were charged, stood trial and were found not guilty.

In the witness box, Constable Murray, who had led the chase, testified:

Justice Mallam: Was it really necessary to shoot to kill in every case? Could you not have occasionally shot to wound?

Const Murray: No, Your Honour, what use is a wounded blackfella a hundred miles from civilisation?

Justice Mallam: How many did you kill?

Const Murray: Seventeen, Your Honour.

Justice Mallam: You mowed them down wholesale …?

Crimes that Brooks may have committed against Aboriginal women were never examined. It was regarded as an insult to his memory, a defamation of his character. No-one wanted a public discussion about Europeans having sex with Aboriginal women.

Another 'pioneer', celebrated at the time as a brave and adventurous explorer responsible for 'taming the outback', was 'Knock-em Down' Tommy Cody, renowned for taking the embers from fires and scarring *'blackfellas to brand them. I don't give a damn if they all get cooked – they're useless'* was his response when challenged, recounts Bill 'Yidumduma' Harney.

Chaining Aboriginal men to trees as punishment was only officially stopped in 1940. Yes, 1940. *'It was humane as long as they were chained by the neck'* rationalised Senior Inspector 'Camel Bill' McKinnon. *'A native who was chained by the neck had complete freedom of body movement. He could walk easily, with his arms free, and could move around any tree to which he was chained at night.'* He insisted it was necessary to prevent escape.

These selected examples – by no means exhaustive, and there are hundreds if not thousands more – are background to the Gurindji walk-off. The walk-off was not just about work conditions and wages, nor was it the start of the struggle for equal rights. It was simply the first time the rest of the country was confronted with the reality of Indigenous dispossession and all that it involved. Until Frank Hardy helped the Gurindji make headlines in the east coast capitals, few raised more than an occasional eyebrow about the racist and discriminatory practices that were breezily dismissed as the unavoidable collateral effects of colonisation. The first recorded strike by Aboriginal pastoral workers had been years before, in 1946 in the Pilbara in WA. That stand-off took three years to resolve and never achieved the same public recognition or made any greater impact like Wave Hill. The cynic in me suggests they needed a better media relations manager, but that observation from eighty years later is not far from the truth. But by the '60s, something had shifted.

Aboriginal rights activists – and there were many from the diverse worlds of politics, religion and medicine who pursued the unpopular cause – had been galvanised by the trial of Rupert Max Stuart, an Aboriginal man, in South Australia in 1958 and 1959. Stuart was accused of the rape and murder of Mary Hattam, a white woman, in Ceduna. The police produced a written confession, even though Stuart was illiterate. He was sentenced to death. He appealed all the way to the Privy Council in London. A brash young newspaper publisher, Rupert Murdoch, campaigned on Stuart's behalf, alleging police misconduct. Public outrage and new evidence forced a Royal Commission, which itself was accused of bias. A junior John Starke, later Frank Hardy's lawyer, had to conduct Stuart's defence solo after the QC walked out, calling the Commissioners 'the most biased tribunal

I have ever appeared before'. Stuart was saved from the gallows, educated in prison, released on parole in 1973, and eventually became Chairman of the Central Lands Council.

These tumultuous times also saw elders from Yirrkala in East Arnhem Land send a historic petition to Canberra. The Yolngu Bark Petition of 1963 pleaded with the Menzies Government to stop a new bauxite mine at nearby Gove. The Yolngu had been granted a reserve but when the site was discovered to be of phenomenal economic value with enormous bauxite deposits, they were forced to move. Their petition – now framed and displayed in Parliament House in Canberra – is an Indigenous Magna Carta.

The Menzies Government refused the Yolngu petition, instead ordering an inquiry into how compensation might be calculated, trying to attribute a dollar value to a claim about spiritual connection to land. The two are incompatible – even opposites.

With the Wave Hill walk-off in the news, the Australian people were asked in 1967 whether to change the constitution to remove discriminatory provisions and to make laws for Aboriginal Australians. Bipartisan support was secured with the strong leadership of Harold Holt, the Liberal prime minister, who recognised the need to bring his conservative party out of the postwar Menzies era. Holt stared down some of his own coalition colleagues, asserted his political authority by joining the campaign, and an astonishing 92 per cent of voters agreed.

Around the same time, activists had been campaigning for an end to an apparent colour-bar for Aboriginal servicemen to be allowed to enter or join RSL clubs. The obvious double standard there was impossible to ignore: if a man was prepared to fight and die for his country, how could he be refused equality and citizenship?

The campaign by the Yolngu from Yirrkala in Arnhem Land persisted when a young Melbourne solicitor, John Little, active within the Methodist Church, took up the cause and with heavyweight QC Ted (later Sir Edward) Woodward sued the Commonwealth and the bauxite miner Nabalco for a declaration that, since time immemorial, traditional owners had enjoyed a form of communal native title, already recognised in New Zealand and Canada.

Justice Blackburn was unsympathetic and in 1971 famously declared that *'the people belong to the land not the other way around'*. At the time, it was seen as the death of the struggle for land rights. Now we can see it became the catalyst.

Woodward advised his clients that the solution to their claim would be found through political action, not litigation. They did not have to wait long for the opportunity, and, shortly after being elected in 1972, Gough Whitlam appointed Woodward a Royal Commissioner, to develop his failed arguments in the Yolngu case into a blueprint for land rights.

Before embarking on their historic strike, the Gurindji went to court in 1965 to try to force Vesteys to pay equal wages. The Cattlemen's Association barrister was John Kerr QC, who argued the industry was unsustainable if Aboriginal stockmen were to be paid equal wages. The Gurindji won, but the Cattlemen argued for and secured a deferral for three years to allow them time to adjust. An exemption from equal pay for 'slow workers' was also granted, an escape clause for any unscrupulous boss. When they learned of their watered-down win, and realised that nothing would change, the Gurindji decided to walk off at Wave Hill.

Eight years passed between the 1967 walk-off and Whitlam's visit to Wave Hill in August 1975 for the symbolic pouring of soil, captured in the historic photo. Eight long years of activism, lobbying, campaigning and protest. There was an element of theatre to Whitlam's visit. Contrary to popular belief, the ceremony did not confer land rights at all, because land rights did not yet exist. In order to make a political point and still commemorate a commitment made, the Gurindji were granted a licence as an interim measure. Just months after, in November 1975, Whitlam was dismissed by Sir John Kerr. Despite enormous pressure from pastoralists and mining companies, Malcolm Fraser finished the job of steering Whitlam's land rights laws through the parliament.

Interestingly, one of the early land rights cases was about Top Springs. In 1979 the Land Claims Commissioner, former High Court judge John Toohey, heard the Yingawunarri (Old Top Springs) claim by the Mudbura people of Top Springs. Thelma Hawks lodged an objection to their claim. Her concerns were twofold – that her mother was buried there and that the airstrip was important for her business. She represented herself at the hearing, speaking in support of her written submission. Commissioner Toohey ruled that she would not lose access to either the airstrip nor her mother's grave and would suffer no detriment whatsoever. The traditional owners satisfied him that they enjoyed a genuine, enduring and continuous connection to the land. There is no record of Thelma's reaction.

Eventually, the ultimate legal breakthrough on native title came from the most unlikely of places. Eddie Mabo from the tiny Torres Strait island of Mer (Murray Island) had commenced his

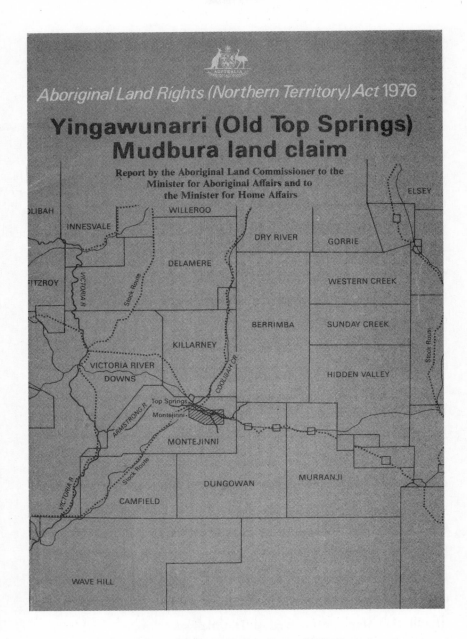

The Report on the Yingawunarri (Old Top Springs) Mudbura Land Claim, 1980.

claim in 1981. After years of legal skirmishes, particularly with the since discredited Bjelke-Petersen government in Queensland, in 1992, the High Court dumped the fiction of the empty land. At last, the shadow of 'terra nullius' was lifted.

Back with Jimmy Wavehill at Kalkarindji, these timelines and this extraordinary decades-long struggle were swirling through my head, a spaghetti of information mixing with the dust and the menacing dogs. Jimmy led us across the patches of struggling grass to the community art centre. We were introduced in rapid succession to a dozen mostly older painters, all head down concentrating over their canvases, brushes dipping into old soup tins for colour and water. The incomplete paintings were magnificent and mostly huge, so T-shirts became our only souvenirs. As with all Indigenous communities, you either stopped for a few weeks and sat down and talked to people in their own time or you remained a blow-in and were treated accordingly. To quote Charlie Ward, local historian, *'whites are like cars – to be used until broken and then replaced with a newer model'*. It was the natural order, and eventually after a cuppa and a chat we jumped back into Stuart's Jeep and headed back the few hours to Top Springs, planning to stop there for the second night. As we got to the concrete forecourt – the broken petrol pump, the bottles and cans under the bushes, the inhospitable welcome – we both agreed we could not face wallowing uncomfortably and eating badly just to indulge my nostalgic connection. Instead, we pressed on to Katherine and a decent pub steak and chips, then the next day back to Darwin. Within a few days Jan and I were in Melbourne, and I was back to my routine, chattering away in a radio studio every morning, in a world so different it was hard to reconcile the two.

Fresh from walking in the red dust, I again read Frank Hardy's *The Unlucky Australians*. This time, my responses were completely different, with the characters, the places, the smell, the light in mind, as if Wave Hill came into our home. I could sense the rusty iron, feel the air and the splinters in my fingers from the dry timber fence posts poking out of the dirt. When our dog nuzzled at my knee, agitating for a walk, it brought to mind the mangy and thin creatures that lounge around Aboriginal towns.

Reading Hardy's book the first time, years ago, was confronting enough. Re-reading it in the light of today's sensibilities is something else again. Why are we still grappling with so many of the exact same issues more than fifty years after it was written? When did we stop listening? How do we pretend that living conditions in remote Aboriginal communities are anything other than scandalous, shameful and a stain on our collective humanity? It is as extraordinary a story from today's perspective as it was then.

Early in *The Unlucky Australians*, we are introduced to Dexter Daniels, the Darwin-based Indigenous organiser for the Northern Australian Workers Union, 'the real hero' of the Gurindji walk-off. '*They know how to wait, those people,*' Hardy learns from Daniels, who '*looks younger than his years early in life and older than his years later in life*'. Upsetting the powerful cattle-station owners and their business interests was not a recipe for popularity in Darwin back then any more than it is today. Lonely as he was, and despite the lack of meaningful support, Dexter Daniels had been given the job of being the 'blackfellas' union organiser' by the NAWU and he more than met the brief. So successful was he that Daniels was first warned, then arrested. In the absence of anything else to accuse him of, he was charged with vagrancy. According to local legal legend, 'he is the only vagrant who went bail for himself' which amply demonstrated the absurdity of the prosecution.

Spending time drinking and yarning in Darwin, Hardy met Robert Tudawali, an Aboriginal actor famous throughout Australia for his pioneering film role in *Jedda*, a story of forbidden love vaguely along *Romeo and Juliet* lines. Tudawali and Dexter Daniels told Hardy about what had just happened down at Wave Hill, and sensing a way to stir things politically while also making some money, Hardy got both the ABC's *Four Corners* and Rupert Murdoch's new and emerging national broadsheet *The Australian* interested in buying some reports – if he could get good copy. He hitched a ride with a delivery truck and headed down the highway to learn more. He was not without insight of the risks – '*The obsessive involvement with the Aborigines could only further complicate the turmoil in my creative sub-conscious …*' – but the attraction was the story, and what a strong and compelling yarn he uncovered.

On arrival at Wave Hill, where the Gurindji were running out of food since Vesteys cut them off, Hardy met the local welfare officer, the remarkable Bill Jeffrey, and his wife, Ann. Hardy wrote, '*Jeffrey is braver than any other white man*' and said he could not talk about him without getting a lump in his throat. Typically, for decades, the 'welfare' people were regarded as being the representatives of white authority and thus on the side of the cattlemen. But the extent to which Jeffrey was prepared to bend the rules and risk his own job and career to support the strikers was astonishing. Jeffrey had legal responsibility to '*provide tucker for lactating mothers and infants. There were a lot of lactating mothers around the strike camp. Some of them were men*'. Jeffrey explained to the Gurindji that the welfare department head office had warned that if the stockmen did not go back to work, the government would stop any supplies getting through. Lingiari replied: *'That's ok, we got plenty fish, goanna, turtle and kangaroo at Wattie Creek. We live on Aborigine tucker.'*

The regular and outrageous practice of white ringers and jackaroos sending black stockmen bush on horses while they had cars *'and could drive back to the main station and use their women'* while the menfolk were away bush is identified in the book as a flashpoint in the walk-off. Hardy reports that *'wages and conditions were a secondary issue – their primary concern was the contempt in which they have always been held'*, in particular the abuse of Gurindji women by the very men who were pretending to be on good terms working with their husbands and fathers.

Hardy inserted himself into the Gurindji negotiations at every turn. He used his networks with church, union and ALP figures in Melbourne and Sydney to advance the Gurindji cause. Critical to the eventual success was an up-and-coming ALP politician, Gordon Bryant, who later became Whitlam's first Minister for Aboriginal Affairs, advised by a young academic lawyer, Gareth Evans. Hardy galvanised support, particularly with student activists. He forged connections with Abschol, the Aboriginal Affairs Department of the National Union of Australian University Students. Their activism had started back in the 1950s, originally offering tutoring and raising funds for scholarships – the first of which was awarded to Charlie Perkins, who led the 'Freedom Ride', a remarkable turning point in Australian awareness of racial discrimination.

As I read more about Abschol, a name jumped at me from the page. The reports named a Tony Lawson as the director of Abschol in 1970 and '71. My mentor at Fitzroy Legal Service when I was a volunteer, and the lawyer who moved my admission to practise in 1982, was Tony Lawson. I had never known of the connection. I called Tony, who laughed and said, *'I joined when I started at Monash in '67 and got more involved over a few years. Tom Roper* [later a minister in the Cain Government] *was my predecessor, and we raised money for a truck, pumps and some housing for the Gurindji. We gave them money for lobbying and publicity as well. We sponsored Vincent Lingiari to come south to talk and raise some more money and support, and he talked about the need to protect culture, not just wages and conditions'*.

It was typical of our western values that the Gurindji dispute about culture, tradition and respect had been turned instead into a simple commercial transaction. The Gurindji told anyone who was listening that their concerns were about wages, conditions, rape – and respect. We stripped away the last two because we did not know how to confront the unthinkable. We instead whittled their concerns down to something we could put a simple transactional value to, a dollar figure that, to our way of thinking, ought to solve the problem and make it go away. But everyone involved, black and white, reinforced that the undercurrent, the build-up to the walk-off was much more nuanced.

Tony continued: *'I accompanied Mick Rangiari to Canberra for a meeting with the minister Peter Nixon; he was a senior minister in Fraser's government and a National Party powerbroker. He agreed to meet us, but Rangiari was scared of Nixon, and in the meeting – it was terrible, he was lording it over him, it was reprehensible really as we look back on it. It was the time of the challenge to apartheid in South Africa and black power in the US, and they were really worried it would happen here too. The miners were scared, the farmers were worried – they all took the same approach. Their attitude was that the land was there to be used up, you leave a mess and walk away. Gordon Bryant* [Shadow Minister for Aboriginal Affairs] *was wonderful – we could use his office when we were there and he would support us whatever we were doing. One time we brought Hardy down to speak at a protest and he was staying at Bob Hawke's place in Sandringham* [Hawke was then the head of the ACTU]. *He was supposed to speak to a demo we had organised outside a Vesteys butcher's shop and I went down to collect Hardy in my car. He kept saying "just a minute, comrade", and I was waiting and waiting. Eventually I said to Frank that we were going to be too late – the crowd would not be there anymore. It took him ages to come out and all because he was putting some bets on a bloody horse race and we were too late for the demo.'* Not for the first time had Hardy got his priorities somewhat skewed.

Vincent Lingiari has many times recounted the details of the Gurindji walk-off, and his well-documented version meshes seamlessly with Hardy's remarkable contemporary account. Lingiari told how they lost faith in the promises being made to them, time after time: *'You promised a lot, promise to build house, big tank on top of hill, big pipe and bore … I'm full of you blokes, don't want nothing out of you blokes no more. Two years of promise – nothing. Bad tucker, no killer, just bones. It was my place before you came over the top of me … this place, this country was mine, he was Aboriginal land.'*

Did the Gurindji walk-off succeed? It depends on your definition of success. What is unarguable is that the attempt to establish a sustainable working cattle station at Kalkarindji, a romantic dream, failed miserably. Valuable stud bulls were killed for meat instead of being preserved for breeding. Vehicles were abused to the point of collapse and valuable farming machinery regularly broke from lack of basic maintenance. The Gurindji Pastoral Company went broke after years of financial support, and for a while, a subsidiary of Vesteys leased back the land until they too decided to pack up and leave. While purporting to encourage autonomy in remote communities, years of interventions by governments, federal and Territorian, in welfare, health, education and land care, among other areas, has in fact had the opposite effect. The cattle operations have ended up in the hands of white managers, with limited jobs for locals and zero community involvement other than for the administration of the townships. Government schemes that were supposed to foster self-management have left the Gurindji more dependent on the indispensable white staff. Depressing stuff.

Hardy was a great storyteller and yarn spinner. Maybe his account from Wave Hill was embellished, maybe he had taken licence, maybe he exaggerated what had happened there. Motivated by resentment harboured from being put on trial for the publication of *Power without Glory* mixed with the attempts by Menzies to make communism illegal, had he mixed reportage with mischief and rebellion?

Far more likely, Hardy saw the Gurindji struggle as the epic tale that it was. As a man and as a writer he knew no fear, and he relished any chance to get into a fight for the underdog.

He boldly tackled the greatest taboo in the land – our racism towards the original inhabitants – and devoted his formidable skills and networks to change this nation for the better, and forever. And he must have stopped off a few times for a beer at the Top Springs pub. Although he barely mentions Toppie, I imagine Frank Hardy meeting Thelma Hawks. They would have got into a blue – you could have sold tickets to a few rounds between the legendary yarn-spinning commie agitator and 'old leather-tits' – the sparks would have flown. Neither would have been prepared to take a backward step. It is even fair to speculate that the absence of more mentions of Top Springs in *The Unlucky Australians* may well be explained by a refusal of the Gurindji and their supporters to patronise Thelma's store or pub except when it could not be avoided.

We cannot pretend the atrocities – the rapes, the murders – did not happen. These unpalatable truths have been avoided for well over one hundred years. We can no longer look away. When Aboriginal men took revenge for the rape of wives and daughters, the attacks by 'wild blacks' were recorded as being about anything except rape. They were instead described as disputes over cattle, land or access to water. There was never going to be candid discussion about that dreadful aspect of remote life. It was air-brushed from our national story.

Truth telling is incompatible with denial. Chasing stories about Thelma, Sid and Top Springs took me on a trip, not just down a dusty dirt road but into my own not-that-distant past. There is no turning back. I cannot 'un-see' these stories, hidden as they have been, omitted from the curriculum as they were.

Apollo was fastidious in boastfully recording and documenting his every feat. Thelma was secretive and left few traces about any aspect of her life, making detection slow and complex. But stories that need to be told have a way of emerging, regardless.

* * *

The birth of Nigel and Rachel's daughter, Rose, our first grandchild, in October 2016, and the steady decline in the health of both of my nonagenarian parents, triggered a rethink of my priorities as I turned sixty. I told the ABC that I wanted to quit and planned my exit. Much as I loved the gig, it could not last forever. I was persuaded to stay a few more years.

I resigned from and finished at the ABC in November 2019. After twenty-three years of 4.15 am alarms and sleep deficits, after thirty years working for that amazing organisation on a range of different shows, I wanted to do other things with whatever was left of my working life. Although talk radio is the perfect job for unattractive people with short attention spans and an overdeveloped sense of self-importance, I dreaded overstaying my welcome. I feared the day when I would forget a name, a date, a detail. I could sense my reactions slowing, like a footballer getting towards the inevitable end. I never wanted to hear someone say, 'He's not as sharp as he used to be'.

It is always better to decide when to pull the pin yourself, rather than someone making that decision for you. I had seen so many amazing broadcasters publicly ripped away from the microphone before they wanted to go, many never recovering from the humiliation and loss. Withdrawing from any drug causes emotional as well as physical reactions, and being on the radio for decades carries the risk that the adrenaline and self-importance becomes addictive. The illusion that any one presenter on one shift on one radio station on one wavelength in one city was somehow important, that everyone saw the world through my eyes, is a trap and I was tired of it to my core. Add the pressure from the organisation to constantly project the brand through the sometimes toxic social media accounts that are regarded as essential parts of being 'on air', and it all amounts to turbo-charged narcissism. The superficiality of what my trade involved – its underpinnings – were the artifice of being a 'personality' or, even worse, being called a 'star'. It was time to reintroduce myself to the real world.

CHAPTER 18
FAME OR FORTUNE?

I only met Thelma Hawks after she died – and it turned out I did not really like her. She may have seemed a lovable rogue to some, but I suspect if we had crossed paths I would not have seen her that way. Just a rogue, forget the lovable bit. I have little doubt we would have clashed. She was selfish, focused on accumulating wealth no matter how, and adopted her own moral code. She showed little interest in the wellbeing of anyone else, including those in desperate need around her. She exploited relationships ruthlessly and with no regard for reputational damage. She undoubtedly was racist, but was hardly alone for that time and place. I am glad I only had to look after her in death, not in life.

When we were introduced, Apollo was just another client, albeit atypical for the entrepreneurial on-the-make types that seemed to be the usual client at Barker Harty & Co back in 1982. He was not a suit, nor a wannabe get-rich-quick, on the make wheeler and dealer. He and his sons were just mug punters sitting nervously in the stuffy reception area, waiting to be ushered in to the swanky office with the jaw-dropping views. The Andersons were beneficiary rabbits in the testamentary headlights, caught in a fight on unfamiliar turf. Although Apollo was an unbeatable champion in a different arena, he was powerless there, and like many, he found out how blunt a weapon, how unaffordable and unwieldy, the legal system often turned out to be.

Looking back forty years, it disappoints me to realise that back then I did exactly what I criticise so many professionals for doing now. I diagnosed the disease and successfully treated the symptoms – but not the entire patient. I saw Apollo and his sons as a discrete legal problem, not complex human beings living difficult lives and needing help. I disconnected them from their story, wrapped their Auntie Thelma's estate into legal bubble wrap, and approached them as if they were just another file on my desk, not a family in distress. I did a technically good job, undercharged them and more than earned my fees, squeezed every one of the claimants trying to get any of Thelma's money, and maximised the payout for her three nephews. But was that superficial outcome in their best interests overall?

Decades later, with hindsight, when all those lives have been half lived and the consequences of decisions taken so long ago can be seen in a different light, it undoubtedly would have been better if everyone involved had compromised early and agreed to resolve Thelma's estate quickly, albeit for a little less. Thelma's money would have been best put to removing the three Anderson boys from the brutal state care they were in and rehousing them somewhere suitable with their father. Even Norman Douglas could have escaped the alcoholic fug of Wanda Inn, banked his payout and headed off to rehab earlier and with more good years to enjoy in his snug home on the riverbank at Katherine.

Sadly, those were not my instructions. Apollo, tight as ever but this time even tighter on behalf of his boys, did not want Thelma's estate to pay out a cent more than was absolutely needed – to anyone. John Flynn was following the rules meticulously, and I was too young and inexperienced to be able to grab everybody involved and shake them out of their habit of simply following the template and doing what lawyers always do – squabble over money. But if confronted with the same scenario today, I would insist on the parties sitting down for a mediation to thrash out an early compromise so everyone could get on with their lives.

But it was not up to just me. Apollo, to his core, was a fighter in every part of his life. Bruce expresses his father's philosophy: '*You are either a wolf or a sheep, and only the wolf survives.*' He was so combative, so competitive that I am not sure he would have accepted an early compromise even if it had been recommended and offered. While he was not happy his sons were in state care, he could not contemplate any alternative. His career and fame were all that mattered. He had always been so single-minded, this smallest son in a large family, the runt of the litter who became a legend and achieved the unimaginable.

'*It was always about survival; pure and simple*' continues Bruce. '*I have NO idea how he could do things. How can someone have an elephant stand on them and survive? And the tram! I just don't know anymore. It is supposed to kill you, that stuff, but he thought of himself as a giant and he thought of the tram as a toy. He would psych himself up in the gym, and he would say "I am the Mighty Apollo, I can do anything". It was like magic; he was a freak. He would challenge guys in the gym to try to knock him over and no-one ever could, not even*

Apollo claiming the world record for sequentially being run over by cars.

the really big guys. He was like a fire plug – solid as, but only a bit over five feet tall.'

Mark has the same reverence for his father. *'He wasn't like normal people. He was a superstar. It's not like he would go every day to the office, then knock off work, come home for tea and become Mr Anderson instead of the Mighty Apollo.'* Paul chips in too. *'It is impossible to imagine him living in a house and us all being a family again. It would have been totally alien to him.'*

Warmly appraising his father's remarkable drive, Mark adds: *'He was always Apollo. He never switched off. He sacrificed himself to his own mythology, and as society changed around him, he just created opportunities, visualising his future and reinventing himself. Remember, he came from pretty humble beginnings and was completely self-made. His self-belief was incredible; in an industry that rewards innovation, he totally reset what it meant to be a strongman.'* Mark is the clearest about how his father extracted commercial leverage from his physical ability and appreciates how difficult it must have been for a short-statured, lightly schooled kid from the impoverished streets of Collingwood to forge his own path through the showbiz jungle.

'All the TV appearances and the endless newspaper pieces – he did all that himself, no-one was hired to do it for him, taught him or even showed him. He had the instinct from somewhere; pretty amazing,' explains Mark. I never thought about Apollo's capacity for self-promotion as a gift, but Mark is correct in his eulogy. Apollo was not just a natural showman but also a natural media performer, back when TV and radio were just starting to provide commercial opportunities. There were few role models and no self-help manuals. Despite all his years of chasing publicity, all his self-promotion and relentless drive, there was curiously scant

commercial success, no evidence of great riches at the end of the weightlifting rainbow.

'The gym was like a mausoleum by the end, and a lot of people were ripping him off. He got nothing for what he did – he didn't do stuff for money. If he had, he would have been a millionaire, but he was focused on fame, not money,' says Mark.

Why had Apollo ended up with so little to show for his glittering career? The business seemed to prosper, yet he lived like a pauper. Where did it all go? *'When Apollo died, we each got a modest sum of cash and that was all there was, along with all those antiques – but there was no property, no shares, he never made serious money,'* says Paul. Apollo worked for twenty years after the separation with Rondahe. *'He had been in hospital for nearly a year when he had the breakdown, and when he came out there were two gyms, rent was owing, he had to close one and start all over again, and there were some so-called friends who ripped him off and stole stuff … I don't really want to go into it, but a lot of men would have just given up. You have to admire him. He came out of hospital and said, "I'm back". He battled on, did well for a decade, then didn't keep up to date. The industry had changed by the '80s, and he didn't, so he never really caught up again. By the '90s, the gym was not really functioning; it was more like his home, and he wasn't really making any money,'* says Paul.

What about the theory aired by Thelma's ex-husband, Sid Hawks, that Thelma was slyly sending money to Apollo to buy a building for his gym? Sid attributed the failure of their marriage to Thelma draining their bank accounts for Apollo's benefit. *'Anyone who says Auntie Thelma was sending him money is talking rubbish. Sid doesn't know what he is talking about. When Incubator*

Apollo's final performance, with Paul junior holding a bluestone block, Bruce looking on.

left, they had a heap of debt and he had to work his guts out to recover. What was he smoking?' scoffs the eldest son.

'At his peak, Apollo was a celebrity and it seemed so glamorous. At the motorbike shops in Elizabeth Street, where all those bikies gather – really tough guys, you wouldn't mess with them – they'd greet him like an uncle. A sea of bikies would part for him when he walked down the street. Towards the end I tried to get Dad out from living at the gym, but he was a prisoner to it by then. He went to live with Bruce in the country but got all depressed, went into the nursing home and was miserable until he died. I would look at Dad when he was old and think, "Who is this stranger?" He was always tough but he was so guarded about himself. We wished we could live with him, but we needed a proper home. He worked from ten to ten, he couldn't be a

parent as well. No wonder I never had kids. I always worried I would end up like Dad did, living in an old gym like a dinosaur – forgotten and ignored, people not giving a shit. He was like an animal in a zoo. People would visit and laugh at him behind his back.'

Paul is still fit, still training clients at his state-of-the-art gym, now one of the biggest and best equipped in Melbourne. He bounces around the space, restless and energetic. His house is as meticulous as his father's gym was chaotic. He displays medals, trophies and certificates from his athletics career, when he excelled as a junior and senior decathlete, hurdler and, later, as a state and national title-holding power lifter where he competed internationally. He attended the prestigious Institute of Sport, recounting that he *'stuffed up the pole vault at the trials for the Edinburgh Commonwealth Games – I used the wrong pole, and missed it completely, and even though I was ahead on all the other events I crashed out. Then the same thing when I was Victorian champion and trialled for the Seoul Olympics. This time I crashed in the hurdles, and hurt my back and couldn't do the javelin, so that was the end of that. It was cruel, and even though I loved athletics and was good at it I could see I wasn't good enough to be the best. I got depressed and walked away – then realised I enjoyed weightlifting more than athletics and got back into it. I bulked up without steroids, did security at nightclubs to make some money and after some detours got back into gyms. Is it my destiny? Dad called me "Little Apollo" and then the "New Young Apollo" as a kid, and I had to break out from that identity. It messed with my head but gave me a path, not a destiny but a path. I always worried about money. I was determined not to end up like Dad'.* Paul's eyes redden for a moment, and he swallows hard as he remembers back twenty-five years to when his father died.

What did the young heirs do with their money from Thelma? Each nephew got a trust account cheque for $77,000 in 1986 and I urged them to buy a house or to make some long-term investments. I steered them towards getting advice from Gavin Anderson, a financial 'guru' who regularly helped clients at Holding Redlich & Co who had large sums to invest after their court cases were finalised. The Andersons were not interested and it was just as well. Gavin Anderson turned out to be a fraudster and ripped off millions of dollars from dozens of people, including members of my own family. To try to recover their money, I acted for my parents and sister, sued him, and after years of tussles where I refused to give up, eventually bankrupted him. In the meantime, he magically had shed all his assets and never repaid anyone a cent. Relentless pressure on the police ensured he was charged; though it was a hollow victory, it was somehow satisfying to be sitting in the County Court to eyeball him and watch as he was sent to gaol.

Years later, chatting to Paul, I asked what he did with his money. Did he take any notice of my advice not to 'piss it up against the wall'? Did he ever invest any of it? Paul grins. *'You kidding? Nah, I blew it on a Mazda RX7 and then handed over heaps of money to a string of pretty impressive girls who never paid any of it back.'* He laughs heartily, and I have to join in.

Back then, Mark wanted to go and work at the Top Springs pub. He was nineteen years old when we first met, and somehow thought he could survive at Top Springs. He laughs now at the memory and explains that he wanted to see if he could hack it in the outback. He thought he could do an apprenticeship or work as a jackaroo. *'I didn't want the keys handed to me … I knew I*

couldn't do that. But I thought it would be a good opportunity to learn.'
He was not long out of foster care, struggling to find work that
suited him. Eventually he took off around Australia with a mate
on underpowered motorbikes. His riotous adventures included a
short stint in prison in the NT for racing unregistered down the
main street of Darwin in the early hours of the morning. *'I'd
been in institutions most of my life so the lock-up wasn't that bad,'* he
shrugs. Eventually, he invested heavily in buying 'state of the art'
video cameras, lights and editing equipment, hoping to establish
a business. More easily said than done, and after a few successful
years the equipment was superseded and eventually became
worthless. Thankfully, those years included capturing many of
his father's stories on what is now priceless video.

Mark is remarkably candid about the emotional scar tissue.
*'I am still dealing with all this shit years later; the wounds have
never resolved. I've never had kids and I would not want anyone
to have to go through what happened to us. But I've had enough.
I learned to suppress my thoughts and my emotions, like you do in
a prison, and to shut off everything to avoid the pain. I got my file
from the welfare through Freedom of Information. It says I was
moody, protective of my possessions and had not been taught to share,
that I did not like to be disturbed when concentrating. Too right.
Apparently, they thought I liked Sunday School. I hated Sunday
School but pretended to like it to avoid being beaten. It was good
to read my file. It proved that all this shit happened, and I wasn't
making it up. I'm better at dealing with it now, but when I was
younger ...'* His voice trails off.

Bruce was the most cautious and used Thelma's money to set
himself up with quality carpentry tools, a classic old Ford and

The Mighty Apollo, Champion of Champions, in his prime.

a house before eventually joining the army. Because he was so young when his mother left, he was in foster care the longest and had a different relationship with Apollo. '*He was far from a perfect father; an amazing man but in lots of ways a pretty crappy father, with no sense of perspective. Everything else was secondary to his sense of himself. There is no point not being honest. I am not bad-mouthing him – just saying it how it was. He chased his fame at the cost of personal relationships and family. He made choices which he said were for the business, and he built that business and reputation all himself, and was this larger-than-life figure. That takes a lot of maintenance. There were no tricks or fakery in what he did – he just devoted his whole life to being The Mighty Apollo, whatever that meant, and there was no room for Alex Anderson, who got left behind. When he couldn't be Apollo anymore there was just this shell of his former self; it was really sad.*'

Twenty-five years after his father died, Bruce sniffs as he sheds a tear talking about him. '*I was in awe of him, but I never knew what to say at school, when people found out he was my dad. I used to say my dad's a brickie or a truck driver or something because otherwise it was like having Superman as your bloody father, and I just wanted to be normal. When I put him on the plane in December a few months before he died, I knew I'd never see him again. If he had to stop being Apollo to be a better father – if he had to be some bloke running a gym – he wouldn't have known how to do that. And he couldn't be both. Although I am sure he would have liked to have seen more of us, he would not regret having been The Mighty Apollo, not even for a second. That was just who he was.*'

Over the years, Apollo assured me several times that Thelma had been trying to sell Wanda Inn so she could quit the Territory, return to Melbourne, buy a house and provide for them both in their old age. Her sudden and untimely death left him stuck in his draughty gym, with only ratty accommodation and noisy plumbing. When his three young sons collected their inheritance, he never asked any of them for money nor sought to impose on them for support. Bruce remembers '*when Thelma died, Dad was really upset and stopped eating. It was a bit like when Rondahe left and he had his big breakdown*'. He realised not only that his sister was gone but so were his prospects of a comfortable old age. The windfall from her estate was an opportunity to reunite with his sons, but none of them saw any reason to chase the romantic notion of living as a family unit after so long apart. They all went their separate ways.

The enduring respect the three sons each have for their legendary father is ample recognition of his positive impact on their lives. Their resentment towards their mother is evidence of the precise opposite – as adults their relationship was uniformly negative and toxic. My own encounters with Apollo left me fond of him, fundamentally insecure though he was. He lived his life inside his own head, determined to prove his worth to himself and everyone around him. He struggled with personal relationships, was entirely transactional and narcissistically self-absorbed. Was his personality because of or despite the allure of showbiz? It is hard to know. His rough charm always overwhelmed the unpleasantness that often accompanies the signature selfishness of the performer.

Almost one hundred years ago, two working-class kids from Collingwood set off into the world. Both ended up as loners after the disruption and aftershocks of a failed marriage. Both put their lives back together and pushed on. He sought fame, she sought fortune. Both found some of what they wanted, but neither found it to the degree they craved.

Thelma made lots of money, many enemies and few friends. She massively overcapitalised Wanda Inn. Her legacy, an oversized folly, still has not found a fraction of the patrons it was built for fifty years ago. There is no recognition whatsoever of her vision, her contribution or even her existence.

There is no Thelma Hawks shrine, nor a memorial, portrait or even a sign mentioning her at Top Springs.

Apollo died with little money but found fame. He entered folklore. For decades, he was everywhere – in the papers, on TV, at charity events, on billboards. But that currency relies entirely on physical prowess and is fickle and transient, like the fame of film stars trading on their good looks. Ironically, as his feats of physical strength recede into the past, his enduring legacy, like Thelma's, is also a building. The Mighty Apollo Apartments and cafe in Hawke Street, West Melbourne, are the brick-and-mortar reminder of the man that was there decades before.

Although Apollo just rented the top floor of the old warehouse for a bit more than a decade, the entire precinct now celebrates him. As long-lasting as its bluestone pitchers, Mighty Apollo Lane will carry his name and memory into perpetuity.

Apollo found the immortality he craved.

AFTERWORD

October 2021

I head to the local post office to collect the mail and plan to ask the manager to witness a statutory declaration. As I arrive, John Morrow walks past. Now a local solicitor, John was the partner at Barker Harty & Co who interviewed me when I was in final year of law school and offered me the opportunity to do my Articles of Clerkship with the firm in 1981. In the more than forty years since, we have bumped into each other from time to time, exchanged pleasantries and the like, but not much more.

We chat for a bit, and he readily agrees to sign the stat dec and ushers me up the stairs to his office. We do the biz with little fuss and then swap COVID stories, a common theme that now passes for normal in all conversation.

'How's retirement post-ABC? What have you been doing?' he asks, as I look around his ordered desk and shelves. Mountainous stacks of files, briefs and lever arch binders are displayed efficiently for the battles either recently waged or still to come. Back in the day, I learned John was a ferocious commercial litigator and, quite clearly, he is still in full harness.

'I've just finished a book – you might be amused to know I write a little about Barker Harty, and a disputed estate file I was given when I first qualified,' I explain.

'Is that the one where you went to Darwin?' he replies, and I am astonished that he remembers. I remind him of just the briefest outline of the Estate of T C Hawks, and he chuckles at the blast from our past. We reminisce about that period, characters of the firm, who had died, who had left the law and so on. He starts telling of his own experience of being an articled clerk, and I nearly fall of my chair.

'I was articled to a bloke in Chadstone, Leon Clancy, but halfway in he shot through to Queensland and I had to get my articles reassigned to another lawyer ...,' starts John.

'What? Stop! Leon Clancy? You're kidding ... did he end up in Darwin?' I interrupt. John nods in agreement.

'He was Thelma's lawyer, who did the will that triggered the entire dispute in her estate ... I've wondered about him for years,' I stumble to explain.

'Yeah, that's the bloke – he was a shocker,' responds John, settling back further into his chair, warming to the always welcome task of reminiscing, grinning at making the connection. 'Despite being a strict Catholic and very churchy, Clancy had a terrible reputation, was widely thought to be shagging a mistress and was pretty rough with his wife Marguerite. I challenged him about it one time and he told me that because he went to confession, he was forgiven his sins each Sunday and could just start again, and keep going! I was appalled. Not surprisingly his wife insisted they leave Melbourne and put it behind them. They moved to Queensland, but his girlfriend followed and the affair continued up there, so they moved again, to Darwin.'

I am chortling, simultaneously incredulous and amused that after so long hoping for information about Clancy and failing so spectacularly, I now belatedly stumble on this connection – not buried deep in the archives, but from someone I've known for years and in my own neighbourhood. It was an incredible coincidence. 'You are kidding me ... did you know he got busted for trust account fraud and went to prison? That's why Thelma crossed him out as executor of her will ...'

'You bet I knew,' John replies, scratching his chin and searching for clearer memories. 'I was working at Galbally's a few years later, and out of the blue I got a call from Darwin. Clancy is on the phone and tells me he's in a bit of a jam, has been caught fiddling the books and he's asking me, a junior lawyer at Galbally's, if Frank would help him as he was probably heading to prison.'

Frank Galbally was the endlessly self-promoting boss of his eponymous firm who had become the 'go-to' advocate for white- and blue-collar crooks alike across Australia in the 1970s and beyond. Blessed with a silver tongue and flowing hair to match, he was a solicitor advocate, a hybrid, shunning the more conventional path and rewards awaiting him as a barrister. Frequently outwitting and out-talking the QCs, he was typically opposed to, despite not having their level of formal training, he cut a formidable figure, grandstanding in the media and through the nation's courts for decades.

John continued. 'Frank went up to Darwin; I think he kept Clancy's sentence down to six months or something, but the poor fella ended up in a mental hospital, and I don't know what happened to him after that. His lovely wife came back to Melbourne and the nuns put her up at Abbotsford Convent for a while until they found her a house around the corner here in North Fitzroy.'

Now I am totally amazed. The Abbotsford Convent is where I have spent the last eighteen months, squirrelled away writing this book, hunched over my screen in one of the former nuns' cells. The deconsecrated convent was years ago saved from property developers by a vigorous community campaign, and has been successfully converted into a cultural precinct. The notion that Mrs Clancy was looking over my shoulder while I wrote about the fallout of her ex-husband's deceit, and that she lived around the corner from our home, is beyond hilarious. We must have been neighbours.

John Morrow and I laugh at the incongruity of life and the twists and turns that catch us by surprise. I thank him for the yarn as well as the witnessing of my statutory declaration and reel down the stairs back to the street.

Thelma saved up one last surprise for The End.

GRATITUDE AND ACKNOWLEDGEMENTS

Reviewing the forty years described in this book and writing down the stories has changed me.

I did not set out to pen a memoir. When I left the ABC, the last thing I wanted to do was start reliving my thirty years behind a microphone. I was looking forwards, not backwards.

Within weeks of my final radio show in October 2019, the joy of publicly acknowledging my parents, with my ninety-three-year-old father Solly sitting in the audience at the Melbourne Town Hall, turned sour when he suffered a stroke, followed by a heart attack, followed by another stroke and worse thereafter. My similarly aged mother, Eva, was already in frail health by then and her slow decline was heartbreaking. Together with my sisters, and with professional help, we had become their carers. In their post-retirement years, they had been transformed, softening their hard edges, and enjoyed life much more. Grandchildren do that and my parents enjoyed their 'third age' until failing health interfered. As they entered their nineties and became dependent, we became closer than ever. They died within months of each other in 2021 while this book was being written. Parents' funerals trigger writer's block, and too often I had to wipe tears from the keyboard and am doing so again as I write these words.

Paul, Mark and Bruce Anderson had been approached before by people who wanted to tell their father's incredible story. A filmmaker spent years developing a proposal for an animated superhero comic–style rendition, but it failed to progress. I sincerely thank each of the brothers for their trust and cooperation, which I hope preserves and promotes Apollo's story for a new and wider audience. He was always so proud of each of you, and quite rightly. For the emotionally gruelling ordeal I subjected you each to, asking you to relive the most traumatic episodes of your upbringing, I am sorry. That many more people now get to celebrate your father is the reward.

Bruce filled in many gaps in my understanding of family history and had rare and valuable insights. Mark devoted days to organising and copying material from his personal collection of memorabilia and generously gave me access to his extensive photo library and wonderful personal videos of his dad. Paul, as unofficial keeper of the Apollo archives, has spent countless hours patiently correcting my errors and mistakes and guiding me through the astonishing historic press books and Apollo's circuitous memoir. My thanks to each of you; this project simply could never have happened without your commitment, contributions and trust.

John Flynn encouraged me for decades to gather yarns about Thelma. Our professional contact became a friendship a long time ago, and no trip north is complete without catching up. From the beginning to the end, even back when the estate was being litigated, his assistance on so many fronts has been vital. As he has proven, the Northern Territory is a bottomless pit of stories and characters richer than any of the minerals mined from the soil. I cannot adequately repay his counsel, his advice and personal generosity.

My thanks to Derek Pugh, Darwin historian and author, who on my behalf, and for modest reward, doggedly dug deep into the NT Archives when COVID-19 blocked my research trip north.

Shirley Hardy-Rix facilitated my visit to Kalkarindji, and judging by the welcome, she must have exaggerated my credentials with the community. She also introduced me to Viv Downes, who has been wonderful in liaison with community Elders. Thank you, Viv and Shirley. To Debra Victor, thank you for granting the family permission to show the iconic images of Vincent Lingiari.

Thanks also to the entire Hardy family for the extraordinary invitation to nervously officiate at Frank's vibrant celebratory funeral all those years ago.

Darrell Lewis was generous in filling in details about the Murranji Track, the history of which has been his particular interest for many years. Its role in opening Top Springs to travellers was new to me, and Darrell gave me access to original materials that provided clues and missing links that would otherwise have been missed.

Ruary Bucknall had a long association and friendship with Sid Hawks and willingly shared his stories, thus fleshing out my own interview with Sid and knowledge of the rest of his extraordinary life. Sid could be another book himself.

To all those who sat down and shared sometimes tragic, sometimes hilarious tales about the NT and are quoted in this book, thank you for sharing your past and putting flesh on the bones of my scant understanding of what life was like sometimes fifty or more years ago. I am grateful you trusted me to let those adventures and misadventures find new ears.

The colonial diarists, oral historians, researchers and writers whose digging has gradually unearthed the true story of the Territory while it was absorbing the spread of white settlers, and who have been prepared to tell the truth – all power to you. When we were taught Australian history at high school, we were provided with a sanitised, air-brushed version of our origin story and it is now well past the time to stop pretending.

The Northern Territory History Awards, administered through the Territory Archives, covered my travel expenses in 1994 to travel to Darwin. I am grateful to Greg Coleman for his assistance.

The NT Law Department assisted me with access to transcripts of Dailly's trial, and documents relating to Thelma's estate.

The Law Institute of Victoria made available their official portrait of Jack Harty, for which I thank them.

Photographer David Johns was masterful and generous in converting much of the archival material and Apollo's personal records into the wonderful photographs that adorn this book.

Publishers and editors exist to save authors from themselves. My gratitude to Sandy Grant for his enthusiasm for this tale, and to the patient and wise Pam Brewster for her gentle guidance through its interrupted gestation. Thanks to Anna Collett and Kate Daniel for steering the book through the editorial process, and to Shalini Kunahlan, Kathleen O'Neill and Kasi Collins for making it known to the world.

To the team who run the Abbotsford Convent, thank you for letting me join your sanctuary. To my neighbours, apologies if the music was too loud. To Sophie Cunningham, your wise counsel at a few crucial blockages was more than appreciated.

For Nigel, Rachel, Rose, Jack and Bethany, thank you for allowing my literary intrusion into your lives, especially Nigel – to whom I will now admit that I ought to have just bought you the Nike Air Jordans in 1988 and stopped my complaining.

There are so many former colleagues within the ABC Radio Melbourne/774/3LO extended family I'd like to acknowledge, but it is impossible to list them all. A radio presenter is only ever as good as the producers and tech team propping them up. From time to time I told a few stories over lunch and to anyone who said, 'You ought to write a book ...' I say thank you. I will single out Sue Howard who was generous as a boss and a colleague and my longevity in the 'Mornings' time slot in Melbourne would never have happened without her gamble to let me take long service leave in 2008.

Mistakes are all mine, and I would be grateful for any contributions that correct errors where they appear.

And my last word is devoted to Jan. Thank you for everything that has been and all that is still to be.

FURTHER READING

There is a rich library of stories about the Top End of Australia, Indigenous biography, the emerging truth of massacres and the colonial settlement of Australia. There are fewer resources about the history of circus in Australia. This is by no means an exhaustive list and is in alphabetical order by author's family name, but these are the books I drew upon to supplement my own recorded conversations with many people over forty years.

Paul Barry; *The Rise and Rise of Kerry Packer* [1993]

Deborah Bird; *Dingo Makes Us Human* [1992]

Doris Blackwell & Douglas Blackwood; *Alice on the Line* [1965]

Geoffrey Blomfield; *Baal Belbora, The End of the Dancing* [1981]

Jim Bowditch; *Whispers from the North* [1993]

Robert Brogdan; *Freak Show* [1988]

Richard Broome & Alick Jackomos; *Sideshow Alley* [1998]

Fred Brophy; *The Last Showman* [2014]

Ron Brown; *Bush Justice* [1990]

Nick Campbell-Jones; *Don't Die Wondering* [2012]

Erika Charola & Felicity Meakins [eds]; *Yijarni, True Stories from Gurindji Country* [2016]

Bruce Chatwin; *The Songlines* [1987]

Charles Chauvel; *Walkabout* [1959]

Tom Cole; *Hell West & Crooked* [1988]

Gillian Cowlishaw; *Love and the Law* [2000]

John Cribbin; *The Killing Times* [1984]

P F Donovan; *At the Other End of Australia* [1984]

Ted Egan; *Due Inheritance* [2008]

Ted Egan; *Justice All Their Own* [1996]

Ted Egan; *Sitdown Up North* [1997]

Ted Egan; *The Land Down Under* [2003]

Elizabeth Eggleston; *Fear, Favour or Affection* [1976]

Bruce Elder; *Blood on the Wattle* [1988]

Elizabeth George; *Two at Daly Waters* [1945]

Walter Gill; *Petermann Journey* [1968]

Neville Green; *The Forrest River Massacres* [1995]

Marc Gumberts; *Neither Justice Nor Reason* [1984]

Peter Hanks & Bryan Keon-Cohen [eds] *Aborigines and the Law*
      [1984]

Frank Hardy; *Power without Glory* [1950]

Frank Hardy; *The Hard Way* [1971]

Frank Hardy; *The Unlucky Australians* [1976]

W E Harney; *Content to Lie in the Sun* [1958]

W E Harney; *Grief, Gaiety & Aborigines* [1961]

W E Harney; *Tales from the Aborigines* [1959]

Thea Hayes; *An Outback Nurse* [2014]

Barry Hill; *Broken Song* [2002]

Ernestine Hill; *The Territory* [1951]

Jenny Hocking; *Frank Hardy, Politics, Literature, Life* [2005]

K S Inglis; *The Stuart Case* [1961]

Barbara James; *No Man's Land, Women of the NT* [1989]

Ricky Jay; *Learned Pigs & Fireproof Women* [1986]

Kurt Johannsen; *A Son of the Red Centre* [1992]

Ellen Kettle; *Gone Bush* [1967]

Phillip Knightley; *The Rise & Fall of the House of Vestey* [1981]

Syd Kyle-Little; *Whispering Wind, Adventures in Arnhem Land* [1957]

Yami Lester; *Yami, Autobiography* [1993]

Darrell Lewis; *A Shared History* [1997]

Darrell Lewis; *The Murranji Track* [2007]

Douglas Lockwood; *Crocodiles and Other People* [1959]

Douglas Lockwood; *I, The Aboriginal* [1962]

Douglas Lockwood; *Up the Track* [1964]

Bob Lunney; *Growing Up Fast in the Top End* [2000]

Pamela Lyon & Michael Parsons; *We Are Staying* [1989]

Colin Macleod; *Patrol in the Dreamtime* [1997]

Jock Makin; *The Big Run* [1983]

Julie Marcus; *The Indomitable Miss Pink* [2001]

Andrew Markus; *Governing Savages* [1990]

Paul Marshall [Ed]; *Raparapa, Stories from the Fitzroy River Drovers* [1988]

Liz Martin; *My Territory, My Life, My Story* [2010]

Maisie McKenzie; *Mission to Arnhem Land* [1976]

Andrew McMillan; *An Intruder's Guide to East Arnhem Land* [2001]

Ward McNally; *Goodbye Dreamtime* [1973]

Ward McNally; *The Angry Australians* [1974]

Jack McPhee & Patrician Konigsberg; *Bee Hill River Man* [1994]

Bob Morgan; *The Showies* [1995]

James Muirhead; *A Brief Summing Up* [1996]

William Murray [ed]; *The Struggle for Dignity* [1962]

'Mulga Mick' O'Reilly; *Bowyangs and Boomerangs* [1984]

Howard Pedersen & Banjo Woorunmurra; *Jandamarra* [1995]

Rachel Perkins & Marcia Langton [eds]; *First Australians* [2008]

Alan Powell; *Far Country, A Short History of the N.T.* [1982]

Charles Priest; *Earlier N.T. Recollections* [1986]

Charles Priest; *Further N. T. Recollections* [1986]

Charles Priest; *Recollections* [1986]

Derek Pugh; *Darwin, Origin of a City* [2019]

Derek Pugh; *Escape Cliffs* [2017]

Derek Pugh; *Turn Left at the Devil Tree* [2013]

Gordon Reid; *A Picnic with the Natives* [1990]

Charlie Schultz; *Beyond the Big Run* [1995]

Anne Scrimgeour; *On Red Earth Walking, The Pilbara Strike* [2020]

Alison Seymour-Bingle; *This Is Our Country* [1987]

Mark St. Leon; *The Wizard of the Wire* [1993]

Gerald Stone; *Compulsive Viewing* [2001]

Justice John Toohey; *Yingawunarri* [Old Top Springs] *Mudbura Land Claim* [1980]

Richard Trudgen; *Why Warriors Lie Down and Die* [2000]

Terry Underwood; *In the Middle of Nowhere* [1998]

Charlie Ward; *A Handful of Sand* [2016]

Charlie Ward: 'Red Truths & White Lies', *Griffith Review* [2012]

Catherine Watson; *The Rabbit King* [1996]

Ken White; *True Stories of the Top End* [2005]

W H Willshire; *The Land of the Dawning, Being Facts Gleaned from Cannibals in the Australian Stone Age* [1896]

Sir Edward Woodward; *One Brief Interval* [2005]

Jan Wositzky & Yidumduma Bill Harney; *Born Under a Paperbark Tree* [1996]

Frank Wright & Penny Goldman; *Telegraph Tourists* [1993]

Mayse Young; *No Place For a Woman* [1991]